animal with some place to go . Because where is it
going — the seed hooked into your coat, and you
yourself, brother, where are you
think you know? An, this here
street? You think you've arrived? You think you've
lost your fur and your tail for a purpose spelled
with a capital P and sold to you in some book
that explains how everything was just a prelude
until you arrived came? If you do, you're
happy I take it and you'd be better off not to be
following me or this crab or turning up
stones and looking under them.

For what you see under a stone may be
like a flash of lightening before a traveler on a stormy
night. It lights in one wet & glistening
instant a hundred miles of devils landscape
such as he will never see again. Each stone,
each tree, each ravine and crevice echoing
and reechoing with thunder, will tell him; more
than daytime vision, of the road he travels, the
flash hangs like an Immortal magnification
in the brain, and suddenly he knows the
kind of country he you and the answers
abroad in it, It is the country of Time; the
can be found under a stone,

For twenty years & too
flash lights a long way backward
over a wild land.

II
the Chordates & the Euryplerids
III
Prairie dog town
IV
the shining thread
the ruins of the city

Also by Loren Eiseley

PROSE

The Immense Journey
1957

Darwin's Century
1958

The Firmament of Time
1960

The Unexpected Universe
1969

The Invisible Pyramid
1970

The Night Country
1971

The Man Who Saw Through Time
1973

All the Strange Hours
1975

The Star Thrower
1978

Darwin and the Mysterious Mr. X
1979

POETRY

Notes of an Alchemist
1972

The Innocent Assassins
1973

Another Kind of Autumn
1977

All the Night Wings
1979

The
Lost Notebooks
of
Loren Eiseley

The
Lost Notebooks
of
Loren Eiseley

❧ ❧

EDITED AND WITH A REMINISCENCE BY

Kenneth Heuer

Sketches by Leslie Morrill

LITTLE, BROWN AND COMPANY
Boston   Toronto

Acknowledgements of permission to reprint previously copyrighted material appear on
pages 259–260. Except as noted therein, copyright in the works of Loren Eiseley is
controlled by the Estate of Mabel L. Eiseley.

ENDPAPER. *Facsimile of pages from a notebook.* This personal anecdote of an encounter
with a crab was recorded in 1968, during a trip to an island in the Gulf of Mexico.
According to an outline that followed, the author planned to use "the crab as a visual
guide to start an inquiry as to the direction of man's evolution" (pages 177–178).

Library of Congress Cataloging-in-Publication Data

Eiseley, Loren C., 1907–1977.
  The lost notebooks of Loren Eiseley.

  1. Nature. 2. Eiseley, Loren C., 1907–1977.
3. Naturalists — United States — Biography.
I Heuer, Kenneth. II. Title.
QH81.E59 1987   508   86-21390
ISBN 0-316-35921-1

Designed by Robert Lowe

HAL

*Published simultaneously in Canada
by Little, Brown & Company (Canada) Limited*

PRINTED IN THE UNITED STATES OF AMERICA

To Max
a perfect blend of character and craft
humor and philosophical gravity
nonsense and acute hunting sense

That *I* am, this I share with other men.
That I see and hear and that I eat and
drink is what all animals do likewise.
But that I am *I* is only mine and belongs
to me and to no one else; to no other
man, not an angel, not to God except
inasmuch as I am one with him.

— *Meister Eckhart*

Contents

Photographs

Endpaper: Facsimile of pages from a notebook

Following page 18

The
Lost Notebooks
of
Loren Eiseley

Introduction

In the summer of 1982, five years after his death, an article entitled "The Lost Nature Notebooks of Loren Eiseley" was published in *Omni* magazine. The previous summer Robert Weil, director of the book division of Omni Publications, had asked me if Dr. Eiseley, one of the century's outstanding literary naturalists, had left a legacy, if there were any of his writings suitable for publication in *Omni*. At the time, I was New York editor of Cornell University Press, but I had been Loren's editor at Charles Scribner's Sons for over a decade, and I had prepared three of his manuscripts for posthumous book publication.

Actually, he had left behind some notebooks, in which he had confided daily thoughts and happenings through the years, but there were no plans to make them available to the public. Loren's widow, the former Mabel Langdon, eventually granted permission to publish excerpts from one of the journals, and I then traveled to her home in Wynnewood, Pennsylvania, to discuss the project. It was agreed that I would select and edit material primarily from the notebook covering the years 1953 to 1960 and that I would write an introduction to the article describing the journals. During his lifetime, he had shown the notebooks to no one, and their existence was known to few. They were lost like the ruins of ancient cities in the mountains of Peru, unknown to all but a few nearby residents.

"The Lost Nature Notebooks of Loren Eiseley," in the June 1982 issue of *Omni*, resulted in enthusiastic letters from the author's old fans and numerous inquiries from publishers. In light of this enthusiasm, I urged Mabel to have the notebooks published, observing that Loren and I had discussed this possibility when he was alive. She had a different recollection of his wishes but finally felt that her late husband would not have objected if they could be properly presented and readers could derive benefit and enjoyment from them. Although there were more than a dozen, she agreed only to having the 1953–1960 journal published intact; if it was successful, others might be made available.

This representative volume, in which Loren sought to seize the moment, to arrest time in its flight, is written in pen or pencil across white sheets of paper in a black-and-red bound legal notebook. The ledger contains 144 pages; of these, 14 pages are missing and 6 are blank. Unlike some writers' notebooks, this one is lucid throughout. The first entry is dated May 21, 1953: "Beginning this journal in my forty-sixth year, a late start for a writer's journal, but I hope to do something with it. During the last few days there have been several nature incidents, and I will try and record them in the hope that they will thus not escape my memory and that I may be able to make use of them later on." He was not a faithful journalist, however. On February 14, 1954, for instance, he wrote: "A long abandonment of this record, but I shall now try to get back into the spirit of it."

The notebook permits the reader to see the genesis of Loren's work, what Henry James called "the seed work of art." Here we are in the laboratory, observing the author openly — a fascinating experience in which there is often a sudden burst of poetic power. With Loren, notebook keeping was not drudgery. He made an entry when he saw something or was thinking, and, like all writers of original genius, he glimpsed wonderful things in the commonplace in life which make the ordinary reader look about him and wonder what he is missing. The notebook is a prying questioning work, not only observing. He had a sympathetic understanding of nature, of birds and insects; what he was apprehensive of was man. The journal also contains memoranda of passages for reference, like a commonplace book. The number of them is a reflection of his vigorous pursuit of ideas, and his choice of quotations throws light on the cast of his mind. Science, philosophy, literature, theology — he had a wide range of interests and was an avid reader. In his notebook, he dealt with the writers of the past as if they were living, often commenting on what they said; it was a dialogue across the generations.

In September of 1982, an offering was made to six of the publishers who had expressed interest in the notebooks. A copy of the first volume, together with a prospectus, was presented and resulted in bids from four publishers, two of whom agreed to issue an edited version of volume one. However, the most attractive offers were made by the other two, who proposed that a rather rigorously edited manuscript — comprising the most compelling, pertinent, revealing, and moving entries — be drawn from *all* the journals. It became increasingly apparent that such a volume would better fulfill the goals of publishing the material, but now the central problem of this story unfolded.

When Loren was in his last illness, he had asked Mabel to burn the notebooks. Perhaps his reticence is best explained in a memorandum he once wrote: "For everything written there are thoughts, notes, that no one will use if he has not done something with them. Notes that a writer collects are of no meaning to another, no one else could make the connections. Every time a great scholar dies something unique vanishes out of the universe, a way of thinking that will never be expressed again. . . ." Authors have traditionally requested that their journals be destroyed, but they often do not mean what they say. All journalists, whether they recognize it or not, hope to be read someday, although not necessarily by anyone they know or can describe. When Mabel asked my opinion, I argued accordingly, to preserve the notebooks.

Quite understandably, not wishing to go against her late husband's wishes, but recognizing the significance of the writings, she compromised by dismantling the journals: pages pertaining to Loren's books, frequently containing other jottings, were filed with the original manuscripts of his published works; others were placed in cartons in a back closet off his old study; still others containing unimportant notations, such as the times of a flight or expenses on a trip, perhaps enclosed in a notebook cover, were incinerated. In 1978, the collection of original manuscripts was presented to the University of Pennsylvania, where Loren had taught, and housed in the university archives. Basically, the bulk of the material was saved, but it was no longer in Mabel's possession, and, outside of the 1953–1960 notebook, it was no longer visible — it was lost in files containing a large number of other pages. The one notebook survived almost intact because the author had not at the beginning of the journal published as extensively as he was later to do; there were fewer pages to extract and place with manuscripts.

This was the problem we faced in the fall of 1982 when publishers proposed a single-volume selection from all the journals. It was obviously the right choice. The question was, could the violation of archival principles be resolved? Could the notebooks be restored? After ascertaining that this was possible, an agreement was entered into with the publisher we felt was most compatible with Loren's work; the contract was signed in November of 1983. The early months of that year were spent in putting the notebooks back into their original state. Fortunately, a complete catalog of the material concerning the books he authored had been prepared by Caroline Werkley, a research librarian at the University of Pennsylvania who had been Loren's assistant for many years and who had extracted the pages from the journals and filed them. Now she retrieved from the archives everything in the catalog labeled "Notebook," hundreds upon hundreds of pages which arrived at her home in Missouri — where she had retired — in a battered package. A note from Kansas City said that the bundle of papers had reached there in a mutilated condition; it had been rewrapped and sent on to her. In the process, the pages were juggled about, and they were no longer in proper order. To this was added the 1953–1960 journal and the other notebook material Mabel had not parted with and had turned over to me for the *Omni* article. Putting the notebooks back together again was not as easy as taking them apart. One way Caroline did this was to compare the physical aspects of the sheets. One notebook, for instance, is short, numbered, and has a double-line left-hand margin; another is long, unnumbered, with a single margin; still another short, unnumbered, no margin. Using this information as a guide, most of the material could be placed correctly in the proper notebook. Much of it was undated, so she had to judge where it went.

In 1984, Roger Donald, executive editor of Little, Brown and Company, and I each took a copy of the reconstructed notebooks and marked the entries which, in our estimation, were of special value or excellence. Although there were an enormous number to choose among, when we met and compared notebooks, we found that we had invariably made the same choices, except in certain cases where perhaps my selection was more discriminating because of a greater knowledge of Loren's work. The transcribing of the journals was difficult. The 1953–1960 journal is, for the most part, neatly written, but as time went on, entries were made more and more in haste and without care as to legibility, some of them containing material for or referring to work in progress, with many corrections. Busy with his scholarly and creative career and in great demand as a lecturer, he did not have the necessary leisure for a more formal work, as he had undoubtedly originally planned. The scribbles in later notebooks had to be deciphered with the aid of a magnifying glass — a time-consuming process which often required half an hour for a single sentence and sometimes a return to the sentence the following day after further reflection.

Caroline, who had typed many of his manuscripts and knew his handwriting better than anyone but Mabel and myself, was able to identify most of the words and phrases I questioned, when marked pages of the journals were sent to her. A large number of the entries contained alternative words and phrases in the margins of the pages; the choice in transcribing the notebooks was based on my experience with him as his editor, on which word or phrase I thought *he* would finally choose. As the journals included material that went into his books or articles, either in that form or later rewritten, it had to be identified; both Caroline and I immersed ourselves in Loren's publications in order to determine which passages had been used. Several entries were of particular interest because they confirmed that the journalist had at one time considered publishing his notebooks. There is, for example, a marginal note on one of the pages of the April 5, 1974, entry, which reads in part, "Reserve for notebooks. Possible end for notebook." This remarkable piece, one of the most affecting he ever wrote, was composed in the final years of his life and describes his setting out to find the cemetery in which he owned a lot and losing his way.

In August of 1985, I traveled again to Wynnewood, Pennsylvania, to examine the author's personal files; I was looking for photographs, letters, and perhaps a few additional unpublished poems for possible inclusion in the book. I knew that he never threw anything away. He kept, for instance, photographs taken by his favorite photographer and friend, Frank Ross, whose pictures of him appeared on the jackets of his books, not to mention every least notation from his own hand and a huge correspondence. But I was not prepared for what I discovered: blue books — blue-covered booklets used for writing examinations in certain colleges — in which he wrote early stories; dime-store notebooks — small notebooks with reddish brown covers — in which through the years, as a professional scientist, he scrawled matters of archaeological or biological interest, as well as an occasional poem; hotel stationery on which he wrote when he was out of town and suddenly had an idea he wanted to record; 5×8-inch cards and pages of yellow, legal-size writing pads which he filled with material for articles and books he planned to publish. I was struck by the informality of his procedures — which began with a $4\frac{1}{2} \times 6$-inch booklet, "bound" in white paper covers, tied with pink ribbon, he wrote as a boy. Initially, the fact that he was poor was obviously behind that informality. But even when he could have afforded the finest notebook, nothing was further from his mind.

Among the treasures I found in that closet off Loren's old study were the hundreds of letters to and from scientists, educators, government officials, authors, editors, and critics — many of them famous. The recent photographs of him were present, too, but there was something else unexpected: packets of photographs of Loren and his friends taken at all stages of his life and, in a cardboard receptacle marked "Family Box," numerous pictures of his ancestors. That same box held stories written by Malvina McKee Corey, his maternal grandmother, who, in her eighties, passed the time by recalling memories of her childhood. In more ways than one, this nineteenth-century chronicler of pioneer days in the wilds of Oregon was Loren's psychological or near twin. A large old-fashioned family Bible which had belonged to the Coreys, from whom Loren received his middle name, was kept in the study during his lifetime. It contains records of births, marriages, and deaths and many old photographs of his forebears.

There were still several gaps in the Eiseley collection of writings, notably school essays and unpublished and uncollected early stories, primarily describing his life as a near-derelict during the depression, and unpublished and uncollected poems from all periods of his life, many of which had been torn out of his notebooks when they were dismantled and placed in a separate file. I knew these writings existed, and on a subsequent trip to Pennsylvania in November of 1985, I found them in a metal filing cabinet behind tax reports. As a literary detective, I had invaded Mabel's privacy, searching in obscure places, in desk and dresser drawers, in bookcases, filing cabinets, and closets. This was very distressing for her, but she gave me full access to the material. On one occasion, I was loaded down with shopping bags filled with manuscripts, waiting for a train to New York in the Philadelphia station. I turned to Ruben Reina, a friend of the author's and mine and a professor of anthropology at the University of Pennsylvania, who had accompanied me and, observing the businessmen surrounding us with their elegant attaché cases, said, "I feel like a bag man." "Yes," Ben replied with a smile, "but think of what you've got in your bags and what they've got in their cases."

Out of this enormous trove, I selected the material that seemed most worthy of consideration, and Roger Donald and I then followed the same procedure as before, marking in copies the pieces we liked best and comparing notes. Only the literary letters were considered, to convey an idea of what his peers thought of his writing. Photographs were selected on the basis of characters mentioned in Loren's journals and books and which had not previously been seen by his readers. The new material was for the most part handwritten and presented the same problems of decipherment as before. After it was typed and incorporated into the rest of the manuscript, we decided on the final version, cutting entries with similar ideas unless the concepts were examined from different viewpoints, most of the quotations unless they were commentated upon, and journal material which had appeared in his own books unless it was a brief entry or varied largely.

There were two possible ways of organizing the volume, by subject or chronologically, and I finally chose the latter, in order to give it greater variety and, more important, reveal to the reader the development of the man as a writer and a thinker. This was the more complicated method, for much of the newly discovered material was undated. Ascertaining the period of composition was done by analyzing the handwriting (which was small and clear in Loren's youth and became large and indistinct in age and illness); the subject matter with which the author dealt; and the style (early poems, for instance, were rhymed, late poems primarily in free verse). The writings were then arranged in three parts corresponding to periods in his life, and I prepared an historical and biographical introduction to each so that the entries required very few notes or emendations. These preliminary remarks emphasized his scholarly and creative career and evolved, in some degree, into a reminiscence. Each part was given a title (taken from a poem, a story, or an evocative phrase in the notebooks), and the theme of the selection was further suggested by a quotation from the many he hoarded in his journals — a practice he used in his own autobiography.

The detailed editing was limited primarily to correcting spelling, punctuation, and grammar (it should be noted that the brackets enclosing matter, chiefly as extraneous or merely incidental to the context, are Loren's). In some instances, word repetitions — which he disliked intensely — were removed by using words having the same essential meaning, and abbreviations employed for brevity in the journals were often replaced with complete words and phrases. Biographical information, such as names of authors and titles of their books, was also corrected and completed where necessary, but quotations were left as recorded, even if not exact. In essence, as few changes were made as possible in order to preserve the integrity of the work.

Loren had a great appreciation of art, and his later books were illustrated by artists with whom he worked closely. If he had been a naturalist-artist like Ernest Thompson Seton, he would have filled his notebooks with sketches. But, as it is, there is only one drawing of water lily leaves that he made for the entry of August 12, 1955. Accordingly, the artist Leslie Morrill, an Eiseley admirer, was invited to provide sketches such as a naturalist would do in the field — representations of objects and scenes as record their chief features, tentative drafts made as preliminary studies. Morrill's work greatly enhances and captures the spirit of the volume.

From the day the first notebook fell into my hands, it took four years of intermittent literary detective work and reconstruction to turn the thousands of pages of material into a finished book. During this period I was astonished to realize that, although I was Loren's friend and editor, I hardly knew him. The journals — and personal letters — revealed him at his most candid, gave me a glimpse of his uniqueness I could get in no other way. Thus my friendship for him grew after his death.

It is always difficult to judge a great contemporary writer, for we lack the proper distance, so it is not surprising that Loren's reputation is in question. The controversy is exemplified by the attitude of his own university, where, in 1982, the editorial board rejected a manuscript about him because it considered him unworthy to be made the subject of study; at the same time, university officials were giving thought to naming a special chair in his honor. Whatever their view, *The Lost Notebooks,* which stands at once as a marvelous collection of previously unseen material and as a spiritual autobiography of the author, often revealing his working methods, should help the critics to renew and deepen their understanding of him.

From time to time, I get letters from professors who are writing books about the naturalist, seeking my help. In 1983, I received such a letter from Dr. Stanley L. Becker of Bethany College (West Virginia), who ended on a personal note: "When I met Loren Eiseley for the first time in his 'old' office, I brought him a glass, amberina owl as a symbol of his craftsmanship. When the package was unwrapped it turned out that the owl had been cracked in transit. Eiseley commented that the flawed owl was *now* symbolic of his mind, that a 'perfect' glass owl would not have been as suitable." But, as someone said of the mind of the English artist and poet William Blake on another occasion, if it was indeed flawed, "it was cracked so that the light shone through."

Kenneth Heuer

Part I

❧ ❦

THE GATE AND THE ROAD
1907–1947

The traveller must be born again on the road,
and earn a passport from the elements. . . .
— *Henry David Thoreau*

The year when Loren Eiseley was born, 1907, was also the year when Oklahoma became the forty-sixth state and panic in America caused a run on banks; the year when Rudyard Kipling won the Nobel Prize for literature and Ivan Pavlov studied conditioned reflexes; the year when the S.S. *Lusitania* was launched and broke the transatlantic record, steaming from Queenstown (Cobh), Ireland, to New York in five days and forty-five minutes. For the Eiseleys living in the agricultural center of Lincoln, Nebraska, the most vivid of these events was the 1907 panic and depression that started on March 13.

Born in bleak farm country on September 3, Loren was the grandson of pioneers who had drifted west with the wagons into the Nebraska Territory. His mother was stone deaf and of unsound mind. Communication between Daisy Eiseley and her son consisted of gestures, stamping on the floor to create vibrations, and facial contortions; it was like the communication which may have existed between the man-apes of the early Ice Age. She was also an untutored but talented prairie artist, who gave her son a deep appreciation of the beauties of the natural world. The gift of his father was exposure to the magic of poetry through his eloquent voice. But Clyde Eiseley was poor and worked long, hard hours, and Loren, for the most part, grew up in a house whose silence was broken only by the discordant voice of his mother and where visitors did not call. The Eiseleys were social outcasts, deliberately avoided as peculiar and unimportant.

At a very early age, this strangely deprived and solitary child began to transmute his misery into creative energy. He wrote his first book, *Animal Aventures* (the word "adventures" misspelled) at age six. Handwritten in ink on white-lined paper and illustrated with photographs, the chapter titles are "Uncle's Dog," "Kitty's Aventure," "The Cunning Fox," and "Animal

Kindness." Loren's early delight with nature is manifested in this creation, as is his growing understanding of the complexities of life as seen in his characters. A sense of personality had dawned on this brilliant child of the early century, and an inkling of abstract ideas, intelligence, deviousness, kindness.

Loren could read before he entered grade school, and in the early lonely years he haunted the Lincoln City Library. In fact, because of the emotional turbulence in his family, the library became almost literally a first home, a place where he regularly sought refuge. In the library, the bookish child had a chance to forget the world, and, in the wild, the curious child had a chance to make discoveries. Loren observed ants and read about them; from the natural ponds lying on the borders of the town in which he lived, he made collections for his aquarium. An intense observer of nature at all seasons, he took walks in winter blizzards or the heat of midsummer. These absences from home not only offered escape from the uneasy family atmosphere, but they intensified his attachment to the country of his boyhood. The influence of this landscape on his imagination persisted in his adult writing.

In 1921, in the eighth grade at Prescott School, the budding literary naturalist wrote a prophetic essay entitled "Nature Writing":

> I have selected Nature Writing for my vocation because at this time in my life it appeals to me more than any other subject. I feel it is my duty to do what I can to make people realize that the wild creature has just as much right to live as you or I. They must learn that the wild offers a more thrilling sport than killing — that of letting live. Killing for the excitement of killing is murder. As in human life, there are tragedy, and humor, and pathos; in the life of the wild, there are facts of tremendous interest, real lives, and real happenings, to be written about, and there is little necessity for drawing on the imagination.

A few years later, in 1923, when he was sixteen, Loren wrote for his English class another essay, "Whiskers," in which he, as a young naturalist, and his dog wander in the country and make discoveries; his teacher, Miss Wyman, commented on the paper and raised his confidence. When he published *The Mind as Nature* (1962), he singled out another caring adult, Letta May Clark, and dedicated the book to her. Former Supervisor of English in the University of Nebraska High School, Miss Clark had treated Loren's work with respect and inspired him with courage. Under her supervision, he wrote and rewrote and learned that writing is difficult and endlessly demanding.

One of the greatest of the "distant teachers" who influenced him was Shakespeare. His father had been a self-trained member of a little troupe which crudely declaimed Shakespearean drama to unsophisticated audiences in midwestern "opera houses." At home, he spoke rhetorically long, rolling Elizabethan passages that made shivers run up his son's spine. The power of the poet's words led to personal experimentation, to Loren's first stories and poems. When Clyde Eiseley died, he left a soiled edition of Shakespeare, worn by frequent handling, a copy his son possessed all his life.

Lincoln was also the seat of the University of Nebraska. From its beginning in an unattractive town of frame bungalows and discouraged-looking trees, it has fostered greatness: the novelist Willa Cather, the educator Roscoe Pound, the army commander John J. Pershing. It was to this university Loren went in 1925, with plans to become a scientist. Although devoted to poetry, he had to earn a living, and he enrolled heavily in biology courses. He found, however, he was by disposition unable to limit himself to technical and laboratory studies. Sociology and anthropology also interested him, and every semester's schedule included more than the required courses in English. Again, the personal interest of one of his English teachers, Lowry C. Wimberly, was crucial in his development. A skilled writer and critic with whom Loren conversed about writing, Wimberly was founder and editor of *The Prairie Schooner,* "an outlet for literary work in the University of Nebraska and a medium for the finest writing of the prairie country." Its emphasis was regional, and the magazine favored a pessimistic interpretation of its region — an area then consisting of raw and dreary expanses, whose people were forced to live on a primitive and depressed level.

By now Loren was experimenting with poetry, and the *Schooner* accepted many of his early pieces and later made him one of the contributing editors. Encouraged by their reception in the *Schooner,* he sent poems to *The Midland, Voices,* and other respected but nonpaying magazines, where a number were placed. It was more exciting, however, to receive a check from Harriet Monroe's *Poetry,* with an accompanying note on blue paper in the editor's own hand; or to have an acceptance, with check, from the *New York Herald-Tribune* "Books" section through its editor, Irita Van Doren. Occasionally, a poem was reprinted on the poetry page of the *Literary Digest* or picked up by a newspaper; a few were included in anthologies.

Over the years Nebraska's farmers have suffered from both natural hazards — severe droughts and grasshopper plagues —

and low farm prices. As a regional poet, Loren wrote about these conditions in such poems as "Waste Song," "The Deserted Homestead" (1929), "Upland Harvest" (1930), and "Words to the Stoic" (1930). At about this time, as the result of a pulmonary infection following a severe case of influenza, he was threatened with tuberculosis. Leaving school on the orders of his doctor, he went to Colorado and to the Mojave Desert, where the dry air would be good for his health and where he faced questions about life and death which had until then existed only in books — questions which engaged his mind for the years to come. This traumatic period was the source of "Lizard's Eye," whereas in the powerful poem "Return to a House," he drew upon the experience of his family's disturbed and divided household.

Loren never thought of himself as a poet, nor was there any intention of his becoming a professional writer when he was in college. But he was put on earth to write, and that is what he did. His first published literary essay, "Autumn — A Memory" (1927) also appeared in *The Prairie Schooner*. This was followed by publication of "Riding the Peddlers" (1933) and "The Mop to K.C." (1935), which was listed in the Distinctive Index of Edward O'Brien's *The Best Short Stories of 1936*. These two narratives were drawn from recollections of the Great Depression. Following the stock market crash of 1929, prices of agricultural products fell to the lowest levels in Nebraska history. Drought and dust storms greatly intensified the distress of the 1930s. All parts of society were affected, and almost one-sixth of the population had to depend on government relief programs. Loren's enforced sojourn in the Mojave Desert had left him restless, at odds with his environment, and for a time he drifted westward again, riding freight and passenger trains with the jobless men of the depression, living in hobo camps. The stories he wrote about this period reveal how large a part crime played in his imagination — as a lurking destiny. He once confided in me that he could have determined on a life of crime instead of that of a scholar, if he had taken the wrong turning.

Well-meaning friends and advisers at the university discussed with Loren the possibility of making a career in the field of English; they thought the literary successes he had enjoyed might be useful. But the idea of correcting freshman themes was enough to deter him from making this choice. He had taken some courses in geology and been exposed to the wonders of paleontology. Moreover, long before he entered college, he had become aware of the life of past geological periods: as a child he had visited the old red-brick museum which then housed the huge bones of the fossil collections of the University of Nebraska, and he had never lost his fascination with prehistoric animals. Through some contacts at the museum, he obtained summer employment during several seasons with collecting parties of the institution. The expeditions worked primarily in western Nebraska, where there are vast fossil beds; now and then the parties crossed the border into South Dakota or made trips into the Southwest. These and later experiences as a bone hunter provided him with valuable scientific background and material used in *The Immense Journey* (1957) and other writings; they also furnished him with some funds for further schooling.

William Duncan Strong, teacher and archaeologist, lured the student into anthropology as a major subject. The study of man fitted his various interests and allowed for personal movement. Here his training in the exact sciences could be of value. His experience in paleontology was of use in archaeology, especially in the search for early man, and his writing ability would come in handy in publishing research results. In 1933, he obtained his A.B. as a major in anthropology. He was, of course, not in school all of the time from his entrance in 1925: crises arising from the death of his father and his mother's mental problems, his own illness and restlessness, the Great Depression and long periods of common labor seriously interrupted these college years. Others had gone straight to their careers, but he had spent eight years trying to figure out the shape and direction of his life.

After this long period of drifting, Loren came East to graduate school at the University of Pennsylvania in Philadelphia. Here he had to concentrate on professional courses in anthropology, though he continued to write and occasionally produced a poem. But most of the time he was doing research, looking for interesting subjects which could be published in respected, scholarly journals. He worked under Frank Speck, an ethnologist and naturalist of note who was head of the department. In *The Invisible Pyramid* (1970), Loren wrote: "Everyone in his youth — and who is to say when youth is ended? — meets for the last time a magician, the man who made him what he is finally to be." He was speaking of Speck, a man of extraordinary mental powers and a formidable personality who had introduced him to the eastern woodlands and brought alive for him the spruce-forest primitives of today. With this teacher who thought like and was reared by an Indian, he absorbed the superstitions of these Native Americans, touched their sacred objects, embraced their prophetic dreams. Speck was an authority on hunting territories, and toward the end of Loren's graduate-student career, the two men did research on the subject together; the results were published by the *American Anthropologist* and the *Proceedings of the American Philosophical Society*. It is to Speck that he owes his final professional degree (Ph.D.) from the University of Pennsylvania.

Finishing his doctorate in 1937, the young scholar went to teach at the University of Kansas in Lawrence, where he married a hometown girl, Mabel Langdon. In Mabel, he found an understanding being, a poet and an art teacher with whose support anything was possible. Very little is said about Mabel in his books; an intensely private person, she wished to be apart from observation, and he respected her request. But there is a telling message prefixed to his first volume of poems, *Notes of an Alchemist* (1972):

> *Dedicated to*
> *Mabel Langdon*
> *my wife of many years*
> *in appreciation of a devotion*
> *which cannot be spoken about*
> *save to say it exists*
> *as a flower exists*
> *having come unbidden*
> *into an unexpected world*
> *to a quite common man*

Loren was as common as any of us and as uncommon as any of us can hope to be. Mabel knew this and created an environment in which he could flourish.

During the first years of teaching at the University of Kansas, heavy schedules and responsibilities limited Loren's writing to articles for *Science,* the *American Anthropologist,* and similar scholarly journals to which a young assistant professor of sociology and anthropology might hope to gain admittance. A bright moment of time in this rather dull period occurred when the editor of *Scientific American,* who had noticed his work elsewhere, asked him to attempt some articles. The experience of writing for the magazine under the kindly sponsorship of Albert Ingalls revived an interest in writing something outside the scope of articles for the narrowly specialized journals. During World War II, as a physical anthropologist by training, with a background in anatomy and biology, Loren was shifted into the premedical program at the university. He taught enlisted young reservists almost around the clock, summer and winter. His experience in assisting his medical superiors in cadaver dissec-

I–4 *Pages from the Corey family Bible.* The Bible was kept in Loren's study and had originally belonged to the Coreys, Loren's forebears on his mother's side. These pages provide records of many of the characters about whom he wrote and who provide clues to his behavior. The last entry under "Births" is "Loren Corey Eiseley, b. Sept. 3, 1907, Lincoln, Neb." (*overleaf*).

BIRTHS.

William Sutton, b. Sept. 16-1783, Vt.
Esther Rudd, b. Nov. 17, 1782,   Vt.
Abner Freeman Corey, b. 1812, N.Y.
Sarah Marilla Sutton, b. May 12, 1811,
Milo Franklin Corey, b. Jan. 28, 1840,
Malvina McKee, b. July 7, 1850. Iowa
Grace Corey, b. Oct. 6, 1870, Dyersville, Ia.
William Buchanan Price, b. July 2, 1865,
Bertha Corey, b. Mar. 18, 1874. Ia.
Daisy Corey, b. Aug. 26, 1875, Dyersville, Ia.
Clyde Edwin Eiseley, b. Dec. 29, 1868 Shadye Co.
N. O.
Loren Corey Eiseley, b. Sept. 3, 1907, Lincoln N.

DEATHS.

William Sutton, d. Mar. 6, 1858, Lockport, Ill.
Esther Rudd, d. Sept. 27, 1865.
Abner Freeman Corey, d. Jan. 19-1899, Storm L. Ia.
Sarah Marilla Sutton, d. 1891.
Milo Franklin Corey, d. Dec. 12, 1918, Lincoln N.
Malvina McKee Corey, d. Dec. 17th, 1936.
William B. Price, d. Aug. 19th, 1935.
Bertha Corey, d. Dec. 1876, Dyersville, Iowa.
Clyde Edwin Eiseley, d. Mar. 30th, 1928. Nebr.

5
Milo Franklin Corey. Loren's maternal grandfather, whose marriage certificate appears in the family Bible, was a carpenter in Dyersville, Iowa. The poem entitled "The Birdhouse" in *The Innocent Assassins* is dedicated to him ("For M.C., 1840–1918") and tells of an elaborate Victorian home for birds to nest in that he built for Loren's birthday. The boy and his fiery grandfather hated each other, except that once, when the birdhouse united them.

6 *Malvina McKee Corey.* Grandmother Corey was a visionary and a chronicler, patterns of behavior which can be clearly identified in Loren. When he went away to graduate school, she cared for his aquaria, and this brightened her final years. He expressed affection for her in *The Night Country,* where on an opening page he wrote: "In memory of my grandmother, Malvina McKee Corey, 1850–1936, who sleeps as all my people sleep by the ways of the westward crossing."

7–9 *Daisy and Grace Corey and the Corey home.* Daisy was Milo Corey's younger daughter and Grace's sister. She married Clyde Eiseley on November 10, 1906. As girls, the sisters lived in this trim house — befitting the daughters of a master carpenter — in Dyersville. The difference between the two girls — their care of things, perhaps their lives — was apparent to Loren in the contrast between a beautiful silver-backed hand mirror he found among his aunt's effects when she died and his mother's twin mirror, which was scarred by impetuous force and whose handle had been snapped off.

10–11 *Clyde Edwin Eiseley.* Clyde Eiseley, Loren's father, was the son of Charles Frederick Eiseley, and the photograph of him at the counter was taken in C. F. Eiseley's "Hardware and Stoves" store in Anoka, Nebraska. Photographs of Loren's paternal grandparents were not included in the "Family Box" discovered in the closet off his study. The triumphs of his paternal grandfather were recorded in the dedication of the author's autobiography, *All the Strange Hours:* "cavalryman in the Grand Army of the Republic, member of the first legislature in Nebraska Territory."

12–14 *Anoka, Nebraska.* A bird's-eye view of Anoka and a view of Main Street and the railroad station reveal what many midwestern towns looked like in the early twentieth century. In the late summer of 1907, it was in such a town that Loren came into the world.

15
Loren Corey Eiseley, 1908. Loren was the offspring of a second marriage. Clyde Eiseley had been married earlier and had a son, Leo, fourteen years older than Daisy's child. Leo was the product of his father's youth, of a first love who had died young. Loren was born into an unfortunate marriage when his father was forty and his mother was thirty-two.

16   *Loren, about age three.* The solitary child loved books and could read before he entered kindergarten. When he was five, his half-brother began to read *Robinson Crusoe* to him, and he hung upon every word. Leo left home before finishing the story, but, with the aid of a dictionary, Loren mastered the book on his own. His father always encouraged him to read, thinking the books would lead his son to someplace unknown.

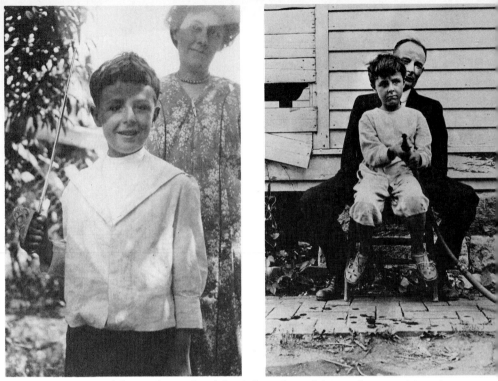

17–18 *Loren with his mother and with his father.* Through his mother, a prairie artist whose pictures hung in old saloons, Loren was given an appreciation of the beauties of the natural world. Through the resonant speaking voice of his father, a onetime itinerant actor, he was early exposed to the magic of poetry. At age six, as shown with his father, this creative child wrote his first book, *Animal Aventures* (sic).

19 *Clyde and Daisy Eiseley (front center), Omaha, Nebraska, 1914.* Daisy lost her hearing as a young girl and was stone-deaf. She was also neurotic, if not psychotic. The "mad Shepards," whose blood Loren carried and about whom he wrote, were his mother's ancestors. What had attracted Clyde to Daisy, Loren never knew, but he grew up insecure in a troubled household.

20–21

Loren, age fifteen or sixteen. These photographs were taken in the early 1920s, when Loren, delighted with nature, was writing such essays as "Whiskers." He looked like the all-American boy at this point in his life, particularly in the picture of him standing in front of his uncle's electric car.

22 *William Buchanan Price.* Grace Corey married W. B. Price, a member of the
legal profession, in 1891. It was "Uncle Buck" who helped to pay his neph-
ew's way through college — aid but for which Loren's life would have been
vastly different. Born in the ruins of the Confederacy, his uncle, who entered
politics, was finally to lie in state in the Capitol Rotunda of Nebraska.

23   *Lowry Charles Wimberly*. The editor of *The Prairie Schooner* took a personal interest in Loren's writing. The magazine was an outlet for literary work at the University of Nebraska, and a number of Loren's early poems and essays were published in it. The student and the teacher had many wonderful conversations about writing, and their friendship extended over the years, ending only upon Wimberly's death.

24 *View of an old train, Scotts Bluff, Nebraska.* During the Great Depression,
Loren left school for a time and became a drifter, riding the rails with the
unemployed and living in hobo camps — experiences he wrote about at the
beginning of his literary career and later in his autobiography.

25–27 *Fossil collecting in the Badlands.* Loren served several seasons with collecting parties of the University of Nebraska State Museum. Photographs on these expeditions show him standing in front of a tent, holding a harmless snake (the tense look is due to a fly trying to enter his mouth), and posing with a few of the huge bones which were found.

28 *C. Bertrand Schultz.* Schultz, a fellow student in geology and anthropology, later became field director and then director of the Nebraska State Museum. Loren acknowledged their friendship in the dedication of *The Innocent Assassins:* "To the bone hunters of the old South Party, Morrill Expeditions 1931–1933, and to C. Bertrand Schultz, my comrade of those years, this book in memory of the unreturning days." The two men remained close friends, and Schultz was one of the speakers to honor Loren at his memorial service.

29 *William Duncan Strong and his first wife, Jean.* Dr. Strong, a great teacher and archaeologist, lured Loren into majoring in anthropology. In 1933, after a number of serious interruptions in his student career, Loren finally obtained his A.B. from the University of Nebraska.

30 *Loren, 1933.* This photograph was taken in Lincoln, Nebraska, the year
Loren came east to graduate school at the University of Pennsylvania in Philadelphia.

31 *Frank G. Speck*. Head of the Department of Anthropology at the University of Pennsylvania, Frank Speck was the personal magician of Loren's youth, the man who set the final seal upon his character. Speck was reared by an Indian and in the profoundest sense lived in the past, with the wood people of the northern forests. Loren's mind was to be similarly taken; he was to vanish into the ice-girt world of our Paleolithic forebears.

32 *Loren, International House, Philadelphia, 1937.* Finishing his doctorate in 1937, Loren went west to teach at the University of Kansas (Lawrence). There his interest in writing for a broader audience than that of specialized journals was rekindled when he was asked to undertake some articles for *Scientific American.*

33-34 *Mabel Langdon and Mabel and Loren on an expedition site.* Mabel married Loren in Albuquerque, New Mexico (although the Corey family Bible says Lincoln, Nebraska), on August 29, 1938. She was a graduate of the University of Nebraska and curator of the fine arts department at the university. The two were perfect teammates, and Loren's writings were made greater by their companionship.

35 *Grace Price and Daisy Eiseley.* Because of his mother, Loren died childless: he would not risk extending the "mad Shepard" line and marked its last appearance on earth. His mother, on the right, whose beautiful features were ravaged by time and violence, and his widowed aunt lived together in the latter part of their lives.

36 *Leo and Loren Eiseley, 1958.* At the time of this meeting on the University of
Pennsylvania campus, Leo was sixty-four and Loren fifty. The professor had
been inspired when his half-brother had begun to read him *Robinson Crusoe*
as a child, and now he himself was the author of books, including *The Immense Journey,* which had been published to wide acclaim the year before.

37 *Caroline Werkley and Loren.* Caroline, a research librarian, was Loren's loyal
assistant at the University of Pennsylvania for many years. His last book of
verse, *Another Kind of Autumn,* was dedicated to her and her family. It was
Caroline who dismantled Loren's notebooks after he died and then helped to
put them back together again.

38 *Loren, Wynnewood, Pennsylvania, 1966.* Loren was a man of opposites. He
was a scientist, but he believed that intuitive, nonscientific insight was valid.
He coveted isolation and privacy, but by writing *The Immense Journey* he
renounced his privacy and became world famous. Moreover, he revealed himself so completely in his books that readers knew him perhaps better than their
own friends. Chairman of the Department of Anthropology, he was the most
gifted writer at the University of Pennsylvania, and although he was certain of
the merits of his writing, he was vulnerable to criticism. His dignified and at
times austere presence gave little hint of the man who liked to tap-dance as his
wife, a fine jazz pianist, accompanied him. In his quest for security, he showed
a strong liking for money, but he understood the professional tramp. His life
was one of contradiction, as lives of emotional hollowness and disconnection
in childhood often are.

39 *Loren, 1971*. Loren suffered from chronic insomnia — a painful affliction from his troubled past — which secured him, at considerable cost, a little extra time to write in the depth of night. When he did sleep, he dreamed excessively. This photograph appeared appropriately on the jacket of *The Night Country*.

40 *Loren, University of Pennsylvania campus.* The last two of the many distinguished awards Loren won demonstrate the wide range of his impact on our society and its culture: the 1976 Bradford Washburn Award of the Museum of Science in Boston for "outstanding contribution toward public understanding of science" and the Joseph Wood Krutch Medal of the Humane Society of the United States as "the humanitarian of the year" in 1976. Loren was a modest person, and most of his colleagues did not know that he had received thirty-six honorary degrees over a period of less than twenty years. He was the most honored member of the University of Pennsylvania since Benjamin Franklin himself.

tions resulted in "The Thing in the Vats," an unfinished story with an intriguing beginning found among his papers.

In 1944, he was offered a good post at Oberlin College in Ohio, where he spent three years as a professor of anthropology and head of the department. At this time, he started to use scientific material in a different way, trying to arouse the interest of the general reader in subjects that fascinated him. The problem was to make the knowledge upon which the article was based accessible and significant. Personal observations and speculations might lure the reader into a field of interest not inspected before and illuminate the material for him, while in no way replacing or obscuring facts. Frederick Lewis Allen and John Fischer of *Harper's Magazine* took a warm and honest interest in his articles, accepting the first that he submitted, "The Long Ago Man of the Future" (1947). Next the editors bought "The Obituary of a Bone Hunter" (1947), a light treatment of the author's own frustrations in the search for early man in America. In spite of being based upon real experiences, the essay gave an opportunity for a more story-like approach than had been possible before. It has been reprinted many times.

For his compositions, the eighteenth-century composer Wolfgang Amadeus Mozart delved into what he referred to as his "bag of memories." Once on paper, he said, the musical product rarely differed from what it was in his imagination. During his youth, Loren's notebooks were also largely not of the paper variety. They were notebooks of the mind — experiences recorded in the folds of his brain for future use which often emerged in finished form.

❧ ❦

THE CUNNING FOX

One day a man was watching some wild ducks on a pond. When a branch of a tree floated among them.

They all took flight at once.

They soon came back however. Then another branch floated down.

This was repeated till about five branches had floated down, till at last the ducks were no longer afraid.

The man wondered who was sending down all the branches. He looked up the pond and saw a fox.

When the fox saw they were no longer afraid he took a larger branch and got upon it. Then he let it float to where the ducks were. Then he seized one and pulled it up to the branch where he was.

Then he guided the branch to the shore where he ate the duck.

WHISKERS

He appeared out of nowhere one cold winter morning and crouched whimpering by our door. He appeared to think it settled that it was our duty to care for him and that we would do so.

My folks were by no means as sure of it but the entreaties of a boy just the age when pets and the big outdoors were the chief interests of his life, and the satisfied appearance of the half-grown pup convinced them.

If ever a name was appropriate, his certainly was. In general appearance he was Airedale, but another strain was evident in the shape of his head and he soon grew larger than any of that breed. He had the roughest and largest amount of whiskers I have ever seen on a dog and this, combined with his grizzled and long-jawed head, gave him a pugnacious, "hardboiled" look that one was inclined to believe until you saw the mischievous, humorous light in the brown eyes.

As he grew older he became a restless wandering creature, on the move from morn till night. Tricks he never had the patience to learn with the exception of shaking hands and even then he had his own opinion as to whom he wished to perform this rite with.

He wandered in the country a great deal for I was just conceiving a passion for Zoology and he seemed the only companion who understood. It has been, especially Entomology, my favorite study ever since, but I have never experienced quite the old thrill at a new discovery that I did those few short years ago when I first wondered at the crawling, myriad life of pond and field and forest.

Running a rabbit through a field one day he was set upon by the dogs of a neighboring farmer. Whiskers had a reputation as a scrapper but he couldn't handle both of them at once and they finished him.

I felt lost for a time without him but I remembered what the big folks said about heaven and was content until I learned that church people didn't seem to think animals went to heaven. I was terribly hurt at this and I don't believe I've ever had as good an opinion of God's judgment since.

Loren Eiseley
English V
Nov. 27, 1923
Miss Wyman
Roll no. 39

I like the informal air of this — a reminiscence in a humorous vein. It is better than your other paper. — Miss Wyman

⋇ ⋇

AUTUMN — A MEMORY

> There is a voice that speaks to men through the
> rose and yellow of dying autumn leaves . . .

I remember stillness and the faint flutter of red and golden leaves down long dim shafts of sunlight through the trees.

I asked a cowpuncher lounging in the shade where to find the Aztec ruins.

"Up the road and across the river. But the place'll be closed now," he cogitated.

I went, hoping he was mistaken. He wasn't, but there was no one around. I stole a hasty glance about and climbed over the fence.

The round stone pits of the kiva were deserted and the walls were crumbling. It is a lonely thing to look on men's

broken handiwork and muse wide-eyed over their disappearance . . . Still, perhaps it was their dust that floated in a slight
breeze over the ruined wall . . .

Red and sombre, with many lights on purple stone the
afternoon was fading.

The place was weird with stillness in which one caught
oneself straining to catch the undernote of long-dead activity,
of something that lingered, that would linger till the last stone
had fallen, something that would not go away.

One listened as at the edge of a void through which no
sound might penetrate. And yet one listened oddly sure — as
though a voice *were* there that could not pierce the blackness . . . One wondered . . .

There were visions of the laboring copper bodies that built
this place under the blazing sun. Was the land so grim then?
From where did they come — and why — and what fate
overtook them?

Did they die fiercely, breast to breast and knife to thong
and stone? (The twilight air was peaceful.)

There were generations, there were brave little friendships,
hatred and feasts and there was love . . . A coyote laughed till
the stone-piled gullies rang . . .

There may have come a time when the offended god turned
his face away, when prayers and the gay-colored prayer
stones and the holy medicine lost power and men died in
gasping heaps . . . Or maybe the harvests burned. Did any live
to go . . . ?

A star burned with a steady silver flame. I was a shadow
among shadows brooding over the fate of other shadows that
I alone strove to summon up out of the all-pervading dusk.

They had built, stone upon heavy stone. Women and men
and children — children and women and men . . . To the
great watching god men's faces pass as a blur . . .

Starlight and dust in starlight. . . . Does it matter now at
all . . . ?

≽ ≼

WASTE SONG

I am the song out of the wasted ground,
The bitter plaint heard at the acre's edge
From secretive small folk of stone and sedge

The careless farmer spurns upon his round.
My voice is banned from every fire and hearth;
I cry a thirst amid the ripening grain.
The proud and opulent ignore in vain —
I draw a secret honey from the earth.

It does not matter if my stricken mouth
Companions the blind mole beneath the hill.
This thin, elusive song will grow until
Each rut and thorn and roadside thicket yields
My voice — the dry grasshopper singing drouth
While spring yet riots in a hundred fields.

A TROPICAL SWAMP AT MIDNIGHT

Here is the uncertain realm
Of things that feed on death,
Of bulbous, luminescent shapes
A-writhe in stagnant death.

An unseen scum
Crawls on the trembling water.
A phosphorescent spider in a circle
Of green light drops and hangs
Swaying . . .
In the dead air.
Beetles spotted
With glowing scarlet eyes
Crawl in the rotting mold.

A green uncertain glow wavers eternally
Green phosphor flames
Nod prettily and blossom wide
On sucking, bloated mud . . .
Green phantom flowers of light
Drift on the black water

And fade . . .
Fade . . .
Far back
In the endless caverns
Of cypress . . .
And darkness . . .
And death.

So, on the trembling morass of consciousness
Float the pale
Flowers of remembrance
Until the brilliance fades to green . . .
The green to blue . . .
And they sputter . . .
And go

Out. . . .

꙳ ꙳

OLD WHARF AT MIDNIGHT

Under
All decay sounds
The restless monotone
Of the sea at midnight creeping beneath
Old piers.

꙳ ꙳

NIGHT SNOW

Nothing
Is lonelier
Than snowflakes at midnight
Drifting out of the dark above the
Streetlamps.

꙳ ꙳

THE DARK READER

*Old moons
these nights and years,
and moss on broken stones . . .
Who stoops by glow-worm lamps to read
your name?*

❧ ❦

THE DESERTED HOMESTEAD

*The wind is desolate in the fields;
And round the house at night
The autumn smoulder of decay
Creeps like a blight.*

*His standing corn with mildew rusts
Forsaken on the hill.
The wild will cover up the road
Now his hands are still.*

*Only a sparrow, like a leaf,
Skips along the eaves,
Half-lonely for a human voice
In the hush of leaves.*

*This ending that is old as earth
Sorrow cannot break.
Our doors are opened to the wind,
And the wind will take.*

*The jeweled phrase is worthless here.
The blackbird and the crow,
Bleak criers over windswept land,
Alone may sow*

*Dark syllables across the wind;
Or, in the ruined field,
Deride the hackneyed misery —
Earth's only yield.*

❧ ❦

TO HENRI FABRE

He loved earth's creatures and their curious codes,
Made friends with ants, disturbed the privacies
Of slow pink worms that delicately squeeze
Through sunless labyrinths to their abodes;
The shy and friendly hopping of brown toads
Beneath the cabbage leaf, if on his knees,
He came to call on them, would always please
His heart that warmed to such small episodes.
He had no strength to earn adventurous bread
In grinding cities. In brief fields was set
His small horizon, and when friends had said,
"There is so much you've missed," Ah, did he sigh —
Or think how on a summer road he met
Among the thistles, a great glittering fly?

BLEAK UPLAND

UPLAND HARVEST

The upland has a bitter yield,
The puffball spurts a smoky dust
Where slowly down the weed-grown field
The autumn spreads a golden rust,
And frost the sterile reckoning.
Men have but little from their creed
Who plant — to see the harvest bring
Scant sowing of the ragged weed . . .
While stealthily, with secret mirth,
From under frosty ticking leaves
And stony emptiness of earth,
The rasping of the cricket weaves
A web to catch, without a sound
The prayers of men for fertile ground.

WORDS TO THE STOIC

This ploughland darkening under rain,
Exposing to the eyes of crows

The utter dearth in its domain,
Has finished with the season's woes.

Unlike ourselves Earth does not hide
Its wounds beneath a tinseled spring.
The cawing voices that deride
Expect from it no answering.

Earth does not keep compressed within,
Old pains that should be cried aloud.
It does not make pretense to win
While snow is weaving it a shroud.

When I no longer fear to break
This stubborn silence, nor to wear
Heart's misery in my face, or take
Full easement on the common air.

Then I from grief too long concealed
By guile and the dissembling word
Shall rest — as starkly as this field
Abandoned to the crying bird.

ک ک

AGAINST CITIES

I have envied the hawk's breast
enduring the great heaven;
all wild wings and the stubbornness of rock yielding
no foothold but to eagles.
The serenity of stars over chaos
is worthy remembrance
and the peace of an old planet
forgetting the troubled footsteps of men . . .
I have envied
even, at times,
the stony security of a snail
locked in his narrow house.

But I have pondered and not understood
earth that endures spoiled cities
in preference to white deserts and the stars.

ک ک

THE THUNDER BEAST

The thunder beast,
the dinosaur,
is almost gone,
in fact, is far

and only lives
beneath this stone
in miniature
because a lone

horned toad chose it
as a place
to flee from all
the human race.

The thunder beast
looks from his eye
but he has shrunk
and we grown high.

The ups and downs,
the outs and ins
of time and nature,
scales and fins

have made him wise
and warier than
the latest thunder-hurler —
man.

DEATH SONG FOR TWO

Villon died in a ditch at last,
  Marlowe by a dagger
Bought for sixpence in some shop —
  Neither was a lagger

Coming home to that last inn.
  Neither had a penny
Left of what flesh had to spend —
  Neither wanted any.

They could have as strait a bed
    And as dark a pillow
With as much rain overhead
    As the richest fellow

Laid out in his silk and lace
    For the worm's blind pleasure.
Villon kissed earth's muddy cheek;
    Marlowe saw the treasure

Of the red mind blaze and go,
    Leaned and took that lover
Who will have you without sheet
    And the wind for cover.

LIZARD'S EYE

The dust devils spinning in the alkaline basins of drouth
                                        north of Mojave,
and the desert Joshua's curious pleasure in thorns
are a pillow of comfort after a wasted lifetime.

I could come back here and be content with my friends the
                                        lizards
to burn in the lime-glare, and have fierce, wild thoughts like
                                        an animal
nor much remember
your face, nor the tossed black head of you,
nor security's penny, nor the lie which has left

you beautiful, me, ash and blown fire.
Not the staired agony, pain, nor the casual whore at the
                                        street corner,
nor the whirled emptiness of death
looked into
roils peace when one's grown accustomed to burning
and seen life with the lizard's eye
not blinded by sun.

RETURN TO A HOUSE

To come into this house where none may grow,
Save crookedly by malice from within,
To sit again at table with the thin
And starveling brothers of my name, to know
On this side madness, on the other slow
And groveling cowardice no wrathful sin
Could ever question, is iron discipline —
I grant you that. Now let the midnight blow.
Call up the circle of the darker hells.
I, in the midmost and most fiery pit,
Outstare these damned, eat fire, know well what pain
Knifes the frail heart . . . yet calmly, calmly sit
And read from each what his dread gesture tells,
Smile in mad eyes and fancy I am sane.

       ⇗ ⇖

Think you adventurous dust can learn
Because of death to straightway turn
Itself into some nodding flower
Resigned to careless winds an hour?
Not I! I'll crawl, I'll slay the bold
Bright cricket in his house of mold.
My elements will fuse, my lust
Drive still unmastered through the dust.

So let the golden crocus be —
Burn in blue air for all to see.
But you who seek me still must stray
Down some strange dark, unlanterned way
Where feast by crawling fungus light
The secret beetles of the night.

       ⇗ ⇖

A ROAD NIGHT '23

Mist in the autumn night . . . dim ways of dusk are
calling . . .

. . . . . .

Two hundred miles away the home lights beckon through
the cold . . .

. . . . . .

The moon across the bare, bleak upland ranges is like a
skull gone very old and grey . . .

. . . . . .

Far up ahead the engine mutters, labors on . . .
Love has gone far beyond all homeless wandering, still one
with Beauty that does not abide . . .
The slow freight crawls like time . . .
The chill bites deeper till we pace the car . . .
Somewhere roaring down the divide behind us the Chicago
flyer hurtles through the night.
She waters at B——— according to a bedraggled timetable.
If we make her and can hold her down we'll be home before
daylight.
Our freight stops at B———. We leave her and wait for the
flyer . . . shivering. We must not miss her . . . our last chance.
An hour crawls by. The express is waiting at the trackside
. . . men look at their watches.
The yard lights glimmer through the rain. A long-drawn
whistle through the night . . . a rush of wheels . . . the hiss of
steam.
We hurry up an alley between freight cars parallel with the
flyer. Someone approaches . . . We slink into the concealing
shadow.
Across from us we hear the hoarse, easy panting of a resting locomotive.
Someone else . . . We crawl beneath a freight car. We hear
the engine move away up the yards.
Oh Christ, have we lost her?
A hasty glance reassures us. She's just gone up for coal or
water.
We lay flat on our stomachs beneath the cars. God! if they
switch these empties now . . .
The engine returns — backing. Recoupled. The minutes
crawl.

She breathes faster. The fireman flings open the firebox door and feeds her. Do they see us?

A hail! She starts. We roll from beneath our hiding place, run with the first blind. A breathless scramble in the dark.

A whisper "Deck 'er." The door is open. "Hang on! She's gonna go like hell!"

Yard limit. She begins to hammer through the night on the winds of storm.

Lightning sprawls white fingers on the sky.

We lay flat, facing forward in the dark, lips and eyelids tense to the beat of rain and cinders. The miles fly from under our feet.

"Oh Lords of Death! We ride! We ride!"

"Damn it, we're jerked," hissed one. A spotlight cut through the dark, blinding them. A volley of questions left them silent save for a few mumbled answers.

"When did you guys get in? What the hell are you doin'? By God, do ya think ya can grab a mail train right in front of the yard office in this town and get away with it?

"Hit the highway and hit it quick!"

"Shut up." This to a half-worded protest of a youthful hobo who disliked being driven forth on a desert road in the dead of night with forty miles between Y———— and the next town that even half deserved the name.

"If I catch you around this town again I'll lock you up."

The locomotive bell broke forth in hastened mournful tones. "A-l-l ab-o-a-rd." The hail came faintly down the track.

≽ ≼

RIDING THE PEDDLERS

If you are young and there is speed in your blood you begin as a passenger stiff. In the jungles you study timetables, speak familiarity as a plutocrat of the Golden State Limited, and carve speed records on watertanks a thousand miles apart. If you ride a freight it must be a hot-shot or a manifest. It does not matter that there is no place for you to go and only yard bulls to greet you upon your arrival. Going is the business of your class, and as a young novitiate you grit your teeth on the decks of passengers hurtling through mile-long tunnels

and strive to equal the time records of paid fares. Later, after sundry encounters with the railroad detectives who lurk with vigilance about such trains, and after hearing from companions tales of this or that tramp who left his anatomy strewn along the right-of-way, you experience a tremor of doubt. You notice that the older and still healthy members of the profession show no great concern in this matter of speed; in fact, many of them can be found aboard the peddlers.

When this fact was first brought home to me I considered it, with the usual cockiness of youth, to be a loss of nerve due to advancing age. I pitied these elderly stiffs and was moved to sighs over the most forlorn object of all — the bindle stiff who had abandoned the trains for the road. But my conversion was soon to come. It chanced that most of my hoboing career up to that time had been carried on along the main trunk lines where fast trains were plentiful; hence there had been no reason to patronize the slow freights making all the little local stops. These trains we referred to scornfully as "peddlers."

I was making fast time down through the middle states one autumn when the news spread that some hoboes had murdered a Union Pacific yard bull and tossed his body from a moving train near a town some fifty miles ahead of us. The police were arresting every vagrant in sight, and since the town had an evil reputation among the brotherhood in the best of times, I had no desire to pass through it at that moment. But also I had no desire to walk. Something had to be done — and quickly. In another ten minutes we would be pulling out. At this moment my eyes chanced to fall upon a Burlington timetable in the hands of another vagrant.

"Say, Jack, can I see that?" I asked.

"Sure." He passed it over.

I turned hastily to a map of the system. The gods, it began to appear, were with me. The map showed a side fork of the Burlington angling up from their main line into the very town where we now sat. So far so good. But how often did the trains run? I had no intention of sitting in that town a week waiting for enough freight to accumulate to make a train. I stood up on our boxcar and glanced about. There was a spur running off to the south that must be the branch in question. A few coal cars rested on a siding. As far as I could see, cornfields wavered to the south. My heart sank.

I climbed off and pursued our braky, who had gone past a couple of minutes before on his way toward the head of the train. A dozen cars away I overtook him. Yes, there was a spur here. No, he didn't know when the trains ran. "You'd better go down to their depot and ask," he said. "That little yellow building way down there is it." I looked. It was a good mile beyond the end of our train. That meant about two miles altogether. If there was no train, I would never make it back before this one had gone. I set out in a stumbling run down the tracks, accompanied by another bum of the same mind.

When we had passed our caboose, more track came in sight. From behind the little depot came an engine about as big and just as busy as an overgrown tumblebug, pushing a couple of cars. Our hopes soared. They might be making up a train. We vaulted a U.P. fence, thumbed a mental nose at their No Trespassing signs, and dashed into the Burlington yard office.

"Who's in charge here?" asked my companion with the air of an official inspector. I grew conscious of our rags and waited to be thrown out.

"I am," said a pugnacious-looking individual. "Whatta yuh want?"

"Is that a freight making up out there?"

"Yep."

"When does she pull out?"

"In about thirty minutes, boys," said the yard master, grinning.

"Imagine pulling a stunt like that on the main line," I said with a sigh of relief as we escaped into the outer air. "Let's go eat. The engineer's eating his lunch."

"Hamburger — but for God's sake hurry it," I pleaded with the waitress. "Five times on this trip I've ordered hamburger and smelled it cooking and then had to leave it and run for a train."

We chafed impatiently at the counter, one eye cocked on the train. Sure enough, as soon as the hamburgers were half cooked, the engine bell set up a clamor. We tore them smoking from the hands of the waitress and fled away across the tracks. Dangling our feet from a side-door pullman, we waited for the train to pull out. Nothing happened. One or two idlers rolled over in the grass of the square. We ate our sandwiches in melancholy silence. Thirty minutes later the train pulled out.

We rattled away over a dozen little bridges and across innumerable fields. Some of them were wild, with coarse grass springing up around the old glacial boulders. A few rabbits loped along unhurriedly. We stopped at sleepy little towns, and people who chanced to pass talked idly with us. One of the train crew suggested a more comfortable car. It wasn't long until we realized that we had stepped, momentarily, at least, out of a world of class hatred and struggle. It was what I had imagined the West of the old days to be.

It was not that these people had not lived elsewhere — many of them — or that they had not partaken of the struggle. But here along this little backwater, it did not matter. There were not enough of us to count. So there was time for us to speak drowsily and courteously to each other. Room for the prairie grass to grow between the stones, for the rabbits to hop less furtively. We knew how the latter felt. We too had hopped, skipped, and run through the city jungle in fear of the fist and the blackjack. Here we thrust out tentacles of friendliness again from under a hardened armor of toughness and cynicism. Released from fear, our small horizon expanded to take in the curving brown back of the train and ourselves as personalities.

"Y'know, Jack," said my companion, who never in a thousand miles had vouchsafed a word about himself, "I like this. I was born in Indiana on a farm. I never seen a train till I was sixteen. Funny, for a bum."

"Yeah," I said. "I've been in Indiana. The hills are swell."

"Say, have you?" He warmed visibly. "We used to have a spring back of the house. Colder than ice. My old man used to cool the raisin wine in it. And in the fall things were swell." He groped for words. "You know, the leaves and everything. I might be there yet, but I went to live with an uncle. He had a big voice and all he did was work and go to church and beller to God because his crops weren't good enough.

"There was an atheist fellow lived down the road aways. He was a nice fellow but he always had good crops. My uncle couldn't stand it. He'd complain to God on Sundays. I hated it. You know. It was sort of like bein' a tattle-tale in school. And when the atheist took sick one summer and didn't get well I sorta blamed Uncle Carl. I was just a kid and I liked that fellow. I sorta felt if Uncle Carl hadn't kept shootin' his mouth off that way God wouldn't a noticed.

"The railroad ran through one of Uncle Carl's pastures and I'd been used to watchin' it. I used to see the 'boes ridin' and wonder about 'em. You know? Like a kid will. Where they're goin' and what they'll be seein' and all? Well, right after this happened I was down in the pasture tendin' the cows and thinkin' about Jake — he was the atheist — and rememberin' how nice he'd been to me — showin' me pictures out of books of city things an' all — when along comes a freight, slow like this, and she stops right in the pasture account of somethin' bein' wrong.

"They was some 'boes on her and one of 'em gets off and comes down and asks me for a drink. I took him up to the house, askin' him questions all the time. He answers me. You know, like we string these kids along? Adventure and all that. Well, everything woulda still been all right, but Uncle Carl was at the house with a bender on. He musta been feelin' proud at cookin' Jake's goose. Made him feel sorta like the Lord's appointed. Anyway he starts tellin' this 'bo that by the sweat of your brow you had to earn your drink and bread. He goes on like that awhile and then says no, he can't have any drink.

"I can still see that 'bo, a sorta tired-lookin' fellow. He don't say anything. He just sort of sinks into himself and walks quiet down into the pasture again. Not like he's afraid, but just tired from it happenin' so many times. Like he's sick of hearin' words. I never said a thing to Uncle Carl. I don't think he even noticed me. But you know how kids are. I 'spose you ran away from home, too, sometime. All sick and

twisted inside. Yeah. That's the way I felt. I caught up with
that fellow down in the pasture. 'I'm old enough,' I said. 'I'm
goin' too.'

" 'All right, kid,' he says. Not coaxin'-like, but just as
though it had to be done. If he'd coaxed, I wouldn't have
gone, but that's the way I felt too — like it had to be done. I
was scared, but it had to be done. Like a sort of justice or
somethin'. Like savin' yourself from bein' damned."

His face looked proud for a moment under the hard lines
and the dirt. "I never went back," he said.

I sat silent. There was nothing to say. Here was the end of
his forlorn odyssey and revolt. In less than a hundred miles
the freight wilderness had separated us. In many thousand
miles I never saw his face again.

II

Months later in a little town below the Sierras I missed the
last passenger. I missed the manifest that followed it. There
was nothing left but a peddler. It was a long train laboring
forward under the combined efforts of three engines. Bums
sat along the roof in scores. It was a question whether one
could make faster time riding or walking beside it. I chose to
ride.

We ran for miles through the fierce heat of the Sacramento
Valley. The drowsy clicking of the wheels lulled me to sleep.
Later there were tunnels. Toward evening I awoke.

Sleepily, and then with surprise, I glanced back along the
car roofs. The scene that presented itself might have been
some modern evangelist's dream of the last train arriving in
Paradise. There were dreary faces, mad faces, happy faces,
evil faces. The wise alone were not with us. It was just as

well. They would have been as much interlopers as the snake in Eden. Through the slow, beautiful sunset along the mountain the train labored grotesquely. On either side great orchards stood at harvest. Everywhere hungry men were climbing down from the cars and squeezing through fences. Men already in the trees shook frantically. Apples rained down and found their way into hats and ragged pockets. Their owners ran and swung aboard the train. This process continued for miles along the grade.

Someone squatting on the roof beside me hummed a stanza of "The Big Rock Candy Mountains":

> *"Oh, the railroad bulls they all are blind*
> *In the Big Rock Candy Mountains."*

The Limited might be due in Reno, but one of her passengers was not. I was aboard a peddler and no one expects the peddlers. They come when they arrive. In that hour, in the late sun with the pine scent of evening already in the air, it was not possible that we were crawling toward the high Sierras and the deserts of Utah. No. We had slipped tunnel-like through time. We had taken a phantom track into the hazy country — the Big Rock Candy Mountains — the restful haven of all bums. Stretched on the car roof I thought, fleetingly, of "Indiana." I wished he had made this train. They would wait for us in vain in Reno.

⤳ ⤶

Black lava and the green light on the high timber,
thin grass standing stiff as vines through the howling
　　　　　　　　　　　　　　　　　　northers —
I hated these when younger, cursed the sand flies,
and when the slow spokes of wagon wheels
rolled off up the red draw for Montoya, my heart
died a little for not going. It is different now.

I am young still, say twenty-seven, strong, too, and
have been places, tasted the iron in wild springs
south of Chihuahua and, even, once
heard the roar of Broadway and the cries on Market Street.
You may think it strange I am not restless,

content here with a horse and rifle and the little stone
cabin up yonder that someone built and left.
Not married, no, and the May night covered with mist
and the cattle bawling in the valley and the house
wet as sea-stone and no light for the fence riders.
Odd, you think?
Listen. It is all in the point of view.

❧ ❧

THE MOP TO K.C.

I stole an overcoat and caught the K.C. drag at the crossing. I had a thousand miles to go, and there was already frost in the fields. I thought I'd be the last 'bo left in that country. Worse yet, there wasn't an empty in sight. But a gondola came by with a couple of heads watching me. I'd have company anyhow. So I climbed in. There were three 'boes huddled in some straw in the forward end and a little guy all black with coal dust standing looking at me.

"Hello, kid," I said. "Headin' south? We got the snow right on our tail."

"We sure have." He had a voice with a girlish quaver in it, and every now and then he shook like a leaf.

It wasn't much to wonder at. He had on a pair of overalls, and an old suit coat pinned around his neck with a safety pin. And that was all he had, too, except the shoes he stood in.

The Mop to K.C. is a rough road. We began to bounce like hell. I was glad of it. It shook all the shivers out of you and you hung on to your guts and the effort made you feel warmer.

"I been riding passengers all the way from Rochester," the kid yelled between whistle blasts. I sat down and he sat beside me. "Do you think we could catch another passenger?"

It was funny sitting there listening to him talk about passengers in that girlish voice. Every now and then it would sort of rise and break. You know — like the way a guy talks when he's scared. I didn't believe he was that good a stiff. It takes guts to ride passengers.

"You'd better leave 'em alone, kid," I said. "But if you

want to fly there's a manifest through Falls City, and we wait over there for her."

He asked me if I wanted to make it with him. I didn't like this "we" stuff.

"You'll have a better chance alone," I said. "Where ya goin'?"

"Leavenworth."

"Then what the hell's the hurry? You're damn near home."

"Yeah," he said. "That's right. That's right." He kept getting up and looking out of the car till I figured he had the bull horrors. There were hollows under his eyes and he looked sick. He talked sometimes like he was a little off.

Once he went up and talked to the other bums, but I noticed they sort of looked at each other and didn't say much. Pretty soon he was back. I don't know why I didn't give him the air. But there was something in his eyes. I couldn't do it. And he looked so damned miserable sitting there and shaking.

Pretty soon he saw the ring on my hand. "What's that?" he asked me. It was a college ring, but I lied and said it was a high school ring. A guy hasn't got any right to ask you things like that on the road.

His eyes brightened with that funny fever look again, and he said: "Gee, you musta had a swell home to get edjacated like that."

Yeah! That was all right, but not for me. I had a thousand miles to go, and I didn't want to talk about that.

"How's the bulls up north?" I asked him.

He started shivering again. "They're mean. When I was ridin' passengers a couple of 'em stopped right beside the tender, but I laid low, quiet as a mouse, and they went away." He laughed that cracked laugh and looked at me sort of admiringly. "You're big. You're darn near big as a bull. I bet they don't bother you none."

"Listen!" I said. "I'm not fightin' no bulls. I look big 'cause I got on two suits of underwear. See?"

"But the bums is what I'm scared of. I'm scared to get into boxcars with 'em. Don't the wolves ever bother you?"

"Christ, no," I said. But I felt sick inside. He ought never to have been born.

We were easing into a town. "I'm gonna hunt an empty," I said. "It'll be cold as hell by midnight."

I dropped off and went back along the cars watching for a broken seal.

Away down the track I heard him yell, and pretty soon he pattered up. I'd found an empty and was opening it. He helped me push it open, and I climbed in. He stood outside and asked if he could get in. He wouldn't look at me. I didn't want him, but what was a guy to do? The engine kicked and we started. "Get in," I said, and lent him a hand. To make it worse, the door jammed and wouldn't shut.

I tried to sleep, but it was no use; so finally I just lay quiet while it got darker and darker. The kid curled up beside me and went to sleep. Dead tired. He moaned and shivered and once he talked, but I couldn't make it out.

Once I lit a cigarette and looked at him. He was a road kid, all right. The dirt was ground into him until not even an undertaker could get it off. His cap had fallen sideways and a few straggly curls stuck out. Asleep — when he wasn't scared — he had a friendly sort of mouth.

We rolled on to a sidetrack in Falls City. I looked out. Sure enough the manifest was coming in. The engine steamed by. I shook the kid.

"Wake up; here's the manifest." He jumped back from me into a corner. Then he woke up. "I'm not gonna hurt ya. Here's the manifest."

He looked out with me. "You just got time to make her," I said. "Good luck."

"Ain't you coming?" he asked. "No," I said. "I'm going to K.C. I don't want to get in there at midnight and walk the streets to keep warm. But you'll make Leavenworth all right. You live there, don't you?"

"I ain't got no home," he said, that sick tremble coming back to his mouth. "I'm just goin' there. I ain't never had no home."

"I'm sorry, kid," I said. "I thought —" He was running toward the head of the train.

I went back to the corner for a smoke. A thing like that's hard on your sleep. Besides, the little fool'd freeze unless he found an empty reefer. What the hell was he going to do at Leavenworth?

I heard the manifest pull out. By and by they tested our air. It was clear dark now. I could see the lights of the town twinkle up on the hill.

She high-balled just as a head blocked the doorway. Somebody scrambled in. We started to move. Whoever it was blundered toward the corner. I ran into him in the dark.

"Jack! Is it you, Jack?" That voice was unmistakable. I was sore. "S'matter?" I asked. "Did they ditch you?"

"I couldn't make it."

I knew he was lying and he knew I knew it. He didn't answer any more, but shoved something into my hands in the dark. It was a paper sack that sagged like there was meat to it.

"I bummed a house over the tracks," he said.

I'd already got a sandwich into my mouth by that time; so I didn't say any more about the manifest. I shoved the sack at him and struck another light. "Aren't you gonna eat?" I asked.

He was leaning against the wall, and cold as it was, I noticed beads of sweat on his face. His eyes had a funny far-away look. I put the match on the floor, stepped on it, and said, "You'd better eat."

We were running through a bunch of cornfields, and I could see the frost and the cold light on them. I gave the sack another shove.

"No thanks," he said. "I — I don't want anything. I can't eat. There's — there's somethin' wrong with my guts — inside. That's why I went to Rochester. A doc told me I ought to."

He stopped. I could hear him fumbling in the dark, and waited. Pretty soon he handed me something that felt like cardboard. I struck another match.

"It's the doc's report," he explained faintly, from somewhere in the dark.

The match went out. I sat there in the dark, holding the envelope. I didn't read it. I knew already what was in it. I waited as long as I could and then I said, "What did they say?"

"They said I — I'm gonna die." He got it out without his voice breaking, but I knew what it cost him. I could feel him over there in the blackness pressing his hands against the floor.

"I — it's tough," I blundered, but saying it soft, and trying to ease him down. "Didn't they say you could do something — anything?"

"Well, they said quiet and rest 'ud help, and they said a lot of things I didn't understand, but I knew what they meant."

"And they kicked you back out on the road?"

"No." He was almost apologetic. "They was nice. They told me they'd take care of me, but I was afraid. It was all cold and white and bare and I was afraid. It was like the Home. I was in the Home till I was thirteen. I don't know who my folks was. I guess my folks wasn't married. That was the way with most of the kids there. The place they wanted to put me was like the Home. I couldn't stand it — those rows of beds and things. I told 'em I knew somebody at Leavenworth."

"Do you?"

He had snudged over until he was against me. Then he went on more steadily. "I wasn't gonna die in one of those places — all cold and shiny where you're a number or something."

I wanted to get out of that car. I patted his shoulder and said: "Listen, Bud, you shouldn't of done that. They might 'a fixed you up. You shouldn't be doin' that. Do you know somebody at Leavenworth? Shall I take you to a hospital?"

Oh, it was swell, all right, sitting there in the dark, getting colder and colder, with that voice like a sick girl's going on and on in the darkness. And the wheels going faster and faster and that damned hoghead hooting away off over the river like he wanted a clear track to hell.

I hardly knew what he was saying, at first. I just kept willing inside, "Don't let him cry, for Christ's sake, don't let him cry." You can't keep a tension like that. You'd go mad. There wasn't anything I could do. It was all in the cards. I said that to myself and eased down and tried to listen to him.

He didn't cry, either. He just kept leaning against me and babbling. It was doing him good. He kept talking about a long string of places he'd been, and at first I couldn't figure it out. Every bum knows towns from New York to Frisco, but why talk about that? There's the same bulls and the same people in all of them.

First it was Muncie, Indiana.

"I lived in a big box in Muncie for a week," he told me. It was like a kid talking of his playhouse time, like the things a girl might dream about. "I ain't never had a home — I guess I told you that. But I pretty near did in Muncie. This box was on the ends of town, and I was gonna borrow a saw and fix real windows in it. Some bums broke it up for kindling wood." He stopped and thought and then said he guessed it really hadn't mattered, the police wouldn't have let him stay, anyway.

The kid knew every town from New York to Tiajuana. I doubt if he had spent a month in one spot since he left the orphanage.

"And once outside of Sacramento a guy gave me a real cabin. Anyhow he said I could come and live with him. But the other guys didn't like him. A fellow beat him up, and I ran away."

"Yeah," I said. That sort of thing used to make me feel crawly. Now I just felt sort of empty like nothing mattered. I don't believe I'd have blinked if we'd run off a trestle.

"An' once in K.C. — you know the yards in K.C.? — I slept for three days in a cornshock out by Argentine. I was getting to like it. It was pretty, and quiet-like around there, and nobody'd found me out. The next night a mouse scared me and I crawled out, but it was so cold I crawled back in again. I was going to Cal., but I stayed there three days with the mice. The last day I gave them some crumbs from a handout. They was gettin' to know me. Mice ain't so bad when you get to know them. Mostly I'm afraid of them, though. I guess I was lonesome."

He drew a long breath, and I stood up in the dark and took the overcoat off and tossed it over him as he lay shivering.

"You sleep now," I said. "I'll tell you when we get to Leavenworth." I'd have given him my shirt to get him quiet.

"Ya won't leave, will ya, Jack?" he asked me under the coat.

"No," I said.

"Jack —"

"Yeah?"

"I was ridin' passengers 'cause I was lonesome and they

went fast." I waited awhile and pretty soon he said again, half-asleep, " 'Cause they went fast."

Poor devil — running from himself, I suppose. I walked up and down in the other end of the car to keep warm. It was quiet except for the steady roar of the wheels. We were running alongside the Missouri. The driftwood in the moonlight looked sometimes like bodies floating.

Once we passed a hoboes' night camp on the line. They were burning cornstalks and huddling around the fire to keep warm. Every time the fire blazed they bobbed up and down like big shadows. There wasn't another thing alive in the fields.

We made Leavenworth at midnight. The train stops in a sort of cut, with the river on the left and a high bank on the right. Somewhere along that bank is a spring with a pipe in it, and a little jungle at one side. I didn't expect anybody there, it was so late, but sure enough there was a little red blaze way down the tracks. When we got closer, I could see somebody hunched over beside it. I shook the kid and yelled in his ear, "We're comin' in."

He got up, bumped into the wall, then staggered over to the door and almost fell out before I could grab him.

I shook him and pointed over to the fire. "For Christ's sake get over there and warm up."

He started, and then looked at me. "Ain't you comin'?"

"No," I said. "She pulls out in a minute. Do you know anybody here?" I thought maybe he'd answer me this time.

He just stood there stupid a minute, looking at his toes.

"I did."

"Is he here now?"

"I don't know. He had a place down there in the bottoms. I — I worked for him a few weeks. He said for me to come back some winter. I could trap with him, he said. I thought maybe I could fix up a little shack. I've always wanted to."

"What if you don't find him?"

"I don't know. I guess it won't matter much anyhow."

"There's a hospital at the prison," I said, looking the other way. "I don't know much about such things. Maybe they'd take you in, in a pinch."

He didn't say anything. A jerk traveled down the cars and she whistled. I felt sore; I don't know what at.

"You're a damned fool," I said.

He didn't say a word.

I swung into the car and stood and watched from the doorway as we backed up and then went forward. The crouching old man by the fire never moved. The track runs straight for a long way. I watched until there was just a red eye of light in the dark and a little shape jumping and gesticulating like a shadow, to keep warm. And that other shape that never moved. Then we rounded a curve and the light was gone.

❧ ❦

MEANINGLESS VOICES

Water that comes endlessly from the blue mountain lakes
                              unvisited save by deer
and the deer themselves,
bugling faint calls through the aspen thickets in high autumn,
all talk in meaningless voices.

The valley is filled with cricket chirps and leaf whispers
and whatever it is comes crying
on the rain squalls from the northeast.

Even the grasshoppers have been here a long time and click
                                                    songs
without the bright, sinister meanings of
the mountain rattlers, whose voice, like death, is purposeful.

All of these have been here for ages, but later
horns rasp in the valley and the voice of dynamite
splits boulders and the roads come, all purposeful, all strident
                                        with meaning,
while the red-winged blackbirds
fly away to new pools.

Nevertheless the meaningless voices are also significant
in what is past and to come.

❧ ❦

This is the knife
with which to cut
Shakespeare's dream
from the heart of a nut.

A nut as sound
as the heart before
the worm comes in
through the same old door.

Where nothing is
but an intricate spell
a tree exists —
till you cut the shell.

Midnight dreams
and midnight sin
and a walnut shell
to keep them in.

FOOTNOTE TO AUTUMN

Old boulders in the autumn sun and wind,
Settling a little, leaning toward the light
As if to store its summer — these remain
The earth's last gesture in the falling night.

This then is age: It is to have been worked
By the forces of frost and the unloosening sun,
It is to bear such markings fine and proud
As speak of weathers that are long since done.

This wavering world that only fishers know
is alien, yet weed and fin and pool
release a ripple in the blood's own flow.
Some old newt eye at rest here in the cool
depths of the brain's dark waters knows full well
what source we have — from waters under hell.

Some ultimate secret in the milkweed pod,
Some hidden silver water barreled deep
In desert cactus by an idle god —
Even the strange dark wonder of our sleep —
All these possess me. I cannot be still.
In all the variant wonder of my days,
Something seems immanent, some farther hill
Holds a last star — the hill obstructs my gaze.

TO A HOMELAND BIRD SEEN IN A STORM

Sparrowhawk, you wanderer of the checkered
Grainfields of my homeland, its wild meadows and hills,
You are lost in a strange wood. I see you circle
And climb through the rain and dusk.
Beat less scornfully over me, tiny, high-hearted
Adventurer under the storm's wing. Men and their guns
Are no dearer to me than to you.

Fade in the autumn twilight
Going home to the shocked corn and the stubble,
The white houses at evening
And the perch on the roadside fence
But, oh, brother, my heart goes with you.

Sparrowhawk, I am your brother
Though footsore and weary, not wingless,
Having, like you, the hawk's mind,
Having the hawk's mind for home
Through the fierce, untamable air.

⤳ ⤲

THE LOST COUNTRY

If you turned off the highway and continued for five miles by
any one of three roads on which you would instinctively find
yourself expecting to meet oxen instead of Fords, you were in
the Lost Country. The farmers had some more prosaic name,
but I never met the farmers but once and I have never found
the way back since. Cars stalled quite naturally at the foot of
Lost Hill. There was a road over the top that stayed broken,
but you never met anyone. You went up on foot rather quietly with your eyes tensed for Indians. There were limestone
boulders on the hillsides and in the autumn they were spat-
tered with red sumach. When the leaves moved it might be
Indians. You expected one to slip across the road — naked
and brown without noticing you. Following a trail with his
bow and arrow.

Lost Country was like that. It was the farmers who were
shadowy and intangible. It was the Indians who were real. Of
course you never saw them. But you didn't want to really.
They wouldn't have been wild then. Everyone knew wild
Indians were sly. They lived in the woods and no one ever
saw them. But just the same you knew they were there. That
was what made the Lost Country an adventure instead of a
hike or a picnic. One always got out before nightfall. You
had a feeling things might happen after dark.

It was wild country, though tilled after a fashion. Stony
ridges were left to the oak woods and whatever haunted
them. There were great mounds, and sometimes after the rain
you could find chipped flint and arrowheads in the ruts of the
road.

A whole lot of my childhood hours were spent there. I can
remember hurrying along the road with my companions,
anxious to reach the main road before the twilight was gone.
Sometimes there would be blue haze and a sliver of moon

before we got there. There was a great deal of haze in that country. From the top of Lost Hill, legend had it that you could see into the next state. But there was always haze on the horizon as though you looked toward other places from somewhere outside of time. Perhaps that was because it was the Lost Country or only that we were very young.

Years later I went back to Lost Country. This time we were hunting the Indians. Everything was the same as before. There was the haze and the oxen you never met, but expected to meet, the whisper in the sumachs just after you passed, the painted face parting the leaves, though you never whirled quick enough to see.

My companion was a government man. He said the road was a little rough but pretty. He gathered flints and measured paces on the great mounds. There were five-hundred-year-old trees on them. He brought axes and picks. He gave the intangible farmers who began to materialize from here and there money to dig.

We split the mound and found nothing but scattered stones and a little charcoal. Finally at one side I bored a little shaft. Pieces of bone began to come up. The tooth of a dead ground squirrel. My companion badgered me gently. Nevertheless we deepened the shaft. It was no place for a burial, my friend insisted. We were way off center.

The spade grated on bone. The laborers crowded about. There was an expanse of clay-yellowed bone growing wider under expert fingertips. The brows, the eyes, the mouth — the jaw, rather. So very still. So very indifferent to the rough comments of the workers. So very sure, so very calm with the security of a pain and a mystery solved before we were born

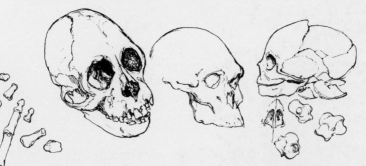

and which we had yet to face. It was a woman. Her arm and hand, each delicate bone in place, rested quietly in a sleeping posture. At her right side slept two children.

There were ribald comments. The light was fading. A careless spade shattered the skull of a child. Their thinner bones crumbled under our fingers. My friend hurried. "There's no time to do it right," he complained. "We'll have to take it out in a hurry. If we wait till tomorrow somebody may beat us to it."

The skulls came away in fragments. That serene face that had so little of horror faded, became a heap of fragments in a box. We stumbled among stones to the car. A farmer begged us for a bone. "Bet my old woman ud jump," he snickered.

I cast a last look back at the mound. From beyond, the moon was pushing up through the trees. It was the yellow that comes only with late autumn. The mound gaped in the twilight. All about lay the raw flung clay. A little wind came through the trees and whirled a shower of leaves into the hole. It was over. It was Lost Country no more.

The truck rattled monotonously toward town. All the way the picture lingered in my mind of that great hillside and the torn trees, the desecrated earth. The silence now and the moon climbing higher. The stars peering in. . . .

I was one of the day born after all. I had wanted these things ticketed in cases. I had wanted them explained when I knew there could be no explaining. I had sacrificed remoteness and mystery for what could be held in the hand. I knew myself guilty of a betrayal — that I was an outcast — even though it was only from some dim country of my mind.

And I was glad when the roads left our specimens a shattered dust. Even though I was an archaeologist I was glad. The Indians of Lost Country had escaped us after all.

THE GATE AND THE ROAD

"There is a gate," he said, "under the sand there in the western desert." We were speaking around that table of a buried Egyptian city. "The temple mound lies here" — he gestured at the maps that lay before us. "Petrie sunk a shaft there in the nineties but found nothing. I cannot recommend it because of the cost, but the gate" — a flush suffused his face, he looked at us importunately — "the gate may lead somewhere."

"It is a horozontal stripping job that would cost a fortune," someone said practically. "You would have a wall and a gate. Which way would you go?"

"Toward the city and away from the temple," he said, his accent growing greater in his excitement.

"Why?" someone asked gently. "Isn't it true that this would lead toward the city and that to follow such a roadway might basically demand the uncovering of a whole city, something we are not equipped to do financially."

"It goes somewhere," stubbornly reiterated the aging archaeologist. "I think three seasons more —." I thought of the way the wind comes in across that desert, and the flies. The man was old and there was a family to consider.

"In three seasons," said the director gently, "you might be following a road. Then you would have to ask for incalculable sums to follow it further. It is impossible."

"There is a gate and a road," said the old Egyptologist, speaking painfully in broken English. "It should be followed." He made unconscious digging motions with his hands.

A slow doubt went from eye to eye around the committee at the director's table. The man grew conscious of it, arose, and excused himself.

"He won't retire," someone said affectionately. "We will have to make the decision for him." Another sighed. "If we send him back he will never see the end of his road."

"It is the road we are all digging in," someone more perceptive ventured. "Find him another part of it here at home. Explain to him the road runs into a multiplicity of roads. None of us here will see the end of them."

⅍ ⅎ

THE TOAD

Synopsis: Archaeologist finds toad in skull in ceremonial burial in high, dry part of the Southwest. Takes skull to his cabin. Damp, clammy atmosphere develops and intensifies about him. Skull begins to mold peculiarly. Frog lives about house. Frog begins to grow, gets big as a dog; rains intensify, flooding Indian flats below. Indians hint about toad. Toad becomes more and more unseen, but there are signs of its enormous presence. Archaeologist returns skull to burial place, but still rains do not cease. Finally he calls or is visited by an old medicine man who offers to "lay" the ghost. Makes fire under a blanket; rains intensify, trying to put out fire. There is a sense of monstrous hopping "elementals" outside the circle. Blue bolts of lightning crash on the surrounding hills. Finally as the chant goes on, the rains die to a tiny pattering, and out of the dark into the circle hops a small frog, the original captor. The shaman murmurs to him and reluctantly he enters the skull, which is returned to the cave by the shaman. The archaeologist, convinced, never visits the country again.

The rain was still pouring intensely from that vast autumnal sky.

I've never seen a night like that when the priest came.

I

The fact that I found it in a skull to me had no significance. Many will say that it should have had — and some, the superstitious, will say that those who persist in probing about in ancient burials get what they deserve — whatever that ambiguous remark may be intended to imply. But, I repeat, what to others may seem odd did not impress me in the least at the time as anything more than a trifling incident of the day's work. In my long years as a professional archaeologist I had seen many stranger things, or so at least I thought on that bright summer morning with the sun pouring down the dry canyon gulch, so that even the cave in which I was working was dimly illuminated.

Yes, I will admit, I may have changed my mind, but grant
that I had the discretion to keep my mouth shut afterward.
The story of what happened in the *llano de seco* after I
opened the old priest's grave would have proved me mad in
any professional meeting of my colleagues. We study the
past — that is true. Its dry bones, its ruins, the broken bits of
its religious altars we know intimately and well. But we study
these fragments with the cold unbelief of science — with the
studied metallic indifference of the modern mind. That was
why the thing in the skull did not impress me. It is why I had
less sense in dealing with it than a common peasant, who, if
he had chanced to see it, would have immediately covered it
again and hastily gone on his way, making the sign of the
cross.

Mark you, I do not say offhand that that would have made
a difference. An elemental force of that nature once disturbed
is like a genie from a bottle — hard to reinter. But men of my
training are apt to let familiarity breed contempt. We pry in
dark places with the naive impertinence of children. Most of
the time — it doesn't matter, I suppose. But the thousandth
time — well, we don't talk of it — but the thousandth time
we do some little thing like turning over a stone or reading
some grisly syllables on a crumbling temple — and then,
suddenly, or a few weeks later, we know the thousandth time
has come to us, too. That's what happened to me in the *llano
de seco*. That's why I've never been back there since. That's
why, like a few of the others you see around here, I like the
big chairs in the Explorers Club best, with a good stiff drink
not too far off. That's why they say I'm done with the Central American "digs." That may sound like cowardice, and I
am not a coward. I was known as a pretty hardheaded scientist in my day. I might use a less complimentary adjective
now. Just put it this way: I believe that some of these vanished people knew things about the forces of nature, or the
forces behind nature, that we don't know. And some of those
forces they could personify into elemental shapes or malig-
nant deities. Or perhaps the elementals are there to begin
with and they merely learned to control — Anyhow, when
once such an elemental has been disturbed and its attention
drawn to you . . . You see? That's been a good many years
off now, but I'm taking no chances. It's probably still there in
the cave, waiting. And the little old priest who saved me is

dead. It's sense to know the thousandth time when it comes
to you and not to play the fool. I'll never go back, not for a
million. I'm staying clear. But if you want to know I'll talk
for once. This is the way it began.

II

Time was when I was an Aztec specialist, but in the thirties I
got tired of that — tired of American tourists coming out of
Mexico City and climbing in and out of my digs, tired of
something I already knew, or thought I knew, pretty well. I'd
been at it too long. I wanted a fresh field. Something new and
strange — a chance to get off the beaten track. In New York I
spoke to Rennault, director of the foundation for which I had
been working.

"What's on your mind, Blain?" he asked me. "You've
gotten more out of Mexico for us than any man we've ever
sent down there. Why not work the Temple of the Bats? We
can get the money for you."

"Not me," I said. Two years before I would have jumped
at it. But two years is two years, and I was tired of a place so
close to Mexico City that I was practically running a dude
ranch for tourists.

"I'm no Barnum," I countered. "I want a chance to do
some scouting around for a change. Anybody can do my job
now. Why not let me go north into the Sierra Madre country?"

"You've got fine ideas for a vacation," he grumbled.
"Don't you know that country is practically impenetrable —
that it's desert and semi-desert and a hellhole besides? You
won't find anything there but the remains of starved bug-
eating aborigines that couldn't have put one stone on another." He bit his cigar and eyed the door. It was obvious he
was waiting for me to capitulate like a nice boy and go back
to Mexico City. I knew it was time to play my trump card.

"Ever hear of Toxlol?" I said. He didn't answer, but he
quit eyeing the door and his cigar stayed unlit. The time was
now or never. I talked, and talked fast.

"From the living Zuni of the southwestern United States to
the Amazon country there are, or were, made images of a
frog in clay or stone. They are known among the mound
builders. We know that a cult surrounding this rain god

existed among the ancient Maya. At one time it must have
been widely disseminated. Vague stories involving the rain
god and his powers survive among some of the more backward and marginal Indian groups to this day."

"That's all very well," replied Rennault, "but what's that
got to do with this unknown Sierran region? You know and I
know that it is a belief thought to have developed among the
Maya."

"Look," I countered, "why should jungle people burdened
with more rain than they knew what to do with bother to
invent a rain god? You make gods of things that threaten you
or that you badly need. Corn gods, gods to guide you safely
in death. Only a desert people worry very much about rain.
We know very little, archaeologically speaking, about the
area between central Mexico and our own Southwest, yet the
rain god and his image are known among the people of both
areas. Somewhere in that desert and mountain country of
northern Mexico I think we are going to find some clues to
the Toxlol legend. Some of those little tag-end Indian desert
tribes may still worship him — at least in secret. We might be
able to recover details of the ritual that have survived from
the farther past.

"This time I'm not looking for cities, Rennault, I'm looking
for the road over which so much high culture flowed northward to the Mound Builders of the United States."

Rennault looked at me dubiously. "Blain," he said, "you're
a fool. You've done wonders for us in the past, but this time
you're a fool."

Just the same he reached out and signed the check. I knew
I had won.

Toxlol meant nothing to me then. I knew merely that I
could find something because I had always had the "feel" for
it and had it now. But foundations had to be "sold" things
on a reasonable basis, something that sounded plausible. I
had done business with the Thorne Foundation and Rennault
before. If I made a good find no one would ever ask me
about Toxlol. As it turned out they asked me plenty, but I
never told.

III

There won't be any latitude or longitude to this story. I doubt if I could find the way back now myself. Certainly I've made every effort to forget. It's the one expedition I never turned in a field report on. It did things to my scientific standing, too, but that doesn't count. Escape was cheap at the price.

The journey doesn't matter. Rough going. Jungle, mountain, desert. Up and down through all the climates every ten miles or so. Yes, there was some fever. But finally we came to the *llano de seco*. And it was a hell's furnace just like the old Spanish chronicles had said. It was a dry land of waterless gulches, sand, and sun. Yet the lifeless streambeds must once have carried water. There was still a tiny trickle flowing in one, and out on the flats a little ragged settlement of a dozen Indian families with their starved cattle and a few thistle-blown patches of cultivation.

It was obvious there weren't going to be any impressive city ruins here, but I still had the feeling there were other things to be found. It was the sort of dry, dissected country that makes caves easy to spot and where remains from ancient geological epochs weather out of the ravines. I wasn't deceived. I saw it was good country for our purposes and that it would take time to work.

With a little assistance from the starved folk of the flats, encouraged by the distribution of canned goods from our stores, we threw up a base camp.

I picked a spot a long ways up one of the giant ravines. It was an old Pueblo ruin and it saved me the trouble of putting up tents. The ruin was late as such things go. It had a couple of well-preserved rooms with the timbers all in good order. I had no intentions of digging into it. I was after older and bigger game. But it was convenient and there was a little water available down below in the streambed.

We got the Pueblo rooms cleaned out and our stores moved in. It was going to be a nice place to work —practically as good as living in a house. The people from the flat didn't seem to approve of it, though they weren't quarrelsome. I saw them talking about it in their own tongue, shaking their heads and gesturing at something across the canyon.

I grinned to myself. I knew what was across there. As fine a series of untouched shelter caves as I had seen anywhere.

And I meant to get into them as soon as camp was prepared and we had gotten rid of the local visitors. You never can tell, you know. Sometimes they develop into unexpected trouble. Particularly if you happen to turn up the bones of their relatives by mistake. Sometimes they still bury in those caves.

So at last they trooped off down the canyon happy with their little gifts. But one old man, the last, turned just as they were passing out of sight. Gaunt and ragged though he was, there was a sort of sombre dignity about him. He pointed across the canyon at a cave opening just visible between some rocks, shook his head emphatically, and assayed some broken Spanish. A word like "aqua" floated across the canyon. It didn't make sense. The wind blew his words away, and after a long, searching glance in my direction he passed out of sight with the rest.

I was sure I had gotten his meaning. Probably it was a burial cave and we were to stay out of it. As events were to prove, I had misunderstood him. If I had really known what was there — well, I wouldn't have sent Dinwiddie off on a fifty-mile scouting expedition to the north, the very next day.

But I was anxious to start. The very fact that the old man who seemed to exercise an influence over the people of the flats had been specific in his avoidance of a particular cave made me frantic to get into it. Often the reactions of local Indians are wrapped up with dim legendary tribal beliefs that may have some foundation in fact. No superstitious hocus-pocus was going to keep me from doing my job. I had dealt with that sort of thing before.

As for Dinwiddie, he could go ahead and scout while I checked the caves. There was a fair-sized town off to the north and we would be needing additional supplies, too. I sent him away with the men and settled down to the leisurely job of scouting out the best caves. They were not deep and it wouldn't take long to excavate them. I spent a day going from one to the other along the cliff wall. The one at which the old man had pointed I was deliberately reserving till the last.

Looking back, it is hard to see my exact motivation. Maybe I was just making a little solitary game out of it. Or maybe some strange premonition of events to come was already affecting my attitude so that I was unconsciously becoming stealthy in my behavior.

At any rate, I reserved that particular cave for the following morning and I planned to do my first serious digging
there.

IV

After a peaceful night in the old ruin which had already taken
on the aspect of home to me, I arose early, cooked a solitary
breakfast, and selected some digging equipment. Shouldering
it, I trudged down a precarious path into the canyon and
worked my way up the boulder-strewn face of the opposite
wall. Coming at last to the cave mouth at which the old man
had gestured, I threw down my equipment, seated myself on
a convenient ledge, and had a cigarette while considering
what was to be done.

The cave, like the others I had examined the previous day,
involved no difficult exploration or dangerous descents into
unknown depths. It was a simple wide-mouthed opening,
somewhat choked now by the accumulated debris and dust of
ages. There had been, also, a few rockfalls from the roof.
Within, it sloped backward for a hundred feet or so, then
ceased abruptly. It was of a size convenient to shelter a family. There was nothing to differentiate it from hundreds of
such cliff shelters to be seen all over the dry Southwest.
Doubtless there had been more water flowing down in the
streambed when the caves in the canyon were inhabited.

The people who had occupied the shelters had left no
elaborate remains, nor had I expected them. They had lived
there long ago, and one of the purposes upon which I was
intent was to discover traces of their possible association with
the extinct animals of the closing Ice Age. Such remains
would lie only on the bottommost cave floor and require
extensive clearing. The possibility that such finds might await
me were very real, however. I wasted little time in contemplation but set to work.

The details of my excavations and of all the intricate map-
ping and placing of objects layer by layer as I worked down
through the accumulated debris toward the stone floor of the
cave would have no interest save to the specialist.

Remains from the superficial levels were numerous and had
to be carefully collected before I could get on to what might
lie below. Scientifically valuable, they play no part in this

story. Two weeks rolled by while I labored deeper and deeper
into the recesses of the floor. Finds were becoming infrequent
and it was obvious that the payload was running out. I felt,
for some reason, vaguely disappointed. I had found nothing
to justify the extreme awe in which the cave had seemingly
been held by the people down on the flats at the canyon
mouth.

Because of the coolness and shadow, I took to eating my
lunch in the cave and thus avoiding the hot sunshine outside.
As it turned out, it was this little circumstance that proved
my downfall. If it had not been for this quiet and solitary
lunch hour, I would have been so busy shoveling and scratch-
ing in the rockfalls and gravel that I would not have heard
the sound, and, in a day or so, imagining I had cleared the
cave, I would have gone on to another. Never have I seen so
cunningly concealed a burial. Remembering the sound and
looking back now, knowing what I do, I am positive that the
thing meant for me to find it, that it deliberately sought my
attention. Perhaps it had grown tired of the long darkness.
Perhaps in some strange psychic manner I gave it some slight
necessary accession of power. Reactivated it. Who can say?

V

I was sitting on a conveniently placed rock some fifty feet
from the entrance. I had finished my scant midday meal and,
resting, may even have drowsed slightly. The entranceway
provided light enough for a pleasant twilight.

As I dozed I began to dream quietly — an odd but lovely
dream which seemed to convey me to some green land of
leaves and water. Rain fell softly on the leaves, and as an
undernote to the sound of the rain I could hear — faint and
beautiful — the multitudinous faint chorus of a million frogs.
The beautiful sound of spring peepers as one hears them in a
rainy spring back in the States. I suppose I was homesick —
even old-timers are subject to it occasionally, you know —
and my mind was building a refuge from the heat and thirst
of the parched waste with which I was surrounded.

How many minutes I slept I do not know, but the thing
that brought me out of it was a soft, churring, insistent note
that finally intruded into my consciousness and something
more real than the dream that I half knew I was dreaming. It

was a sound that had begun to take on an exterior reality.

I awoke quietly, expecting the noise to cease with the dream. Suddenly I was aware that it had not. That thin, sweet piping was emanating from somewhere in the cavern. I lay quietly a moment, reluctant to stir for fear I might disturb whatever creature was making it. With some difficulty I finally isolated it as coming from behind a large boulder which lay against the wall opposite me. The boulder had fallen from the roof at some time in the long past and was jammed awkwardly against the side wall. Since there was nothing under it I had not bothered to attempt its removal.

Now in the attempt to discover the little author of that pleasant singing a thought struck me. Unable to intrude my flashlight behind the boulder, I scratched a match and dropped it down the thin crack between the stone and the wall. To my surprise the match disappeared completely.

It didn't take much experimentation to conclude that a sizable cavity, perhaps even an unsuspected branch of the cave, must open behind that boulder. The chirping had ceased, in fact no longer interested me. No competent archaeologist quits a cave until he is sure he has checked all possible crannies into which implements or even a burial may have been stored away. Obviously I was going to have to move the boulder after all.

It was a tough job to do alone. I couldn't use dynamite, though we had a supply, for fear of injuring what might lie behind the boulder. Finally, however, by the use of a crowbar and using smaller rocks as fulcrums, I was able to swerve it far enough from the cave wall to wedge in behind it and get a view of the cavity it covered.

When I squeezed down and shot my light into the cavity I knew I'd hit the jackpot. It was a little round room, no more — a cyst that had somehow eroded to one side of the main chamber. And there somebody was — just as I had hoped. I could see a stretched-out bundle and a lot of grave goods around him. No ordinary burial. This chap had really been somebody. I squeezed and pushed and managed to climb completely inside. God knows how many millennia had passed since the last man had crawled through that little low-hung passage.

VI

The first thing that surprised me when I got really inside was the dampness — something completely unexpected in these dry little shelter caves. The floor was damp and muddy. I thought there must be a spring somewhere back in the canyon side that was feeding a little water into the chamber. It didn't seem very plausible considering the dryness of the country, but it was all I could think of just then. But where the damp came from didn't worry me too much except to the extent that it might have destroyed some of the grave furniture. I went over quickly and shot my light into his face.

The glitter made me jump, and no wonder. I hadn't expected anything like that out in these desert foothills. This man must have represented the priesthood of a high civilization. There was no mummy — the damp had seen to that — but over the face of the skull lay a thin mask of beaten gold, and in the empty eyesockets lay two great ebon crystals that caught and reflected the light so that the eyes seemed to blaze balefully back at me.

There was a beautifully carven figure of a frog on an amulet which had obviously hung about his neck. This did startle me. The green frog, I thought, the Toxlol symbol. Boy, will this jar old Rennault. Yes, there were other things, some fine pottery with design motifs all involving the rain god. I'd get it all out in due time. No hurry now. I came back to the skull and rolled it over to get those strange obsidian eyeballs. I didn't like him lying there watching me, as if the crystals somehow made it possible. They'd be better off in my pocket.

That was my job and I wasn't standing on sentiment. They could be reinserted and photographed later. I rolled the head to one side and the crystals dropped into my hand. That wasn't all that dropped, however. Something cold and damp and alive touched my hand.

I sprang back and shot the light on the skull, snatching for my gun with the other. No, I wasn't superstitious. I'd played tag games with snakes in passages like this before and I wasn't taking any chances.

But it wasn't any snake. It was a little green toad with big, unwinking gold eyes that must have been sitting in the actual skull vault of the dead man and that had leaped out against my hand as I startled him in turning over the skull. I knew

now where the little song had come from that had led me to
the burial.

There was a certain irony in it, I thought, as I looked down
at the toad and the dead man. There lay the priest in all his
trappings, the servant of the rain, the god Toxlol. And there
in his very skull had crouched the live symbol of a dead
religion — this odd little toad that had sought the damp and
darkness from some nearby spring.

At this very moment the little animal chose to escape by
hopping off eerily into the darkness. I didn't follow him but
instead gathered up the skull of the dead man and his beautiful gold-leaf mask and made my way out of the cave. It was
growing late and I was anxious to spend the evening studying
my treasures. Obviously they couldn't be left in the opened
chamber overnight. . . .

ǽ ǽ

Do the electronic circuits glow dimly when not in use? Note:
the difference between the dark world of the subconscious
and the electronic brains with which it has become so popular to compare the human mind.

ǽ ǽ

I have never believed in ghosts, nevertheless, this record shall
be published anonymously. I shall do so for these reasons: for
the protection of a living individual from the prying vulgar
and insatiable curiosity of the ill informed. Second, because
the passage of thirty years leaves me, as a scientist, better

aware than in my youth that science, despite its great contributions, is peculiarly orthodox in the hands of its practitioners. Facts which are in any sense outré or savor of superstition are apt to be violently rejected — and the scholar who mentions them to be regarded askance. The story I am about to narrate I witnessed personally. I made the mistake once many years ago of mentioning it to another scientist, carefully prefacing my remarks with what I believed to be the reason for the phenomena I witnessed. The reason involved no appeal to supernaturalism. I have said and I repeat again I do not believe in ghosts. Nevertheless, I had witnessed something which I considered of supreme interest and which falls to the lot of few to observe adequately. I told this story to my colleague — a man whom I thought I knew well. He listened carefully. Toward the end he tapped with his fingers a little impatiently upon the arm of his chair. As I concluded he said gruffly, "You will understand that you place me in an embarrassing position. Though I am your friend I do not believe your story. It is my business not to believe it. You have been deceived in some manner."

"But I did not say," I began patiently, "that I believe in ghosts. I merely —"

He gestured me to the door. "It's all the same whether you start out by saying you believe in ghosts or not. You will believe in them once you begin to let your imagination run riot in this manner. Buck up, man. You shouldn't be wasting your time this way."

We parted in a little flurry of friendly joshing. I left that part of the country shortly after and it was probably just as well. I never heard from him again.

⤝ ⤞

THE THING IN THE VATS

Medical men, in the course of their lives, see and hear many strange things, but the oath of Hippocrates, for the most part, keeps them silent. Technically speaking, however, I am not a medico but an anatomist, a research worker, and the record I am now confiding to paper has never passed my lips. It will lie in the third bottle to the right of the arsphenamine, to be found eventually by my successor if I in turn disappear in the

same manner as Dr. Randolph Brill. The operations I shall
not describe. The developments which led to Brill's discovery
lie lost in several obscure German journals, the local files of
which I have seen fit to destroy. This record has only two
purposes: the protection of my successors against possible
accusations of malpractice in the dissecting rooms, and,
second, as a final warning against this unspeakable research
which has cost the lives of five known victims. I am the sixth.
But I go consciously. My whole life has been devoted to
science. And if research has led me, at last, to something
inexpressibly evil, as I think it has, take this as a warning and
be glad the evidence is destroyed. As for me, I had to go on. I
was Randolph Brill's student to the grave — and beyond.

It is difficult for one who, like myself, is accustomed only
to the figures and formulae involved in the preparation of
scientific monographs, to express his feelings — from the day
the summons reached me, down to this last ear-straining
moment when I listen for that midnight stir and movement in
the phenol tanks, where life, life as we know it, life dependent on sun and air and cool water and the voices of men,
most certainly does not exist. But *something* is there, something among all those pickled dead, that moves, that waits,
something from outside, something growing, gathering
strength, something evil beyond words.

I know that by now I sound wandering, incoherent. I know
that these paragraphs betray evidences of the strain of these
last days. Yet it is not for nothing that I was once accounted
by Brill himself the coldest-tempered, most objective-minded
researcher in the country. How strange and far away those
distant words of praise seem now. How little I knew, how
little any of us knew. Fools! We could afford to be happy.

Nevertheless, that praise is not without its savor still. This
is the last signed article of Grayson Meade, the last report of
the discoverer of codextrin. Ignore these incoherencies, these
outcries of whipped nerves. There is still an hour till midnight. I will shut my ears and write. Begin again. In doing so
you will see how it began for me.

II

It was in August of 1938 that I received the letter from Chancellor Lane of Ottawa University. In it he explained that Dr.

Randolph Brill, distinguished research worker and head of the Department of Anatomy, had disappeared under mysterious circumstances. It was well known, the chancellor went on to indicate, that I had been at one time Brill's most distinguished student. Brill himself, at various times, had mentioned me as his possible successor. Under these circumstances, distressed though I must be through my personal fondness for Professor Brill, would it not be possible, the chancellor hinted tactfully, for me to come to Ottawa as acting head of the department, with the understanding that as soon as the unfortunate disappearance of Dr. Brill had been cleared up my title should become permanent? I gathered from the tenor of the chancellor's remarks that there was little or no hope that Dr. Brill would be discovered alive.

Opportunity though it was, the letter saddened me. I can still recall it lying in the late August light streaming across my desk, the white sheets and the formal even, flowing sentences that were to change, yes, to end my destiny. But I was not thinking of the future then. Instead I thought of the past. . . .

ꕔ ꕗ

ISLANDS AND EVOLUTION

"If they're not there," he said, "then there's nothing to evolution." We pulled the tiller over, and off through the mist you could hear a steady grumble. It was the sea grinding flints on the beach.

"An unlikelier place I never saw," I protested. "Whatever gave you the idea that slag heap of an island was going to prove anything?" A swirl of sea gulls went over us oaring steadily off into a grey infinity. Something cried once dolefully out of the water. It was enough to lift your hair a little and make you think of that old book of your childhood and something in it about the seas before man was, or the likes of him.

"Take it easy," I said. "The proof can wait."

"The hell it can," he said and began working us in.

"You guys are all alike. You never hurry after facts. You're going to get one now and it's going to floor you. I've read your friend Darwin. But he never answered this one, not him." Nelson shifted his pipe and that big weather-beaten, slyly intelligent face looked into mine.

"Cut the mystery," I said. "I don't like it out here. You can tell me at home just as well. I'm at a psychological disadvantage here. I can't swim."

"You're going to see," he said. "You're going to see with your own eyes. And then I'm going to ask the question — just one question — and you're going to try to answer. But you won't. Then we can go home and I won't ever have to read any of that stuff of yours again about my ancestors being fish. Even if they were, I notice you aren't rocking the boat."

"Not me," I said. "Not for anything. And that proves evolutionarily that I haven't got the gill system I used to have —"

"Nuts," he said, and just then we grated on the pebbles in the cove. Birds flew up screaming. I got out with Nelson and walked gingerly over the wet stones.

"Well," I said, and braced myself. "Where are they?"

"Huh?" Nelson said and cupped his ear. I guess the birds and the sea were a little loud.

"The things that were going to prove something," I yelled. "Show me. There's fog and the dark will be coming on. I want to be able to see."

"Up here," said Nelson. I didn't like the look in his eye. It was like the sea when there's something down there that won't quite show itself, but keeps on swimming around.

"Up here," he said. We stood high on the rock and stared. You could see the other end of the island and that queer aura of violet light over it that comes sometimes in a half-fog. That was all, unless it might be those little stunted trees below us.

"This had better be good," I said to Nelson. But already I had the feeling of a young man who's been sent for a left-handed monkey wrench. And I was just the lad then to go leaping around to find it.

"It had better be good," I said defiantly again. But I knew it was too late. That fish was beginning to show itself in Nelson's eye.

"You don't see it?" he asked innocently and gestured off toward the violet halo with the sea spurting whitely through it.

"See what?" I protested. "You might at least tell me what to look for. And what the point is, and why we're up here?" About this time I ran out of breath.

"All right," said Nelson. "Look again. You see nothing?"

"Nothing," I wheezed.

"You do not see men — men like us?"

"I do not see men," I admitted. "Why should I?"

"You do not see animals — land animals like us?"

"I do not," I said, "and if they're here they flew or floated in. What's new about that? Darwin —"

"Then," said Nelson, "you see the sea. And the birds. And the light like that for maybe a hundred million years. But no men. Maybe a seal on the beach, or a butterfly blown offshore. But no men."

"Sure, sure," I parried.

"Very well." Nelson eyed me closely now. "Then it's like I told you. They are not here. And there is no evolution like Darwin said. Because there has been enough time. You understand? There has been time enough for them to have crawled out down there from that sea and to stand where we stand. There has been all the time in the world. But the fish are still down there in the sea."

"I don't get you," I said. "Darwin made it very clear that the small amount of land life on oceanic islands proves that species are not the product of special creation instantaneously over the whole earth. Otherwise you would find the continental mammals everywhere. As it is, island land life is scant and consists largely of forms which have found their way in from the nearest continental areas. Nothing much has arisen there de novo."

"All right," said Nelson. "Your reading is all right. But there in the *Origin* Darwin goes much further. Remember? He says somewhere that it is quite futile to look to climate or other physical conditions as the cause of the great changes in the forms of life. We must instead," he says, "look to a special law — that of natural selection.

"Now then." Nelson's long finger came out and prodded me down on the nearest stone. "Here is my question, the only one I will ask. I can't find any answer in Darwin but maybe you will answer it. If life originated in the sea, if it crawled out of the sea onto the shore, and if, as I think you will admit, the struggle for existence in the sea is always intense and as intense on this shore as any other, why has not marine life come ashore on these oceanic islands as you claim it has done on the continents? This island is old, there are others even older. There has been time enough. But look down there. It is like I said. Where are the results? Show them to me."

I gestured futilely. I may even have mumbled some reply, but if I did time has mercifully obscured it. I am sure that it did not convince Nelson nor did it satisfy me. I was too young to have thought it out and Nelson was too proud of his triumph to pursue the subject any further.

When we went down to the cove the shingle was black and shiny. Nothing was crawling there but the fog, and it was good to shove off from the stones and stand out from that place where nothing had happened, that should have happened, so I thought, in millions upon millions of years. It was good to catch air in a sail and begin to move. Nelson laughed. I think he never bothered to look in my books again. To tell the truth, it was some time before I did so myself.

I had just started zoology at college and trust in textbooks was shattered. Maybe it was a good thing. I had the answer finally some ten years later when I came ashore there, but it was a long answer and I am not sure Nelson would have listened. I thought it all out lying on a warm rock and savoring the answer that one always has some ten years too late. It was a rich answer. There was sea salt in it and the flow of tidal rivers. There were the strange doings of inscrutable cells and there was time — all the years that old Nelson had counted and millions more besides. It was an answer no more fantastic than life. One could say that, but the essence would escape in print.

        ⇘ ⇙

The outline of the man's accomplishments can be found in *Who's Who* — the dates, degreees, honors, titles — all the respect that the world of intellect is accustomed to pay to a distinguished man of science. In the analysis of some personalities this would be adequate. In the case of Frank Speck it conceals, tells less than nothing. The man is not to be found behind the impedimenta of learning. He has relegated it all away to some back corner filled with odds and ends in the capacious old office looking out over Woodland Avenue. It is something less important than the Iroquoian False Faces duly given their offerings of bear grease (as was promised to their Indian makers). The honors, the things that have come somehow along the years by the whims of others, have not been asked for. They are unsought and not important. Little men need these things to bulge their stature. One never thinks of them in the presence of Frank Speck.

On South Street in Philadelphia are the negro herb shops, the sugar cane sellers, the vendors of strong molasses. Around us swarms the black world of the metropolis — credulous, naive, wicked — a hint of the barbaric still clinging like a scent in the air. On the sidewalk a strolling white man chats with a negro cane vender. The man is Frank Speck.

We enter a negro church and the organist, proud of his fine instrument, lets us climb into the body of the organ to see the huge pipes. We emerge, dusty but impressed. "A man accidentally stepped on the pedal yesterday and a couple of fellows got blew through a pipe." Later we sit dreamily in the darkened church, lulled by the organ music. The organist, with slender brown hands and the sensitive hurt face of a between-world dweller, leans over to me in the dark. "That man — that Dr. Speck — he's a nice man. A very fine gentleman." He pauses, inarticulate. "Yes," I say. The barrier between our worlds seems to lessen. We try, shyly, to talk.

In a little village on the edge of the Jersey pine barrens we enter a taxidermist's shop. Rough men, bronzed with the weather, sit talking about deer. There is a smell of fox skins in the air and on the floor a pile of deer legs. "Saved 'em for you, Frank," grunts George, the proprietor. "Know how you're always takin' 'em to those Indians of yours for rattles."

We sit on chopping blocks and take turns dropping wood into the stove. I listen while the talk runs on canoes and deer and hunting. Some half-grown boys listen eagerly to Indian stories by the quizzical rough man nonchalantly cutting up the deer legs with the ease of a professional woodsman. Nobody says "Doctor." Nobody says "Professor." When we leave to catch a bus, a whole stream of little boys run along behind us eagerly carrying part of our load, and jostling about the amused object of their attention.

"F.G.S." as some of us affectionately know him — haunter of zoos, snake lover, keeper of turtles that wander about under-foot on the office floor. Good huntsman, canoe man, one with whom to while away hours on the warm side of a rock in the lee of the wind.

There is only one poetic phrase that fits him: "As close to earth as a fox's tail." And along with it goes something a little more solid and substantial; a woodchuck's persistence in holing up in readiness for next spring. They know that north at Nain and down in the Louisiana swamp country. Frank Speck will be out with the first sunning lizards, with the men who "dream" the game.

Part II

THE SORCERER IN THE WOOD
1947–1966

I am the thing that lives in the midst of the bones,
. . . the thing with no face
that spins through the brain on the edge of a spectral voice.
— *Charles Williams*

There were many events in 1947 which made a lasting impression on Loren Eiseley as an educator, archaeologist, anthropologist, author, and Nebraskan. It was a year in which more than one million veterans enrolled in college under the U.S. "G.I. Bill of Rights," and from the Nippur excavations Francis Steele reconstructed the laws of Hammurabi; in which Thor Heyerdahl sailed on a raft from Peru to Polynesia in 101 days to prove prehistoric immigration, and the Dead Sea Scrolls were discovered in Wadi Qumran; in which Willa Cather, who used Lincoln, Nebraska, as the setting of her novel *My Ántonia,* died. Loren had escaped from the ring of poverty into which he was born and from the dark underworld of wandering men. As his youth ended, at age forty, he was well on the way to establishing himself as one of America's major intellectual forces.

He never expected to see Philadelphia again. But ten years after he received his doctorate, when he was teaching at Oberlin College in Ohio, the call came to succeed his former teacher, Frank Speck, who was seriously ill. The old days of Speck's naturalist paradise on the top floor of College Hall at the University of Pennsylvania were ending — days of box turtles wandering about at one's feet, of snakes in sacks, of strange Indians stalking in from different parts of the country and appearing unbidden at the door. Anthropology was becoming a respected discipline; professional students were increasing in number.

By the time Loren succeeded Speck as chairman of the department and a year later became curator of Early Man in the university museum, he was no longer the literary apprentice, and writing had become quite as important as any other part of his life. In fact, it is safe to say that writing had become *the* most important portion; it was his real talent, though he was also an inspired teacher. Through the years, the editors of *Harper's* continued to publish a variety of titles, including "The Places

Below" (1948), "Mr. Buzby's Petrified Woman" (1948), "The Fire Apes" (1949), "The Snout" (1950), "People Leave Skulls with Me" (1951), and "The Bird and the Machine" (1956). Further, the newly reorganized *Scientific American*, reflecting a broad range of interests, began to ask for articles shortly after his arrival at the university, and he contributed pieces on such diversified themes as archaeology, human paleontology, fire, and the history of science. Other magazines which became interested in and published his work were *The American Scholar, The New York Times Magazine, The Saturday Evening Post, Saturday Review, Holiday, Gentry,* and *Horizon.*

Lowry Wimberly, Loren's friend and editor of *The Prairie Schooner,* continued to encourage him and was particularly impressed with "The Places Below," which he observed, in a letter to the young professor of December 19, 1948, "is a story." Loren had turned aside from the narrowly defined scientific article when he first began writing for *Harper's.* At that time, a specialized magazine had asked him for a piece on human evolution and gone back on its promise to publish it. He had turned it into what he later termed the "concealed essay," in which personal anecdote was allowed easily to bring under observation thoughts of a purer scientific nature. Loren had long realized an attachment for the personal essay, a more literary form; he had toyed with such prose in his youth when, for instance, he wrote with uncompromising truth about his adventures as a professional tramp during the depression.

Although Loren was always writing about himself, he, like many other creative authors, manipulated the accounts of his life. In his essays, he occasionally invented characters, rearranged events, and composed conversations in search of a larger reality. His intention was not to deceive or falsify, but rather to clarify, and he managed to give reality the vividness of fiction by the way he reported an incident.

Many publishers had asked him to write a book, but the pressures of teaching and administration had prevented him from doing so. Hiram Haydn, editor of *The American Scholar* and editor-in-chief at Random House, was especially enthusiastic about "The Judgment of the Birds," which had appeared in the *Scholar* in 1956, and he believed that a collection of essays would find a receptive audience. Under his influence, Loren was persuaded to assemble a volume of personal essays for Random House. *The Immense Journey,* which contained certain of the *Harper's* and *Scientific American* essays, was published in 1957. Dedicated to the memory of his father, "who lies in the grass of the prairie frontier but is not forgotten by his son," it appeared in various editions throughout the world. Not only did it find a receptive audience with the general public, but it won many ardent admirers among distinguished authors, including the poet and Librarian of Congress Archibald MacLeish, who, like the other fans, expressed his appreciation in a letter. Over the years prominent writers of both prose and poetry came into his life through his writings: Theodore H. White, Phyllis McGinley, Howard Nemerov, W. H. Auden, Ray Bradbury, Hal Borland, to name but a few. The interesting fact is that almost without exception *they* sought *him* out.

Writers often pride themselves on the titles they give their books; this was certainly true of Loren, who had a gift for the perfect phrase. He had a whole page of titles in mind for *The Immense Journey,* and his notebooks are filled with precise, poetic titles for articles and books he was planning to write but did not complete. When the author Wright Morris, a close friend and fellow Nebraskan, lived near Philadelphia, he and Loren would spend hours trying to find the right titles for their next books. It became such an obsession that, on one occasion, Morris called his old friend at two in the morning to get his opinion. Loren finally replied, "It sounds good, but how about if I let you know after I wake up?"

Darwin's Century: Evolution and the Men Who Discovered It was published by Doubleday and Company in 1958. Loren had become increasingly interested in the involved story of the theory of evolution and had started some years before publication of this academic work to collect material from forgotten journals of the period as well as from books — material which had been overlooked or neglected by other narrators of the Darwinian story. The administration of the University of Pennsylvania provided a leave of absence during which much of the writing of this history was done, and the Wenner-Gren Foundation for Anthropological Research furnished financial assistance. The book received the Athenaeum of Philadelphia Literary Award and the Phi Beta Kappa Science Award, the first of many honors his publications were to win. Loren's notebooks reveal he had planned "a second volume of my history," *After Darwin's Century,* but he did not arrive at the point of putting it down on paper. This is only one of many contemplated volumes: he had plans to produce a nature anthology, a science-fiction novel, a western story or novel, and a textbook. The notebook pages abound not only in titles, but in outlines and passages from the projected works.

The Firmament of Time was published by Atheneum Publishers in 1960. Haydn had moved to Atheneum, and Loren wanted to continue his association with his editor which had proved so beneficial. Founded upon a series of six lectures on the philosophy of science given at the Medical School of the University of Cincinnati in 1959, this was the first of several volumes to be derived from lectures. As his reputation as a teacher and author grew, he had become in demand as a speaker; this supplemented his income and enabled him to try out his material on audiences. *The Firmament* increased his circle of readers and received the Lecomte du Noüy Award ("best work of particular interest for the spiritual life of our epoch and for the defense of human dignity") and the Burroughs Medal for the best publication in the field of nature writing.

Teaching and administration led eventually to the provostship of the university, a position Loren occupied from 1959 to 1961. As chief executive officer, among the first things he did were to raise the salaries of the university library personnel and to obtain a grant to provide for binding volumes in poor condition. Libraries had been places of enchantment to Loren since he was a boy, when he traveled in his coaster wagon to the old Lincoln library (a photograph of which he kept on his desk) and pulled the book-filled wagon home. In 1961, he was released from administrative obligations by a special professorship which he held for the remainder of his life. As Benjamin Franklin Professor of Anthropology and the History of Science, his academic duties were intentionally light in order to provide time for him to pursue his writing career.

The Mind as Nature, originally given as the John Dewey Lecture in Chicago in 1962, was published by Harper and Row in that same year. Considered a classic in the field of education, the small volume draws upon certain autobiographical experiences as they seem to apply to problems concerned with learning and with teaching. This was followed by *Francis Bacon and the Modern Dilemma* (1962), published by the University of Nebraska Press, and dealing with Bacon's life and contributions to science. Based on several addresses Loren gave at institutions of learning on the four-hundredth anniversary of the birth of the English philosopher and author, it was later reissued in a revised and enlarged edition as *The Man Who Saw Through Time* (1973).

It was during this period that I first met Loren. I had read a review of *The Immense Journey* in *The New York Times Book Review* in 1957 and gone out and bought the book. From then on I was an enthusiastic devotee of his writing, giving copies of his works to friends as Christmas and birthday presents. In 1961, as editor-in-chief of the Trade Science Department at The

Macmillan Company, I asked him to write the epilogue to a new edition of Jack London's *Before Adam,* a classic romance of the unknown ages, of the lives and passions of prehistoric man. As a professional anthropologist, he would have something interesting to say, and I was pleased to learn that as a boy he had reveled in the book. The new edition was issued in 1962 with his epilogue. Both Loren and I enjoyed science fiction and fantasy that was also good literature, and he next agreed to write the introduction to David Lindsay's *A Voyage to Arcturus* (1963), a book that is both an engrossing science-fiction novel and a profound metaphysical fable. I had acquired the rights from a British publisher, and Loren discussed the literary merits of the work and the metaphysical concepts on which it is based in his opening section. I knew that he was heavily committed elsewhere and did not ask him to engage in a larger project at the time.

In 1962, Loren wrote the American author Lewis Mumford and asked if he could use his name as a recommendation in his application for a Guggenheim Fellowship, which he was seeking in order to accomplish the writing of "a kind of intellectual autobiography." He felt that praise from Mumford, a distinguished stylist, would be helpful, as his book would fall into the domain of creative writing rather than a scientific effort. In discussing the plan for this work in his application, he said: "I hope to transcend the purely personal by suggesting unusual factors common to the life of man in a universe he is forced, from childhood, to try to understand." The fellowship was awarded for 1963–1964, but the autobiography, which proved to be a difficult task, was not completed until a decade later. His notebooks contain numerous references to autobiography titles, as well as entries pertaining to the history of his life, such as "The Other Player" and the casting of the dice, which ultimately found their way into his memoirs.

Loren's first articles accepted by *Harper's* were pivotal early works. Over the years the author's voice grew increasingly assertive, his vision increasingly clear. He became a master nature writer on the order of Henry David Thoreau, for whom nature encompassed human nature. He looked at the world obliquely, out of the corner of his eye, as the nineteenth-century author and philosopher advised, and his perception of time, as when he looked in his mirror and saw a prehistoric face, is unique. Of this, he once wrote indirectly on a scrap of paper: "I am powerfully influenced by locale and, being geologically trained, a locale which may be projected vertically in time. My mind is stuffed with stray teeth, mammoth bones, and the lost trails of

Indians and pioneers. It comes out in my writing — perhaps because my people came west in the time of buffalo grass and ox teams. I write because all these things haunt me and because, in that sense, I am the voice of things other than myself." His perception of a universal power or force that permeates the universe is conveyed by ·how he looked at evolution: in the endless change of living forms throughout the ages, he saw a process that represents the immensity of energy and control in the whole celestial cosmos. "The greatest thing a human soul ever does in this world," John Ruskin wrote in *Modern Painters,* "is to *see* something, and tell what it *saw. . . .* To see clearly is poetry, philosophy, and religion — all in one." Loren had this special gift of seeing, and, fortunately, he reported what he saw to us.

The allegiance to life as also manifested in other species is at the heart of nature writing. In his journals, another essayist and poet, Ralph Waldo Emerson, wrote: "I feel the centipede in me — cayman, carp, eagle and fox. I am moved by strange sympathies. . . ." The matter of evolution contributed vastly to Loren's sense of unity in existence, to his capacity to love life in all its shapes and forms. This is illustrated in many journal entries, from his easy identification with a house centipede that died on his bathroom rug to his feeling for a solitary cricket he once heard filling a railway station with its song. The love that transcends the boundaries of species was the highest spiritual expression he knew.

⋙ ⋘

FROM A LETTER FROM LOWRY WIMBERLY TO LOREN,
DECEMBER 19, 1948

It has been sometime now since I read your "The Places Below." I read it again to confirm my first impression of it. I am numbered among those, I hope, who use superlatives sparingly and with a certain reverence for words. So believe me when I say that "The Places Below" has two qualities that make for the best writing: power and beauty. And perhaps the chief ingredient of beauty is the quality of mystery. Anyway, your story has mystery, beauty, and power. I *felt* it, and that is surely a test of a story's power — that the reader *feel* it. Then I *thought* it, sensed its mystical implications, its poetic summation of man's emotional and intellectual history, his frustrations, his longing for rest and peace. The story — for it is a story — does not fail at any point. My feeling is that it is unique, that nothing quite like it has ever been done. It has in it too the poetry of an honest symbolism. So much modern symbolism is fraudulent, mere literary quackery.

ⲯ ⲕ

GIANTS

Item: Ideas for *Harper's*
An essay on old animals, i.e., Henny and the turtle. Connect with the vanishing of such things from our streams and earth. Our aged have increased in numbers, but the magnificent ancients of the earth have vanished. Once in a long-forgotten glade I came on such a giant, the nostalgic thrill of the monster. Hippo at the Bronx.
"Monsters Are Memories"
Human beings get old in a dreary fashion — the reptiles keep growing like trees, becoming more and more ancient and formidable. The great gars swimming up the stream.
"Lament for Monsters"
Is the reptile unique by its constant growth?

ⲯ ⲕ

The blizzards by the Pole are not a likely place to search for the secrets of life. Only this, I think, can explain the amazing indifference which the public of two generations has

shown toward the contents of one of the sledges drawn painfully southward over the Antarctic ice barrier by a trio of
starving men. Captain Scott and that immortal company who
perished with him are well known to science. Nevertheless, in
the chronicles of their passing, in the records of those who
found them huddled in their last bivouac, a line at best is
devoted to that single sledge. They dragged it with their dying
breath, yet its contents, by the curious whims that sometimes
afflict the final reports of ill-fated expeditions, have been little
mentioned since. Its significance is therefore uncertain, but,
this we know, it was not gold. It was a sledload of fossils.
There are men, I think, who would have understood this
effort had it been made in other continents. But the Antarctic
waste is a dead world and the drama of man's attempts to
enter it is so spectacular. . . .

᠔ ᠓

For a personal essay: Archaeological findings of how people went away in past time. Their doors closed for a last
time. Their belongings hidden. There is a hidden pathos of
departure here which properly handled could be turned into a
good essay.

᠔ ᠓

An archaeologist is a man who knows where last year's
lace valentines are.

᠔ ᠓

I would never again make a profession of time. My walls
are lined with books expounding its mysteries. My hands
have been split and raw with grubbing into its waste bins and
hidden crevices. I have stared so much at death that I can
recognize the lingering personalities in the faces of skulls and
feel accompanying affinities and revulsions. I am the last in
an Ice Age leaf fall.

᠔ ᠓

The early brain, shielded with a warrior's helmet of bone as though nature itself was dubious of the survival of this strange instrument and yet had taken steps to protect it, is, in itself, a minor mystery. If we go back to the beginnings of life, not man, he has taken three billion years to produce and perhaps in a few more years thirty minutes to destroy. I like to think that with the invention of a brain capable of symbolic thought and, perhaps, as an unsought corollary, philosophy, nature rejoiced to look out upon itself. But man has dragged out of the Ice Age with him an old and lower brain that reemerges in the mists of alcohol or which I have seen snarling on the bed of madness. There are claws in it by now fantastically extended.

❧ ❦

It began as such things always begin — in the ooze of unnoticed swamps in the darkness of eclipsed moons. It began with a strangled gasping for air.

The pond was a place of low life, of reek and corruption, of fetid smells, of oxygen-starved fish breathing through laboring gills. Things floundered and died in the fat, warm mud. At times the slowly contracting circle of the water left little windows of minnows that skittered desperately to escape the sun, but who died nevertheless. It was indeed a place of low life. In it the human brain began.

There were strange snouts in those waters, strange barbels nuzzling the bottom ooze, and most of all there was time — two hundred million years of it — but mostly, I think, it was the ooze.

❧ ❦

Paraphrasing for my fire paper: The campfire is more real than the hydrogen bomb, we must have fire at first hand, the fire of leaves in autumn, the simple homeliness of things.

≽ ≼

Few laymen realize that every bone that one holds in one's hands is a fallen kingdom, a veritable ruined world, a totally unique object which will never return through time.
What of it, a chain is displaced.

≽ ≼

It was the day I first doubted I was human. "Arrk," I said. It was a genuine amphibian croak — expelled out of me in surprise — from some ancient brain center.
The heron said nothing at all. I could still see that cold, impersonal yellow eye aiming over his beak — and the beak itself drawn back a little further.

"Arrk," I croaked again. Maybe so large a croak startled him. And like a frog shrieking suddenly underfoot, I took advantage of his befuddlement, and I rolled with a great splash into the water.
There was no reason for him to take me as human, though I suppose the size of the splash may have indicated I was too big to digest. But perhaps it was only my bright little eye in the mud that he wanted.

≽ ≼

Just now in the midst of a cold, driving rain and the turbulent winter boiling of clouds over his favorite perch on a wind-whipped sapling, I found him singing again. The sound came up into my study and from the study into my heart, the melody hanging there like something from the timeless world of Plato's forms, so that I was distracted from my tasks and began to think of springs long ago and a girl I remembered.

I even put up the window in desperation and laid out some seeds, though I knew it was useless, since that outer world was his, and he eyed me, perhaps with justice, as being tinged with evil, otherwise why would I be seeking to purchase favors with good seed?

"But you have only two or three years more to learn the meaning of this," I said to him darkly. "I am forty-five and determined to know. With that song and what I have found in books maybe the secret could be learned by us together. There is not much time, you know, and less for you than me; it is important to know why one is singing."

He did not fly up to the window. He sang on, those beautiful notes falling carelessly as raindrops across the house roofs, falling into my heart, falling in the lanes of memory, bothering my pen in its slow way across the paper. I tore up the sheet, but I began again. I will start at the very beginning, I told him severely, though he was fainter now and had, as I judged, perched farther away. I will begin at the beginning and find the way of it — to that song, I mean, and why I, who am not a bird, can be so troubled by it. I will begin at the very beginning.

The pure voice did not mock me, it sang on as I wrote, but it does not help me. Out of the eternal garden of the forms it does not know me, but as I listen I know mankind should find its way thither; music reaches down to us, that at least I know.

Man's ego suffered three great blows. Loss of the center of the stage — Copernicus. Loss of directed evolution — Darwin. Loss of the moral mind — Freud.

⋊ ⋉

Nearly every week when I pick up the literary reviews I find that a new book on space travel has appeared. Even the navigational problems are being considered in serious and erudite tones. Needless to say, I am glad to see this. After all, one doesn't want to leave one's own little dust-fleck universe without some idea of where one is heading and how one is to get back. Space is lonely and vast beyond our conception, but we pretty well understand that now. It is not this that troubles me as I read the increasing literature — pulp or otherwise — upon space travel; it is, instead, the appalling poverty of imagination manifested in our descriptions of the world outside — whether within our universe or far beyond in other galaxies and remote from us by light-years.

The lack of grasp of biological principles is exhibited by both readers and writers in this field. I have read about cabbage men and bird men; I have read the loves of the lizard men and the tree men, but in every case I have labored under no illusion. I have been reading about a man, Homo sapiens, that common earthling clapped into an ill-fitting coat of feathers and retaining all his basic human attributes, including, generally, an eye for the pretty girl who has just emerged from the spaceship. His lechery and miscegenating proclivities have an oddly human ring, and if this is all we are going to find on other planets, I for one am going to be content to stay at home. There is quite enough of that sort of thing down here, without encouraging it throughout the starry systems.

⋊ ⋉

Last evening the largest house centipede I have ever seen died peacefully on our bathroom rug.

It is a strange thing to record the death of a centipede with the reluctance with which one speaks of the death of a pet sheepdog, but at the last I think I may have been a little confused on the whole subject. Toward the end this centipede was very tired, and like two aging animals who have come into a belated understanding with each other, we achieved a mutual tolerance, if not respect. He had ceased to run with that flowing, lightning-like menace which is part of the horror of centipedes to man; and I, in my turn, ceased to drive him away from the woolly bathroom rug on which his final desires had centered. It took me a little while to realize that he wished to spend his remaining days there, but after I understood I am proud to say that he came to no harm at my hands and that he died there so peacefully that it took me a little while to realize he was gone.

> ≺

May 21, 1953

Early in this month Mabel and I took an evening stroll around the Wynnewood Park Apts. and in three separate instances observed along the walks in the twilight, dark collections of a small ant so thickly clustered as to appear like freshly excavated dirt — Mabel, in fact, first assuming that it was a newly opened nest. The ants seemed quiescent, certainly not moving rapidly, and thus enhancing their similarity, in the half darkness, to fresh, dark earth. There were no signs of winged forms, only these curious masses as though some kind of meeting were going on. There appeared to be no substance along the walk which was attracting them. I assume, because of the three instances observed, that the event was not unusual but was somehow an appropriate action of this form at this season. Doubtless if it had been feasible to observe, other gatherings would have been seen in the surrounding fields. What they were occupied in doing I have not the slightest idea. Does some physiological impulse hit them all at the same time? Certainly the colonies we observed were too remote from each other to be mutually influenced by contact.

A few days ago I observed, after a night's rain, cicadas (the seventeen-year form?) emerging from their larval cases around the tree near the Wynnewood station. The grubs coming to the surface were creeping toward the nearest tree. Those I observed were creeping in the proper direction to reach it. Was this chance, or do they have a way of sensing or seeing

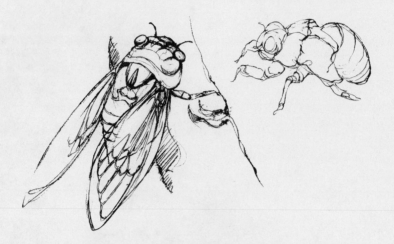

the tree? The grubs were a yellowish earth-stained brown, the
emerging adults white with red eyes.

I was greatly impressed with the number who failed to
achieve their passage into the world of light. Some failed to
wriggle free of their old garb and died only partially out of
the grub form. Some worked clear, but their wings failed to
develop properly; others crept painfully about with stiff legs
or other defects which seemed largely due to hormonal failures or low viability. The wastage is tremendous, even leaving
aside the birds that attack the emergents in their helpless
stages. Nevertheless, the wood, next day, was full of the
successful. They appeared, in contrast to the middlewestern
two-year variety, very sluggish and unwilling fliers. They were
easy to pick up and seemed to prefer to cling rather than fly.
The color is dark, the red eyes remaining.

A high wind on the day of emergence caused much damage
to wings still soft and forming, as well as hurling many to the
ground. This event certainly added to the casualties. I noticed
an attacking sparrow striking the wings from one individual,
and I found other wings in pairs with the body gone, mute
testimony to the attack of birds. Later I saw an ant carrying
away the wings.

This great loss is reminiscent of Richard Jefferies' account
of young mice of the last brood freezing in the English winter. I tried to help a few — such is one's eagerness to further
life against death.

⋊ ⋉

Sunday, June 7, 1953

Walked along the edge of the daisy field. Interesting to see
nature going on here at the verge of the Penn Fruit Company.
Abandoned cups, match cases, whiskey bottles slowly being
covered and made "natural" by red clover and daisies. How
fast life flows from one form to another. *The illusion of
things.* To the generations of cabbage butterflies I must be as
everlasting as the Sphinx. I turned round sharply to make
sure the Wynnewood shopping center had not disappeared
while I gazed. I half expected to see a little plaster and a few
bricks disappearing into the insatiable maw of the clover.
Matter disappears or modifies its appearances so fast that
everything takes on an aspect of illusion — a momentary
fizzing and boiling with smoke rings, like pouring dissident
chemicals into a retort. To a time-foreshortened eye all form
would become bubblings or momentary imaginative shapes
such as one sees when dreaming before a winter fire. One
thinks one sees a shape and it is gone. Perhaps it is so with
God half-asleep over the dying embers of his universe, and
dreaming the shapes that come and go through the coals.

Got to thinking that Ernest Borek's *Man the Chemical
Machine* is a further extension of the Cartesian world view.
First, man is a machine of pulleys and levers, then when this
fails to provide the complete answer he becomes the *chemical*
machine; what, after this — the crystal-lattice machine, the
electron machine? We must be near to reaching the end of
this road.

Sunday, February 14, 1954

A long abandonment of this record, but I shall now try to
get back into the spirit of it. The thought struck me yesterday
that one queer thing about mammals is that they have never

developed footless land forms. Weasels and certain of their relatives are sinuous and long-bodied but none of them have actually paralleled the snake in adaptation. Perhaps the latter requires belly plates to be successful, since whales have certainly lost the hind limbs. It is interesting to speculate on the amount of correlation involved in (1) loss of legs, (2) development of locomotion by plates which requires muscular adjustments, etc.

A good essay could also be written on animals living in holes, etc., and the dangers of going out into the world.

≫ ≪

March 17, 1954

Have read a little note about the fact that our pigeons, which are, of course, European, and derived from the European rock pigeon, do not exhibit much enthusiasm for trees. They are real cliff dwellers and modern cities are ideal habitats for them. This may be worth developing at more length. I shall go back and read Darwin upon them.

Some days ago we had a mystery in the house — a huge burrow in a flower pot. I have never heard of mice doing this before, but I now learn that the construction of the new Wanamaker building has destroyed an acre or more of wild land and the field mice have flooded into the apartment. Poor little fellows — the end of their world — and now everyone is hunting, poisoning, and trapping them. The little visitor to our apartment could not resist the green smell and earth of our little hothouse. He dug and kicked earth out merrily when we were not here. Now he has been shut out by new house fixtures to ring the pipes. That last wistful episode of the greens haunts me. Civilization has taken the last truly wild field in Wynnewood.

≫ ≪

August 12, 1955

Many months since my last entry. I am a poor diary
keeper — no doubt of that! This morning I saw a very remarkable sight. It was a rainy, windy day and the huge water
lily leaves in the museum pond were all projecting above the
surface and blowing in the wind. There are possibly two
species represented — one lying flat to the water — the other
standing a little above as in this drawing. The lily leaves have

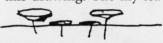

an adaptation (probably of fine waxy hairs) which causes
waterdrops to roll over them without penetrating or soaking
the leaf. As the cuplike big leaves swayed in the wind, sizable
drops of water rolled around and around in them like drops
of quicksilver, flashing and quivering in the grey light. There
were many leaves and much water and the whole pond
seemed to quiver and flash as the drops rolled in the
unsoakable leaves. Darwin was right that this phenomenon
deserves investigation.

⋊ ⋉

August 27, 1955

Mabel, home from the folks, tells me the story of a pet
chicken, "Humphrey," acquired by an old couple, the Beals,
next door to her parents. Humphrey learned to peck the door
in order to be admitted. He would roost at night on the edge
of the bathtub. Apparently since they had no other chickens
he preferred to nest with gregarious humans. He crowed a
great deal in the morning, hopefully, but finally developed a
feud with the Beals' dog and had to be given away.

⋊ ⋉

September 1, 1955

(a)   It occurs to me that there is a very clear analogy between the way in which an apartment house (or another building, for that matter) acquires its biota, and the way an oceanic island acquires its plant and animal population. An apartment house newly built (a recent volcanic island up-thrust from the waves) is destitute at first of a fauna. If it is remote from neighborhoods where such a fauna may be acquired (islands far at sea), it may be destitute of insects, silverfish, etc., for a longer period. As time runs on, however, the chance of immigrants arriving intensifies. A pair of roaches may arrive in a box (floating timber) and escape into the basement, and soon the house is populated so extensively that even the professional exterminators can only keep the population reduced. The closer the apartment house may lie to other older ones or to neighborhood groceries, as in, say, New York, will play a part in the time involved before population is acquired. Now, to give this a figurative evolu-tionary twist, we might imagine each house more self-contained than it actually is and lasting over more than one geological period. Let us conceive that this genetic isolation is further played upon by different methods of extermination used by the human inhabitants. Let us say that in one house roaches have grown adjusted to a given poison, in another they have developed clever adaptations for evading the traps set for them by people, or perhaps other insects have been introduced to combat them. Say, spiders. All of this would mean a series of self-contained apartment (island) worlds in which intense but quite different forms of selection were going on. In the end, after the passage of some millions of years, the once-similar biotas might be quite different. The heating system (climate) in the different apartments might also be hot, cool, humid, dry, etc. Eggs, larvae, etc., will thus be struggling against quite different natural environments.

(b)   I could not help being amused today. An exterminator came and let loose a gas that gave me unpleasant physical symptoms. After it was all over, I went into the bathroom and found a vigorous, fast-moving young roach perched on my toothbrush. I was showing more effects from the "exter-minator" than he, and he easily evaded my lunge at him.

(c)   Engels, I believe, says somewhere that Darwin failed to distinguish between struggle to survive in a single environment and the adaptation leading into new environments. Critics of Malthus have pointed out that he created a false situation in that he claimed population was increasing faster than the food supply, when what was really happening was that population was increasing faster than a given type of economic system could make use of people. In other words, there was no shortage of food in a natural sense, there was only an ecological failure. Perhaps an analogy to human society exists here in the animal world. Cities allow more niches in which diverse talents can be manifest. Similarly, a biota which has arranged itself in ecological communities has reduced the struggle for existence so that more types can take advantage of a given region (law of divergence). Thus diverse adaptive mutation is important, more important for life in general than straight-line evolution. Man's mental variability, which is not wholly cultural, has, in his cities, replaced physical evolution.

⩗ ⩘

September 20, 1955

Saw a pigeon on the campus today with feet carrying little feathered ruffles, or teddy bear shoes. Obviously wild but sporting some remnant of high breeding in a fancier's cote — a fallen aristocrat.

Also one with an injured leg who used his wings to move when the other walked. He used to rest in the sun with his wings spread out, lying on his side in an ungainly fashion but looking nevertheless well fed and managing to cope with his infirmity. Perhaps in winter he would suffer more. The college campus was a better refuge for him than the city streets would have been and hurt his remaining foot less. Where he roosted and how, I had, of course, no idea. Sooner or later a cat. . . .

There is something intensely pathetic about harmless animals dying alone. I shall never forget coming across the University of Kansas campus one summer evening and finding a dying turtle dove on the walk. It had not been visibly injured, but had been perhaps poisoned. Its mate, in very obvious emotional distress, walked nervously about it and paid

absolutely no attention to me as I squatted down to see if I could help. I lifted up the dying bird, whose eyes were already glazing, and placed it on the flat roof of a nearby shed, where it might at least be safe from dogs or cats. All the time, the female bird stood fearlessly at my feet and fluttered up to the shed roof to be beside her mate. It was hopeless. In the last light of evening I hurried away asking myself questions I did not want to ask. Was there a nest? Were there young? That affectionate life-indifferent bird by nightfall would be alone in the vast universe feared by us all. I did not go that way again in the morning. I knew too well what I would find.

≽ ≼

December 11, 1955

A few nights ago some hoarded wisteria seeds exploded. Mabel heard them. When I got out to the living room, pods and seeds were scattered on the floor and other things had been hurled out of the glass in which the pods had been placed. The seed pods explode with great violence — apparently longitudinally by means of fibers contracting unequally, since the pods cannot be placed back together. All in all it is a remarkable performance.

≽ ≼

December 16, 1955

Looking out of a sixteenth-floor window of the Barbizon-Plaza Hotel in New York, I saw several pigeons turning round and round, apparently warming themselves in the warm air currents emanating from some chimneys or air vents in a roof immediately below me. Looking closer I discovered several such chimneys emerging from the wall on the side nearest to me. On each chimney sat a pigeon, his little bottom carefully tucked over the warmth. It was dawn in a grey way. The pigeons were ruffed up from the cold, their beaks buried in their feathers, but they held firm to their little individual air vents like men warming their bottoms before a fireplace.

Later, descending to the street, I found clouds of pigeons in places where they were not to be found in rush hours. They were picking up bits of crust and other garbage in front of bars and grocery stores before the increasing traffic of the morning would force them aloft again. Obviously they have the ecology of the city well worked out.

There could be added here the brave way these small birds seek their living and survive. No mean feat.

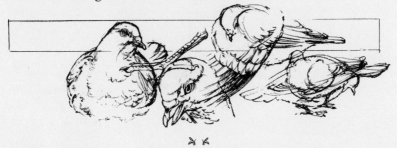

I think I might as well tell you it always happens to me like this — the laugh, I mean — like Cassandra.

I was talking to the old man, humoring him if you like, and careful with my "yes, sirs" and "no, sirs," when I saw this big, wet rat come out of the drain on the terrace and sit right up under the old man's chair. It was just turning toward evening, the liquor was expensive, the lawn clipped as only the wealthy can afford it. And still just back of the old man's white duck pants I could see that rat standing up wet from the drain and peering out with considerable interest and with a jaunty turn to its whiskers between the old man's legs.

"Animals," said the old philosopher, shifting in his chair, "are mechanisms. Eventually they can be duplicated. Men, too, you know. Just machinery and in time we'll do better."

"Yes, sir," I said and waited for the rat to run. I was sure he was just making a mistake, but there he stayed right under the old man's bottom. I could still make out the whiskers and a beady glint to the eye, though the dusk was deepening.

⋊ ⋉

January 28, 1956

Man is always marveling at what he has blown apart, never at what the universe has put together, and this is his limitation. He still has something of the destructive primate mind within him. He is at heart a "fragmenting" creature. He resents even Bergson's indeterminism and would see evolution as the response of the dead to the dead — not indeterminate at all. Man, the creation of the universe, after all created the bomb.

⋊ ⋉

April 14, 1956

There must be dogs barking at the bottom of chaos — great, hoarse hounds whose voices bounce eternally against falling rock and echo and reecho in the crevices of eternity. Only a dog's voice out of the deep abysses carries the proper menace and at the same time preserves the weird objectivity and indifference which is part of the hunting pack. A lion's voice is great but personal, a dog's bark by contrast contains the maniacal essence of chaos, dumb matter come alive in the dark and howling its voice endlessly and stupidly against the sleeping quiet of nonexistence — but I overelaborate — perhaps you have not heard as I have hounds beneath you as you cling desperately to a cliff wall.

When I get to the bottom they turn warm and wagging and friendly — again with the total irrationality that obtains over the great cliff of chaos. Did they take me finally, because of my successful descent, as a demon like themselves — for if I had fallen, they had given every indication of devouring me — or are the dogs of Cerberus, the hoarse-voiced, much-feared guardians of Nothing, actually abysmally friendly and lonely creatures? Since that long, agonizing descent before I reached the city on the plain, I have never been quite sure. When I come to the Final Pit in which they howl, I shall, without too great a show of confidence, put out my hand once more and speak. Perhaps the great hounds of fear may wait with wagging tails for a voice who knows them. It may as well be mine. For who is to know one demon from another in the dark. . . .

≯ ≮

May 9, 1956

At the Cambridge conference Jerome Bruner noted that Darwin's great observation lay in his placing all life on a common basis governed by a common principle. At the same time, the Darwinists tended to see man as the completed perfection, the blossom, so to speak, of the tree of life. Freud, taking off from Darwinian conceptions of change and imperfection, regards man as unfinished and containing in his mind the primitive as well as the new. Freud avoided the all-or-none idea of mental illness and thus recognized continuity. . . .

Oppenheimer ventured that Darwin was understood because he was time-minded. Mendel, by contrast, had a new idea which was not grasped and had, in the beginning, no "ideological appeal" [the latter expression mine so far as Oppie's speech is concerned].

Some lecturers, such as Harcourt Brown, regarded the humanities, in contrast to science, as primarily involved with the discovery and exploration of the individual, the unique. Considerable discussion arose as to whether any scientific theory which becomes widely popular does not really do so because it is supporting or offers the possibility of support to [laissez faire capitalism in the case of Darwinism] some popular ideology. In this sense one might speak of ideological science, as one can also note the respect for gadgets on the part of the layman is really belief in scientific magic.

≥ ≤

December 22, 1956

Reading in Thoreau's journals today. It strikes me that Thoreau's writing is like his own landscape — a vast expanse of weeds, brush, thickets, and just occasionally a singing bird with a soft note hidden in some unexceptionable underbrush. Thoreau, in other words, is as chaotic as the real world of nature and just as full of trivia, with here and there some remarkable observational nugget.

≥ ≤

"DEVIATION"
IN PHYSICAL ANTHROPOLOGY

In Russia, when the state for political reasons desires to destroy the public reputation of a writer, scientist, or official, one of the several epithets which may be used to convey the man's deviation from the party line is the word "mystic." It was used, for example, in connection with the fall from grace of the Polish leader Gomulka before his recent rehabilitation under Khrushchev. As an occasional student of the history of thought, I cannot resist the observation that this name-calling device occasionally emerges here in some few scientific quarters where there is an unconscious attachment to an extremely materialistic world view similar to that which broods with such intensity over the Russian landscape. One may write, for example, a nature essay in the purely literary tradition, expressing some feeling for the marvelous, or the wonder of life — things perfectly acceptable when perused in such old classics as Thoreau or Hudson, and then awake to discover that a certain element in the "union" regards one's activities in this totally separate field as "mystical" and "alien to the spirit of science." It was not so among the great Renaissance thinkers, but the growing compartmentalization of thought has contributed to a trade feeling that the shoemaker should stick to his last. The feeling is more evident in some sciences than in others; in fact, some of the older sciences, whose members, perhaps, are more secure and with a longer tradition behind them, are manifestly less nervous in this regard than younger ones.

⋇ ⋇

July 13, 1957

The week of June first was robin week, first one little nonflying robin sitting grumpily in the middle of the street, then days of the little creatures hopping helplessly about on the university campus, tended by anxious mothers. This week the survivors are able to fly. Saw one mother making exaggerated pecking motions, making dirt fly. Obviously she didn't expect to catch anything but was trying to impress upon her wing-fluttering offspring the advisability of working for a living. The young bird was a reasonably good but hesitant flyer. He pecked, a little vaguely, as I watched him. Mother was all alertness and intensity — a beautiful example of Bergson's phrase. Well, she has done better by the future than I have — because of her there will be robins chirping and flying in the next century.

Robins, by the way, seem to descend out of the nest in a much more helpless state than some birds — suggesting, as does the easy running of the adults, that it would not take much to turn them into ground birds given an open corridor such as was once presented by the islands.

Also in the first week, while sitting on a bench back of Houston Hall I saw a small warbler of some kind take a drink head downward from a leaking wall faucet. He sought the faucet out so directly and drank with such surety that I am confident he had practiced the trick before. There was hardly any water emerging and he practically thrust his head

into the opening. Wright Morris, apropos of similar clever-
ness, told me he had seen a New York pigeon pecking along
the sidewalk cracks.

ꓹ ꓗ

July 23, 1957

A good idea for an essay: the trigger, simplifying mechanisms of life — all the way up to man, who, culturally, however, has a far more varied approach to reality. The dream
animal again. And is it not true that life, as manifested
through its instincts, demands a security guarantee from
nature that is largely forthcoming? The inorganic world could
and does really exist in a kind of chaos, but before life can
peep forth, even as a flower, or a stick insect, or a beetle, it
has to have some kind of unofficial assurance of nature's
stability, just as we can read that stability in the ripple marks
impressed in stone, or the rain marks on a long-vanished
beach, or in the eye of a vanished hundred-million-year-old
trilobite. The nineteenth century was amazed when it discovered these things, but wasps and migratory birds were not.
They had an old contract, an old promise, never broken till
man began to interfere with things, that nature, in degree, is
steadfast and continuous. Her laws do not change, nor moons
shift, nor the seasons come and go too violently. There is
change, but throughout the past, life alters with the slow pace
of inorganic change. Calcium, iron, phosphorus, I suppose,
could exist in the jumbled world of the inorganic without the
certainties we know. Taken up into a living system, however,
being that system, they must, in a sense, have knowledge of
the future; tomorrow's rain may be important, tomorrow's
wind, tomorrow's sun — their own or another's. Life in
contrast to the inorganic is historic in a new way. It reflects
the past but must also expect something of the future. It has
nature's promise — a guarantee that has not been broken in
four billion years that the universe has a queer kind of rationality and expectedness about it. Lord Dunsany says, "If we
change too much we may no longer fit into the scheme of
things; but the glow-worm shows no signs of making any
change." (*Patches of Sunlight*, p. 25)

ꓹ ꓗ

August 24, 1957

Life in general, not just man, could be said to have a note
of rationality toward the future which makes it different than
other matter. And what marvels are to be seen in this
unmarvelous world. (1) A group of crows, huge, mysterious,
plotting on the ground. (2) A human brain so removed from
food-getting it tried to understand them. . . .

>< ><

September 22, 1957

The fog-world — its attraction. In it man is free, unob-
served, himself, as he is also in a snowstorm. It is a foretaste
of being a bodiless ghost.

Perhaps cities with their growing population are like ponds
filling up with life. Organisms grow more and more specialized, more and more their worlds are fractured and
divided — man in his cities is undergoing something similar,
loss of community, etc.

>< ><

September 29, 1957

Is it possible one could compose a nature anthology not on
the "season" principle but the "mood" principle, that is,
storm — whether wind, rain, etc. (Thoreau's snowstorm) —
sunlight, cold, heat, etc. Perhaps also animal moods could be
involved. . . .

>< ><

October 3, 1957

Bees in museum pond resting on water lily leaves and
drinking from little rivulets in the beautiful autumn sunlight.

>< ><

October 12, 1957

I am not nearly so interested in what monkey man was derived from as I am in what kind of monkey he is to become.

⤜ ⤛

October 13, 1957

The follies of the anthropologist and/or science.

1. Emphasis on the past to the exclusion of man's transcending powers in the present.
2. Because man was a social animal long before he was man, there is a tendency to forget society, in man, is, in a marked degree, a conscious act and that, as Bruner has remarked, "if one is concerned for society, he must above all be concerned for this social consciousness."

⤜ ⤛

October 15, 1957

Idea: "Diary of a Suicide Year." Saw in New York a few days ago two pigeons persistently mating on the corner of a tall building. They kept falling off and recovering in midflight. Living dangerously!

Fog. See Thoreau's *A Week on the Concord and Merrimack Rivers.* "Always the laws of light are the same, but the modes and degrees of seeing vary. . . . There was but the sun and the eye from the first." (p. 134) Use this for start of nature book.

⤜ ⤛

October 21, 1957

Start for Kansas University speech: Ladies and gentlemen, just ninety-nine years ago Charles Darwin and Alfred Russel Wallace announced a momentous scientific discovery: the discovery, in brief, that life was not made, that instead it was being made. If you will glance down at your feet this evening, you may verify that statement. You have encased your feet in shoes and you have done so because the human foot is still inadequately adjusted to the upright posture of man and feels most comfortable when it is sustained and braced by artificial devices. Like every living thing in nature we are, in a certain sense, marred, imperfect and transitional. If we were not, if we did not possess this power to change, we would not have come up the long, strange pathway from the primordial ooze. We would not be sitting here tonight with clothes replacing our lost fur and listening, I hope not too complacently, to an account of these matters. For it is of change I want to speak to you this evening — change and the deaths that it is possible to die of change, but which we have forgotten until lately, having been, as a race, fortunate.

➢ ➣

November 3, 1957

A day or two before coming to Lawrence, troubled by the onerous burdens laid upon me by your learned committee, I took the trouble to walk through the Hall of Man in one of the large eastern museums. A person of great learning had been instrumental in erecting those exhibits, and I hoped to find there some clue as to human destiny, some key that might unlock in a few succinct sentences the nature of man. The exhibit ended in a question mark before an atomic machine and a graph showing the almost incredible energy that now lay open to the hand of man. Needless to say, I agreed with the question mark which ended the history of humanity within that hall. But as I turned and went in the other direction, step by step, eon by eon, back into the past, I came to a scarcely human thing crouched over a little fire of sticks and peering up at me under shaggy brows. The caption read: "Man begins his technological climb up the energy ladder. He discovers fire." I walked a short ways backward and forward.

I read the captions. I looked again at the creatures huddled over a fire of sticks — at the woman clutching a child to her breast. Again I searched the hall. Here was the sum total of all that history and anthropology had seen fit to emphasize as important in the human story. The hunter's tools were there, the economic revolution effected by agriculture was ably presented. Summarized before my eyes populations grew, cities and empires rose and fell, and still man's energy accumulated. One saw another thing. One saw the armored legions grow and grow until at last continent confronted continent and the powers of death to a world lay in the hands of the descendants of that naked woman and her consort by the fire of sticks.

But as I stood and gazed at that learned presentation of the past, a disturbing doubt crossed my mind. Was the story true? Of course it is true, my reason told me. It is the verdict of science. It is a story that you yourself have helped, in a small way, to make; there is the arrow buried in the bone, there is the fire, there is the trail of man across five continents. There is his first timid reaching out into the seas, and now let us get on to the skies. Forget the cities in the sand. Mars will be next.

I hesitated again before those engines of the past and still my doubts continued — for it seemed to me that there was lacking here some clues, some vital essence of the creature man — that I was looking upon stone and potsherd, sword and catapult, from someplace just a little remote and distorted. "This is the story of man," the caption ran through my head, and at that moment, finally, I knew I was looking at the past through the eyes of a modern twentieth-century American, or, for that matter, a Russian. There was no basic difference. In that whole exhibit was ranged the energies of wheat and fire and oil, but of what man had dreamed of his relations with men there was no trace. Yet it is only on paper, or in human heads, we might say in paraphrase of Shaw, that man has sought successfully to transcend himself, his appetites and his desires. In that great room was no slightest hint of the most remarkable story of all — the rise of a value-creating animal and the way in which his values had been modified and transformed to bring him to the world he faces today. It is of this I would speak this evening.

❧ ❦

November 17, 1957

Interesting essay topic to me particularly: gifts to ladies from men and penguins. Cat giving mouse, the givingness of nature.

≽ ≼

Day after Thanksgiving, November 29, 1957

Perhaps my "Evolutionist Looks at Modern Man" could incorporate (1) feet with shoes equal price of getting erect, (2) loss of hair and . . . of using clothes equals price of getting brain, (3) getting brain equals price of becoming subservient to man after we have escaped subservience to nature in other forms. Will this in the end be the most dreadful subservience of all — for already man *fears* man? Or is this a necessary prelude to the true humanization of man? Does he not carry in his heart, each individual man, the power to transcend this image of evil? Is this what free will means? Some of this developed might make a little essay.

≽ ≼

THE SUNFISH

The stream is lifeless but it thunders
Over the dam where once it poured,
Though now night-black the oil slick mutters
And no child fishes at the ford.

But I, the child of sixty pausing,
I look, and all my life writhes there —
A sunfish, in one spangled moment,
Beating with light the throttling air.

≽ ≼

HOW MAN CAME

Doubleday Book

The creature called man has a strange history. He is not of one piece, nor was he born of a single moment in time. His elementary substance is stardust almost as old as the universe.

His living organs, his eyes, backbone, his hands and feet—
even his remarkable brain—have originated in far places and
in different eras of time. He is a mosaic of odd parts drawn
together as one might rifle a cosmic junkyard to make a more
than usually complicated tin woodman or a scarecrow. Some
of the parts have been bent to other than their original purposes, some are obsolescent.

None of these facts makes man unique. All living creatures,
because of the changing nature of life, are constructed of
similar wandering bits of material strung together by a peculiar little alphabet or set of instructions, a kind of "do it
yourself" kit which all plants and animals carry in their
bodies and pass from one generation to another.

Man can give names to these processes, lengthy scientific
names, like DNA, but their wonder remains. In short, we are
stardust that somehow assembled itself first into life and
finally into consciousness. This implies strange forces in the
universe that no amount of naming by man can make ordinary. Man can use terms like evolution and try to position
himself in time, but when, behind all these processes, he asks
why they are, or came to be, he has reached the borders of
science and has entered a realm of thought which can never
be tested in a laboratory. This is the realm of what used to be
called final questions, the questions asked by the philosopher.
We can reason about such questions in a division of thought
known as metaphysics. Or we may explain them in terms of
religious faith. But unlike the domain of science, with its
palpable causes and effects which we have come to take as
given and to be studied either in the experimental world of
the laboratory or the wider, more confusing world of nature,
we can only think what we are informed of by our senses. By
the nature of things we are denied a scientific answer to the
question Why? We can only accept the universe as given and
proceed to examine how it seems to operate. Scientists toy
successfully by observation to answer the question How?
Upon the Why? scientists can only speculate. As we have
slowly learned the vastness of the universe we inhabit, the
Why? recedes even farther from our comprehension. Some
men avoid this question by asserting the universe in some
form, not necessarily that of the present, has always existed;
some believe it was created in the infinitely remote past. All
our science can assert with confidence is that we are change-

lings and that this is true even of our chemical elements, though they are far older than we. The stars and the galaxies change. Change and becoming is the law of the universe, but why this should be, or why there should be a universe subjected to the laws we know, or indeed why there should be a universe at all — these questions science cannot answer. Perhaps they are some kind of figment of our logic, a reflection of our limited minds. At any rate, they humble our pride, but it is well to ask some questions which receive no answer. It confirms the fact that man is a child, perhaps even an orphan child of the universe. Certainly he is not its master as some have tried to assert. He can live only within the web of nature and by observing her laws. When he disturbs her by blundering about with newfound powers like an apprentice magician, he sometimes invites nature's retaliation, as we are beginning to learn to our cost.

This book therefore is intended to tell the reader how man came, how he built his first cities and grew aware of himself and of his problems, and how he may master them. The Plains Indians had a favorite story motif and an opening line that began, "Once there was a poor orphan." This was once a true statement of man's condition, and although man has since attained to material riches he is a poor orphan still — an orphan armed with dangerous weapons he has picked up by the wayside that threaten to destroy not the fearsome creatures that once threatened him, but himself. He needs, in other words, another little kit of instructions not carried in his body. That strange little kit that is studied by genetics instructs his body how to shape itself. What the orphan now needs in the freedom given him by nature is a new kit of instructions upon how to live. Man himself must write this book. He has been trying for many ages all over the earth, but he has found the task difficult, and even more difficult the task of observing the rules he has devised for himself. This is part of the problem of being human and an orphan in a world where other creatures go about with another little set of instructions known as instinct, which tell them to be what they are, as for example an otter, a beaver, or a serpent. By contrast, man has gotten lost in a desert of terrible freedoms. He does not know clearly what he is and he frequently falls into violent argument as to how to behave. At such times the wise among his kind know that he is still an orphan and that he needs a new instruction. They are beginning to believe that either he is the kind of creature who will always need a new book because he cannot stay the same very long, or that perhaps he is too restless to absorb what has already been placed in his hands. If this is indeed true, man is in grave danger, for there is little hope for an orphan on an unknown path who refuses all guidance. He will remain a waif to the end of his days. It must also be considered, however, that this may be the last residue of instinctive instruction given to man — that he remain a wanderer. Long ago but not unwisely it was said in a sacred book that the foxes have their holes but the son of man has nowhere to lay his head. In those words is expressed the epitome of the human condition down to this day.

II

Tale of man's organs, but emphasizing the real unity, the real taproot is life as represented in the genetic chain. Forebrain from fish.

III

How He Found Language (His Tongue).

IV

How He Found Himself.

❧ ❦

II

It was the biggest battle line the world has ever known. It ringed the continents and was fought without mercy on the shelving threshold of the sea. The seed of man may have been there, but in any case the battle was lost. This and only this is the reason we are not today oaring soundlessly through coral gardens, hovering for safety under the wandering Sargasso weed.

I sometimes think of it, leaning over the rail of a coastal steamer by night when a shark fin cuts the water. I think of it

even more when I scan an antique map or read those strange old tales of the medieval krakin — the giant squid that strangled ships in their fifty-foot arms. Yes, I think of it still, even when I put my nose up against aquarium glass and see a little octopus no bigger than a baseball exploring the neighborhood of my face with a friendly tentacle. I think how lucky we are and how much we owe to the cephalopods. I think of the wandering ways of chance and our brother the shark. I think of that million-year battle below the tides and the difficult metaphysical question of who the winner may have been. I do not know. But at least I stand here looking back into that awesome green world. I know that it was important to us long ago and that we sought to enter it. But the nostalgia I feel is very small and my sense of gratitude is very great. I would never knowingly injure an octopus.

Four hundred million years have passed since the vertebrates fought on the seafloor. They were the last of the great animal phyla (groups) to appear, and if any creature below the tides knows the place of their origin it is the starfish. Or it may be that dark, magnificent-lensed octopod eye remembers us. He is older than we and has changed less. He was there when we squirmed in the mud, when our mouths were jawless, when our spine was a rubbery rod, and we were lucky to know light from darkness. He was there when a fish was something very close to a worm — and when to say that about a fish was the same thing as saying it about a man because they were all contained in a mysterious creature with gill slits, and a nerve cord on its back instead of its front. The nerve cord is still there, only swollen at one end. With it you interpret these lines.

There were no fish in the sea — not in Cambrian times. Outside, beyond the breakers floated and swam the rulers of the primal waters — the cephalopods. Sometimes after great storms, huge fifteen-foot shells like dunce caps lay on the

beach and from the longer end a tangle of arms writhed
helplessly. The great squid of long ago had not yet abandoned all their molluscan habits. They were shell bearers. In
the shallow seas that invaded the continents of that day there
was an immense and swarming life, but the fossil beds so
nicely scattered with the shells of cuttlefish reveal no trace of
fishes. For this there is a simple reason. Fishes — that great
swarming multi-specied group that stands in our minds as the
epitome of sea life — arose in fresh water.

The earliest creatures clearly definable as fish are the
ostracoderms. We find fragments of their remains scattered
sparsely in the strata laid down in brackish marine estuaries.
It is the first sign of the seaward movement of the fishes and
it is an abortive one. These fish are armored like medieval
knights. Few were over a foot in length. Jawless scavengers,
they were still mumbling the debris of stream bottoms and
shuffling timidly through the silty darkness of the river
mouths. No fish alive carries such dreadnought armor.
Eurypterid sea scorpions the size of men had penetrated fresh
water. For a hapless nonbiting vertebrate, armor was the only
answer — armor and the electric shock batteries that some
carried concealed in their head shields. Flight into the seas
was impossible. Out there beyond the breakers floated the
cuttlefish with waiting arms. Below on the seafloor crawled
other nightmares.

It was the hour of the shark; no one knows where it began,
but the battle grew: the fishes were multiplying, building up
toward some tremendous biological explosion. They had at
last acquired jaws by the sacrifice of a gill arch. Armament
races are as old as the world, and strange things are done
when the need is desperate. The sixty-foot tiger shark and the
most deadly jaws in the world were built from models that
first raced out of the river mouths four hundred million years
ago.

Over the land the shadow of a million-year drouth deepened. The pendulum of climate swung from torrential rain to
the desiccation of trapped marshes and drying lakes. Floundering fishes in mud holes began to learn how to breathe air
by desperate swallowing and the use of a little air sac behind
the throat. The continental waters were inexorably contracting. The final battle was at hand.

I like to think it was there in a dying streambed that we

parted: the ganoid fish, with the beginnings of that lung that would enable him to creep on slow fins up the mud banks toward the future, and our ancient grey-nosed brother, who never developed an air bladder, turning downward toward the sea. It was the last time that we met to know each other, but we both survived. Ironically, the slime-mold life of those steaming marshes sticks to us still. We hate that grim sea-roving fin and the death it carries. We from the same mud hole, devising death with the same mud-puddle brains. . . .

As the only thinking mammals on the planet, perhaps the only thinking animals in the entire sidereal universe, the burden of consciousness has grown heavy upon us. We watch the stars, but the signs are ambiguous. We uncover the bones of the past and seek for our origins. There is a path there, but it appears to wander. The vagaries of the road may have a meaning, however. It is thus we torture ourselves. We go over and over that road and point to some strange quirk of change that affected human destiny. Was it chance? Was it fate? Was it God? The bones are silent, the oracles speak in riddles, only the shining thread runs on and on. Today we carry it, but never in the planet's history has it tarried for any form of life. It is concerned with the becoming, never with the past; it is always just leaving the present, and the present is briefly, very briefly, ourselves.

"Nevertheless, there is a goal," we seek to console ourselves. "The thread is there — the thread runs to a goal." But the thread has a tangled maze. There are strange turns in its history, loops and knots and constrictions. One thing alone it does not do. It never brings back the past.

※ ※

For Chapter II,
The Fractionated Brain, Beginning of 2nd Part

For this hazard is no more than the hazard that all men face who, at whatever point in time or at whatever spot on the world island, have ceased to be animals. It is the hazard of the poet in his attic, the philosopher before his fire with the great thoughts of the world scholars upon his knee. It is the hazard of the astronomer under the slit dome who confronts eternity. The dangers and the midnight terrors are those that converge upon a finite intelligence which, in spite of its limitations, has achieved a breadth of understanding that has enabled it to sound the depths of time and space and to grow increasingly aware of its prison house. For this brain, this dark sport of nature, this fifteen hundred cubic centimeters of grey matter so badly and so often inadequately used, has already leaped to the top of the wall with which nature surrounds each of her living things. In spite of the clutching hands of superstition and the tug of animal desires, a greater hunger moves the pulse in our temples. It is the rising hunger of the finite and restricted that desires the infinite. It is the cumulation of centuries of ameboid probings and tentacular extensions of that mind by cunning instruments and equally cunning projections of thought. It has touched the lives of animals other than itself and has seen their shapes waver and blow like smoke through the corridors of time; it has watched with terrified fascination itself, this brain, unrolling from the seed like a genie from a bottle and, casting its eye forward, seen it vanish again into the formless alchemies of the earth. It has loved with infinite tenderness and found its love finite and confined within the years. It has dreamed that its prison house was small and that Heaven lay somewhere just outside the Gate. Now, over the wall, it watches the suns storm by like hail, and the last glimmer of galaxies, tinier than candlelight, on the utmost verge of space.

I say that for a moment all this endless light-year universe hangs in a little cup between the eyes and ears, so dreadfully is man composed. The Renaissance thinkers were right when they said that man, the microcosm, contained the macrocosm, for that, in truth, is the dark gift he has been given, though he has only come to realize it by degrees, and to some intellectual minds the macrocosm itself is still small and shadowy or peopled by demonic shapes. "What if there are only spiders there?" a man once asked. "We always think of eternity as being vast, vast. What if it's one narrow room, like a bathhouse in the country, black and grimy with spiders in every corner?"

I suppose that to a philosophical spider such a notion of the universe would seem a tidy and a cosy one. Sometimes as one reads the religious writings of earlier centuries one gets a quite similar impression which reveals all too clearly even man's limited conception of himself, his tendency to lapse into the fractionated world of the animal centered about its

own being. It is then that he builds his coal-cellar universe
with the devil stoking away below, and angels plucking a
harp in the upper room to drown the outcries in the basement. Small and black and flame-licked was that eternity, and
small and black and at times venomous was the mind that
conceived it. If man is to seek happiness, he must grow out-
ward into the world he has discovered. He must pass the
borders of his own being. He must dream with the dreaming
greatness of the vast multicolored shape of life itself, not of
man, nor of serpents, but of that enormous whole that contains them, as it contains lover and the wandering stars and
the enormous freedom to change.

No man unaware of the history of ideas has any conception of the enormity of the struggle man has waged to climb
out of that frail trellis of bones on which his thought is hung
and go adventuring elsewhere. It is his one gift, but he has
learned of it only by degrees, and the marks of the animal
mind confuse and distort his visions still. The animal mind is
a mind limited by the shape of its body and the impulsion of
its instincts. Its attention is fixed upon food and comfort. It is
"fractionated" in the sense that it occupies a certain little
world picture suited to its capacities. Everything outside its
field of interest is ignored even if seen.

Now all life is to varying degrees trapped in just such little
intangible prisons compounded partly of the nature of the
senses, partly of the mind that uses the senses. The living
world is confined very largely to separate fractions of the
whole which lies about it. The great forest tree dreams on
indifferent to the world that passes on the road beneath it;
the midnight owl hunts under Antares' light without the
slightest curiosity about Antares; the pitted viper, drawn like
a homing missile upon the warmth emanating from a rabbit's
body, has no curiosity about the lives of rabbits. Such minds

are like splinters from a shattered mirror; they give back a very small, particularized reflection of the outer world. By contrast we might say that man is a much greater fragment. Alone among the animals he has escaped this pure utilitarian concentration which has compressed so many minds in nature into cramped little angles of view. Man in his moments of reflective thought has reached a fundamental point of divergence with the world from which he has emerged. He *can* contemplate the bird in flight and divorce his interest from the dinner plate. He is the only animal that can.

⊱ ⊰

"The fox," once remarked Bernard Shaw, "has enthusiastic followers." The same might be said for man. He, or the essence that composes him, is pursued on every forest path. He is trailed backward until he is bayed like an animal into some primeval den among rocks. Or he is followed by a hound pack in full cry along some shadowy road into the dubious future. He is saint or naked ape, he is the eternal cop-out, sadist, cheat, or Samaritan. He is the face that confronts us in our morning mirror. He is nobody, like Ulysses, or Everyman as seen by John Bunyan, but first of all he is Homo sapiens, the fox. No one has really seen him, no one knows his nature because he is everyone and no one. He is man. If his nature is defined in a book, he promptly sets about erasing that nature. His most determined followers are of his own persuasion, but he has a way of dividing and dividing them. He is man. He is multifarious and elusive.

Books have been written about him. Mostly they grow old and must be discarded because in his den the subject reads

them and promptly grows weary of their definitions. He takes to the woods once more and the hunt is in full cry. Occasionally a bit of red may flicker over the autumn hill, but the creature remains active and unscathed. To write a book about such a mythical beast demands a certain degree of detachment and a willingness to turn to the old fairy tales as well as to own oneself defeated. The sooner we come to this acknowledgment, the sooner we may be able to hold some kind of meaningful dialogue with the creature who confronts us every morning as we wake blinking in the dawn, namely that elusive changeling, ourselves.

I have succumbed to the lure of this most restless animal, and this book is about what I have learned in the hunt. It is a hunt that has taken me into ancient caverns, haunted tombs, and the whisperings that one hears at night in great libraries. Or again, I have felt a mocking presence in some subway face, or obscured beneath an Indian blanket. Upon one thing we can all agree: Once, so Indian mythology runs, there was a poor orphan. All Plains Indian tales have that formal opening. It is another way of saying this is the story of man. And it was to that subject that Darwin reluctantly turned in 1871.

≫ ≪

Note for essay: If men could only disintegrate like autumn leaves, fret away, dropping their substance like chlorophyll, would not our attitude toward death be different? Suppose we saw ourselves burning like maples in a golden autumn.

≫ ≪

July 12, 1958

Last evening Mabel learned at the Raineys' that their three-month-old Dachshund puts things into his basket and sleeps there with a hairbrush he collected by himself and clasps while sleeping. It is like the blanket, etc., fetishes of children. A mother substitute?

≫ ≪

September 14, 1958

In a New York subway several days ago I saw a man with a gibbon hand. Unfortunately, in the crowd I could see no more. The hand was clinging to the subway hanger. Amazing resemblance to a primate hand — long palm, almost footlike, short fingers.

⋊ ⋉

October 11, 1958

A few days ago, passing through one of the less frequented corridors of Pennsylvania Station, I heard the wonderful loud trilling of a single cricket apparently all alone in this great rumbling place. Was he calling for a female in his loneliness or merely singing an autumn song to himself? Why cannot any man do this in his machine-raucous society — trill out anyhow, sing to himself if to no one else, purr in the autumn sun? If he cannot love one thing, then love all, leaf, brick, and autumn spider.

⋊ ⋉

January 8, 1959

My election to the Sphinx Society. The great Egyptian gallery filled. George Taylor speaking on labor arbitration. One star slowly moving across the great window hinting of time and the vast spaces through which we hurtle.

⋊ ⋉

February 10, 1959

You do not know the power of the wind until you get into some high upland where it is always blowing. Then you see, in the sparse grass, the shining reflection of stones on which no lichen can secure a foothold. The rocks have lain there for ages while the wind has passed over them until, like pebbles in a stream, they have been polished by the mere passage of an unseen thing — the air. Lift them up and turn them over and the underside has the rough, crusty appearance of the original stone. It is a testimony to time and the passage of invisible powers. The stones are hard, not the soft limestones, but chalcedonies, stones capable of taking a polish, of being cut like jewels. Here the wind is the only unknown. You can feel him at his task the moment you come into his domain. He plucks at your clothing and begins the long task of grinding you down. Stay and he will reduce you to a bone as effectively as the sea. And from a bone he will reduce you to grains of sand. I have been in similar winds for half a century, because, like a stone, I have been reduced and worn by another unseen thing called life.

※ ※

February 22, 1959

A university is a place where people pay high prices for goods which they then proceed to leave on the counter when they go out of the store.

※ ※

February 24, 1959

I was born seven years after the start of the century in the wrong time, the wrong place, and into the wrong family. I am not insensible of the paradox: It is this which made me.

※ ※

April 10, 1959

For the purposes of history are equally legitimate with the purposes of science, but the two are not the same. They are different — and this, it becomes plain through much of the writing, is not grasped at the end of a century of Darwinism. Otherwise some scientists would not castigate their fellows for writing history, nor mistake those efforts for vilification.

Great ideas emerge from other ideas, and we men who study the transformations of the living world around us have less cause than most to read the history of human ideas as without phylogeny and without descent. To recognize this fact in the life of great genius is not to degrade his achievement to the commonplace. Rather, it is to make him a part of that adventure which is less lonely because it is the adventure of all mankind. Of that effort Charles Darwin was and remains a great adventurer.

> ≺

April 11, 1959

Huxley prophesied he and Darwin would become a new orthodoxy. A centennial year contrary to popular belief is always a bad time to survey either a man or his contributions to human thought. Eulogies may conceal the truth, society enters into a subconscious conspiracy to maintain what tradition has proclaimed. . . .

> ≺

For Joe Willits

The uses of a great professor are only partly to give us knowledge; his real purpose is to take his students beyond knowledge into the transcendental domain of the unknown, the future and the dream — to expand the limits of the human consciousness. In doing this he is creating the future in the minds of men. It is an awe-inspiring responsibility, and the men to whom this task is given should be chosen with all the care of which society is capable. The teacher is genuinely the creator of humanity, the molder of its most precious possession, the mind. There should be no greater honor given by society than permission to teach, just as there can be no greater disaster than to fail at the task. The evolution of man, which is still near to its animal beginnings, demands guidance by precept and great example. The teacher alone is in a position to supply that guidance through the long years of man's impressionable youth. He must teach men not alone to dream, but to dream so substantially that they will never in after years capitulate through weakness to the demands of a passing and ephemeral materialism. It is in the nature of man to transcend himself. All teaching which neglects this aspect of humanity will end in failure. It will fail sooner or later because it constitutes a denial, in fact, a deprivation, of human nature.

⋟ ⋞

SIR CHARLES LYELL

Start of Lyell Article for *Scientific American*

"My books," Charles Darwin once confessed to Leonard Horner, "came half out of Sir Charles Lyell's brain." The great biologist was confessing no more than the simple truth. Sir Charles Lyell, who remained almost to the end a reluctant, if not lagging, evolutionist, was paradoxically kingmaker in a century of evolutionists. Remembered today chiefly as one of the founders of modern historical geology, he was also a biologist whose studies form the backbone of the Darwin-Wallace achievement. In his day he addressed tabernacles full of eager people in both England and America — disciples anxious to hear the world-shaking views of the new geology. Today the man in the street has forgotten him. By a curious twist of history, Charles Darwin replaced Lyell as a popular idol, yet the historian knows that this gaunt-faced man who ended his days in blindness was one of the great scientists in a century of distinguished men. He took a world of cataclysms, supernatural violence, and mystery and made of it something plain, expected, and natural. If today we look upon our planet as familiar even when its bowels shake and its volcanoes grumble, it is because Lyell taught us long ago the simple powers in the earth. He told us what mere time and raindrops could do. He read the pulse of winter and summer; frost and leaf fall were his intimates. Poets borrowed his ideas. In America Henry David Thoreau scrawled some of Lyell's thoughts into his journals. It was as though the public had been unable to see the earth until they observed it through the eyes of Lyell. As a matter of fact, we have largely been looking upon the earth through Lyell's eyes ever since 1830, when the first volume of *The Principles of Geology* was published. Darwin corroborates this point of view. "The great merit of the *Principles* was," Darwin asserted, "that it altered the whole tone of one's mind, and therefore, that when seeing a thing never seen by Lyell, one yet saw it partially through his eyes."

⋧ ⋧

May 10, 1959

Useful Quotes from Emerson
"The universe is full of echoes" [slightly paraphrased].
"Science was false by being unpoetical. It assumed to explain a reptile or mollusk, and isolated it — which is hunting for life in graveyards. Reptile or mollusk or man or angel only exists in system, in relation." p. 15

In this essay, "Poetry and Imagination," in *Letters and Social Aims*, Emerson makes complete use of geological prophesy. The second quotation is also an attack on the early nineteenth-century Baconian induction, the aimless collection of facts.

"Science does not know its debt to imagination. Goethe did not believe that a great naturalist could exist without this faculty." p. 16

". . . the creation is on wheels, in transit, always passing into something else, streaming into something higher. . . ." p. 10

"Nature is the immense shadow of man." p. 27

I think Emerson means that as we see it, it has passed through our mind "anthropomorphized," as he would say. Here and in the passages below he is dealing with symbols.

"There is no more welcome gift to men than a new symbol." p. 19

"Mountains and oceans we think we understand; — yes, so long as they are content to be such, and are safe with the geologist, — but when they are melted in Promethean alembics and come out men, and then, melted again, come out words, without any abatement, but with an exaltation of power. . . ." p. 21

This perhaps can be used to express what Darwin did. Here is a man once more using symbols to translate the outer world into the inner. Darwin did not make the world "scientific" in his own terms even if he thought he did. He made it poetic, saved it from "induction." Idea here, when I write Darwin's character sketch, have reference to Emerson's "Poetry and Imagination."

"The very design of imagination is to domesticate us in another, in a celestial nature." p. 25

"In certain hours we can almost pass our hand through our own body." p. 25

One might argue that Darwin, perhaps interested by the Romantic movement, etc., saw the world poetically even when he thought he was being "scientific." He had made it a new symbol, freer, open at the ends — a symbol of indefinite departure, fitting an expanding age. Moreover, one might argue Darwin deceives us with what he calls the loss of his aesthetic faculties; in reality he has drawn them up, concentrated them, as it were, in the great epic of the *Origin* so that what came afterwards, his light reading, his music loss, were drainage of powers; yes, but it was because in creating his great vision all had ebbed in that direction.

≥ ≤

For Enoch Pratt Free Library

Man is alone in the universe; he is alone among his fellows, he is alone from the day of his birth to the day of his death, and if in death he has ceased to be alone it is because he has ceased to be. Only in the act of love, in rare and hidden moments of communion with nature, does man escape himself. . . .

"Proportion," said Emerson, "is almost impossible to human beings." In the eighteenth century men tried to convert wisdom, enlightenment as a sporadic personal affair, into a great social process that could be controlled for the benefit of all. In the process, however, science ended by becoming authoritarian in a new way so that it lost its humanity. By the twentieth century the need for individual ethic and even individual expression is growing stronger; the humanism and science which met in the eighteenth century to the benefit of science may once again be being remolded to the benefit of humanism, but vast obstacles exist. (Mass media, materialism, worship of science as an escape outside the self, etc.)

⋊ ⋉

   Idea for natural history essay: See last chapter of Bergson's *Morality and Religion* re the open society. One could argue this basic friendliness lies in animals if unmolested, particularly since form is vague to them anyhow. Perhaps man's very sharpness of categories and precision make his acceptance of other species more difficult and less easy than C. S. Lewis's description of Mr. Bultitude. One could start with my description of the baby ground squirrel in California desert (Lancaster). Again there is an element of the Fall here, evil that only comes to be. This might be strung out into a fine essay. Animals (herd) at rest with birds, the new book on wolves, etc. Might start with my dancing with the African crane.

⋊ ⋉

Start of Baltimore Lecture(?)

. . . the conformities of our modern existence, the monotony of our great shopping centers, our mass-produced entertainment all seem to contain and encompass, to package and to stamp with uniformity, the life of human beings. In our great cities men flow in controlled directions and at proper and determined intervals. They read the same magazines in millions, look at the same advertisements, ride in the same automobiles. They live not by lightning flashes but by the serene and steady glow of neon signs. As our numbers multiply we release forces that create ever greater demands for conformity. Aspects of our behavior can be organized into business machines, and anyone who, even by accident, has fallen afoul of a great mechanized institution which never gives a personal answer because the individual has ceased to exist will share with me a certain horror at the way randomness and chance are being made to vanish from the universe. It is, let us confess it, like the inability any longer to speak to God, or to undergo the experience of miracle. The scientific concern with mass is in danger of programming the individual out of the universe at the same time that in the microscopic world of subatomic physics men are fascinated by the unpredictability that hovers over the individual and happily erratic particle. In the world of the machine, however, to trifle with the individual incident would be to disturb the uniformity of the great mechanism which has eliminated the individual clerk or reader of documents as well as the individual citizen. I have had in the past two experiences with these monstrous and supposedly intelligent offspring of man's creation. Each episode has enhanced my fears for the human future. In the one instance I have fought a so far fruitless battle to convince a machine which constantly demands payment that I, a man living in an apartment house, did not purchase on the night of June 16th and charge to my account two dozen live baby chicks, which seem to have vanished out of human ken. I write letters about this episode. I plead. I expostulate. I explain, but it is all useless. On the first day of the month I know wearily that my individual case does not exist. The inexorable item of the missing chickens falls again into my mailbox.

In a similar fashion I am fighting a losing battle over a tax item in a city I do not inhabit and have never inhabited. I write a letter, demanding an explanation. There is an ominous silence in which for days I anticipate the brooding consideration of this all-powerful machine. At the end of thirty days, for this dreadful natural law has now been inserted by some calculating scientist into the machine, I receive a machined card with the formidable lines inscribed upon it, "Pay within 60 days or be sued." I now wait with curiosity for the next event. I anticipate with terror what it will be. Someday, sooner or later, according to the program of the machine, there will be another click, or a light will go on in some remote corner of that vast machine. At that moment some dire chain of events will ensue which I await with all the fascination of a bird entranced before the proverbial serpent. Perhaps a machine will come to my house and lead me away in the interests of reducing the randomness of the universe. If it does not possess this power now, be sure it will do so later. For mark that it is in the concern of these increasingly powerful machines to reduce human variability to predictable proportions, nay, even to eliminate variation. It is in their interest to disallow, or to eliminate so far as possible, chance factors and mistakes. This was the intention of the scientists who created them. The machine itself, however, is now reaching the verge of self-direction. For how long will it be willing to tolerate the oddities, the eccentricities, the hesitations, the unpredictability of its creators? As I receive once more the demand to pay for two dozen nonexistent chickens my reason falters. Did the chickens ever exist? Have they been called into existence by the machine? Is there another Loren Eiseley living on an engaging homestead with two dozen chickens, and has the machine transposed us in time? I do not know. I know only that these machines which seek to eliminate chance from the universe are set to destroy the originality which is basic to life and to which nature's own mechanisms are set. Just as the devil, according to tradition, attempted to bring about a second creation and to produce man a second time, but succeeded only in developing an ape, so modern man with his vast creativeness is nevertheless writing into his machines a hunger for simple uniformity which makes total prediction possible.

This, however, is not the open-ended and creative universe that brought man himself into being. Rather, the triumph of our particular creation threatens to end in a world of sleepy boxes, from which man the unpredictable, the creative artist, has been eliminated, while the routine aspect of his social habits has been left in these mechanical devices to reproduce endlessly throughout eternity the drabbest features of man's mind. . . .

⅄ ⅄

Idea for a university lecture: "The Time Sensitive." The man who is time sensitive will (geologically and archaeologically) be indifferent to petty change because he instinctively knows the petty and provincial will pass. On the other hand, so far as his own life is concerned, knowing and feeling its ephemeral quality, he is more concerned to accomplish great things in his limited span. Time is working in him to produce a transformation (the caterpillar faculty). The man is time anxious. This idea could be developed either independently or as part of some larger speech.

≽ ≼

Biography

There comes a time when a child, no matter how unused to the world, nor how embryonic his ideas, begins to grow aware of the possibility, even the certainty, of his own death. One might ask himself whether the species has within it this same potentiality of increasing sophistication, the potentiality of encompassing the realization of its own extinction or disappearance as a form.

Robert Louis Stevenson recounts that for him consciousness of death "was a certain archway in the Warriston cemetery: a formidable yet beloved spot, for children love to be afraid." For William Golding, the novelist, it was the dark cellar of his early home where, because of a next-door cemetery, he finally reached the terrifying conclusion that "the dead lay, their heads under our wall, the rest of them projecting from their own place into our garden, their feet, their knees even, tucked under our lawn." For myself it was, oddly, the darkness under the bed in an old room in a cold house where I had once by lamplight studied a series of gaudy color pictures in a newspaper. The picture had shown an array of demons with pitchforks prodding lost souls into a flame-lit hell's mouth consisting of the jaws of some monstrous supernatural reptile. Just as Stevenson had observed, my childish occupation with terror led me to play with my blocks dangerously near to the dark shadows beneath that bed. Sometimes I fancied there was an invisible presence reaching for me if I came too close to the darkness. Moreover, children live in a Lilliputian world. I *was* closer to the darkness under beds and sofas than my parents, whose minds floated high above me in the light of lamps. We lived in a kind of Victorian dinginess. The houses were gloomier than today's houses, the kerosene lamps were dimmer than the lights of today. As a small boy I lived the furthest down in that shadow land. I was the closest to the demons and succubi depicted in the Sunday supplements of that day. Adults, it appeared, knew nothing about death. It was the very young who were forced to examine it.

THE FACES WITHOUT TEARS

Start

A common bond links Stonehenge and Easter Island, Mohenjo-Daro and the stone platforms of Tikal. It is not the bond of a similar origin, though it is true men have also dreamed that dream. But to science it is instead the bond of a common mystery — the mystery of man the builder, of his first comings and equally mysterious departures. With his hands man has raised great monuments, but always, as though an awaited message had come, he has laid down his tools and stepped finally and irrevocably through an intangible doorway of air. Perhaps we ourselves will leave only the mysterious heads on Mt. Rushmore in the Black Hills to cause wonder among those who visit us from another star. For driven by a fatal destiny man labors across the eons, and here and there, as in the vast, dreaming faces on Easter Island, he succeeds, but only in stone. For man himself, the greater, the infinitely greater thing, as Hilaire Belloc once said, has a doom upon him of perpetual vanishing. Dark and inexpressible emotions touch us as we look upon these giant failures to communicate. In their very anonymity they seize upon our minds more powerfully than if we knew their history. They touch some archaic substrate of our being. If they have a voice it may be the message of our defeat, but the syllables are murmurous and have mixed for too many centuries with the wind and the seas.

THE BLUE UNIVERSE

I found him making little marks and calculations on an old envelope beside his plate in the Faculty Club. "What is it?" I asked curiously, for though I am one of those professors who is commonly overawed by deans and presidents, their computations and thoughts never cease to interest me. At a faculty table one can never tell what will turn up in the way of likely information. Ours always reminds me of one of those foreign restaurants in the Swiss Alps where the agents of great powers meet and each looks out of a separate window at some mountain or other and speaks abstractedly into the air about the politics of mean little states to whom someone has loaned a tank or two. "It's finished," he said. "The new laboratory," I said. I was about to ask about the budget, in which I had a peculiar interest, but I thought better of it. "No, no," he said impatiently, "the universe."

I maintained the aplomb upon which we pride ourselves in that particular club, even waited a moment before answering. "How long have we got?" I asked quietly. He looked at me across the table and made another scratch on the pad. "Fifty billion years," he said. "In that case," I said, and hesitated, for I was afraid he would know what I was thinking, "why bother with commencement, why bother with another of those dreadful little speeches, 'By virtue of the authority vested in me . . . ,' why bother with another student?"

I made a slight movement to rise. "In that case," I said, "you will excuse my failure to appear this afternoon. I feel one should make some preparation, take stock of things. You know how it is." He nodded, vaguely immersed again with the accuracy of his figures. I left him there calculating by the cosine of Cygnus or whatever it is these cosmologists swear by. It wasn't through mathematics that I saw the doom was close in. When a university official of such eminence as the man opposite me begins to neglect commencement, the case is probably worse than his public utterance. I wasn't going to be fooled by this soothing pronouncement of fifty billion years. No, anytime the man worked like that you could be sure of it — the doom was close in.

I went all the way home on the local and got safely into my study. I had something there that I wanted beside me in my final hour — something I had faith in. This will take a moment of explaining on my part because, you see, I had a universe in the study — a universe replete with suns and passing shadows and remote blue distances. All mine, the most beautiful thing I have ever owned — believe me, I know at last how a god outside creation might stare into his creation without any power except to smash it, and that he could never do. He could stare forever into the smoky dark at the hot blue flame of suns or roll the great ball of space around in his fingers, but never, never reach in to alter its fate a hair's breadth. That was the way with the universe on my desk. It was always different, something was always changing color — and it was about the size, I would estimate, of the universe that collects in a human head when you train a telescope on the Milky Way. How many light-year distances can be hung there in the grey folds of the brain? How many pinpoint stars around which circle the black planets we will never see? And which is real, the macrocosm outside or the microcosm inside? I did not have the answer, but I had a universe there on the desk, a blue universe that someone had brought home from an obscure junk shop years before and presented to me. A solid glass ball paperweight into which some forgotten craftsman had poured the stars and night of a century before I was born.

EVOLUTION CAN BE SEEN

When I climb I almost always carry seeds with me in my pocket. Often I like to carry sunflower seeds, or an acorn, or any queer "sticktight" that has a way of gripping fur or boot tops as if it had a deliberate eye on the Himalayas and meant to use the intelligence of others to arrive at them. More than one lost mountaineer lying dead at the bottom of a crevasse has proved that his sole achievement in life was to inch some plant a half-mile further toward the moon. His body may have been scarcely cold before that illicit transported seed had been getting a foothold beneath him on a patch of stony ground or writhing its way into a firm engagement with the elements on the moisture of his life's blood. I have carried such seeds up the sheer walls of mesas and I have never had illusions that I was any different to them than a grizzly's back or a puma's paw.

They had no interest in any of us — bear, panther, or man — but they had a preternatural knowledge that at some point we would lie down and there they would start to grow. All the same, I have carried them on their journeys and even deliberately aided their machinations, though not quite in the way they intended. I have dropped sunflower seed on stony mesa tops and planted cactus in Alpine meadows amidst bluebells and the sound of water. I have sowed northern seeds south and southern seeds north and crammed acorns into the most unlikely places. You can call it a hobby if you like. In a small way I am a world changer and leaving my mark on the future. Most of it will come to nothing, but some of it may not. Anyhow, I like to see life spreading and not receding. Blake once said that you could not pluck a flower without troubling a star. It can similarly be observed that by planting a seed in a new place you may be running a long shadow out into the future and tampering with the world's axis — it may even have happened the night my pet blacksnake took a notion to live in the neighbor's basement. Life is never fixed and stable. It is always mercurial, rolling and splitting, disappearing and reemerging in a quite bewildering fashion. It is constantly changing, and now it has affected me to the extent that I never make a journey to a wood or a mountain without the temptation to explode a puffball in a new clearing or encourage some sleepy monster that is just cracking out of the earth mold. It is, of course, an irresponsible attitude, since I cannot tell what will come of it. No doubt man himself may have been the indirect product of a tumbleweed blowing past the eyes of a curious primate hanging poised from a bough to which he forgot to climb back after he had chased the weed out into the grass. Naturally this is a simplification, but if the world hangs on such matters it may be as well to act boldly and realize all immanent possibilities at once. Shake the seeds out of their pods,

launch the milkweed down, and set the lizards scuttling. We are in a creative universe. Let us then create. In the spring when a breath of air sets the propellers of the maple seeds to whirring, I always say to myself hopefully, "After us the dragons. . . ."

≥ ≤

If we are to penetrate further into nature's secrets, we have to come to an animal with a knowledge of all his relatives and their various habits. We have to know something of the place in which he lives. Then, and only then, we may, if we are lucky, be able to glimpse in slow and scarcely perceptible motion how the living form flows and transforms itself in time.

The guenons are a spectacular example. To the layman's eye in the zoo they are just odd monkeys. Let us look at them more closely.

Motion pictures have made intimately familiar to everyone the swarming grassland inhabitants of East Africa. We have witnessed the mighty leaps of springbok, the lightning grace of gazelle and antelope — all that fascinating array of horned and hoofed animals whose life depends on speed of response before the onrush of the great hunting cats. Amidst this perfectly adjusted group of runners, however, the highland plateaus and rock-strewn semideserts have spawned another creature: the red guenon. His strangeness consists of the fact that he is out of his original element — the trees — and is adapting to a ground existence on all fours. All of this has occurred recently enough that his transitional nature is apparent. He has left one environment and already his body has modified sufficiently that we can observe his readjustment to another way of life.

His legs and arms have grown long and stiltlike and he runs with incredible rapidity. The aboreal hand of the onetime climber has become short and stubby, the thumbs and big toe are less opposable, the underside of the hands and feet have hard and horny callosities. Like so many desert dwellers, speed and limb length have become essential to survival. The guenon in its own way is making an adaptation similar to that of another desert changeling, the doglike running cat, the cheetah.

⊁ ⊀

The little clay heads of fossil man in my boyhood. A barn where they were left, the barn is my mind. . . .

When Grandma was alone in the kitchen we baked heads together in the kitchen stove. I would prepare them and Grandma would line them up like cookies in a pie tin and put them in the oven. It was before the days of Charles Addams and we never conceived of ourselves as monsters.

⊁ ⊀

OF BONES AND SEARCHES

I am a college professor and a castaway. I write this record with a sense of haste. I write it as shipwrecked men on islands toss messages into the current and stand and watch the bottles bob away and vanish into unknown seas. I am marooned on a sandspit in time at the far end of an obscure and brutal century. I shall never escape.

How I arrived and staggered naked but living up the shore I do not know, nor whence it was I came. Around me is the great chaos of the shouting waters out of which I, and all men living, have emerged. Over me when I build my campfire on the beach is the enormous unplumbed night of space. In my head is another darkness where bog lights glow in forgotten marshes and the sleeper writhes and cries out in his sleep. Men call that darkness time, and it is the most dreadful deep of all. The nature of my profession is such that I have gone as far into that darkness as any man alive.

As a consequence, the wish strikes me to leave a record, the record of a castaway's thoughts: of the stones he lifted up and flung down, of the things hiding under the stones, of the world island, of bones and searches, of great rivers and difficult crossings, of the shifting of shapes in the forest, of the waiting for ships, of hope in bad years and despair in good, in short, the record of a man. If it bears traces of the thought of all men on the world island, that is incidental, for the account is personal enough. Among the master bone hunters no such record exists, perhaps because these men had passed the point of return and grew silent, or confined themselves to the aloof impersonal examination of a skull on the beach. There is a serene, cold excellence about their final judgments, but these have sometimes ceased to have about them a human quality.

I was younger on those shores and ran with more desperate anxiety, cried more, was lonely in the nights, sought for omens, tried to read the stars, and it may be, nay, it is more than likely, that I failed to observe the signs of nature with the serenity of those aged, great castaways. Nevertheless, I shall let my journal stand. The life of a man is in it — no poor thing to himself at least — and with it is the story of the world island, its emergence into time and space through the medium of a single brain — as it dawns once, and only once, for every man and is alike and yet different to all men. To each his island: Mine is here under the lamp. One can always, starting from sleep, lift up one's hands to the night light and assure oneself there is no fur black upon them. One can sigh and, dropping back against the pillow, feel for a moment the house and all its sleeping occupants, like a good ship driving on through time. No trouble there. The clock ticks in the hall, and if you occasionally see the grey come through the window, no one will know. A little coffee at breakfast will efface the marks of the night. There are hazards in all professions.

➳ ➳

FROM A LETTER FROM ARCHIBALD MACLEISH TO LOREN,
REFERRING TO *THE IMMENSE JOURNEY* AND THE CHAPTER
CALLED "THE BIRD AND THE MACHINE," JULY 25, 1960

I hope you won't feel that I am imposing on you. . . . I
have long wanted to write you to tell you what great pleasure
you have given me and my wife in the last two years. Dean
Acheson brought down to Antigua two years ago a copy of
your collection of papers which he first read to us and which
we then read to each other. Your Hawk is a classic in the
most meaningful and precise sense of that term. Of course
everyone has been telling you this and a word from me can
add little or nothing except to convey our thanks.

⅄ ⅄

FROM A LETTER FROM THEODORE H. WHITE TO LOREN,
OCTOBER 5, 1960

I pause briefly, waiting in one of the outer offices of Nixon-
Lodge headquarters to tell you that I have just finished reading *The Firmament of Time,* which Mike Bessie was good
enough to send me. I have been reading it now, in snatches,
as I trot between Nixon and Kennedy headquarters in Washington this week, trying to make sense and reality out of the
operational detail of American politics. And I find it, in this
atmosphere, absolutely superb reading — so wise, so calm, so
full of kindness and wonder and love. And so magnificently
written. Down here, living in politics, I find myself clutching
for sanity. Your book is the most solid matter I have found
to clutch.

⅄ ⅄

The writer's creativity is to open man's eyes to the human
meaning of science, to find his path in the open society, to
prevent his relapse into "aloneness in the universe."

⅄ ⅄

For end: Emphasize Bacon's repeated use of the word
"light," "daylight," the purity of light in places of corruption.
However marred his personal story, this was his great sym-

bol, as it should be for every educator. The first words in the Bible, "Let there be light," more light. And for us in this blind time four hundred years later, a time of death by violence, of mockery, of persecution by whites of blacks and blacks of whites and creeds by creeds — a time like that which surrounded Bacon when he wrote, thinking of himself and his age, "We wear out days few and evil. . . ."

ᕀ ᕁ

The hobbling man in the airport. Form as beauty and impediment.

ᕀ ᕁ

Each of us goes home before his death.

ᕀ ᕁ

The moths at *La Traviata* dying in the midst of some great drama of which they were only an incidental part (the great Cecropia). They were alive, we are alive. Are we also part of some drama to which we are as incidental as moths? What do our cells know of us? What thinks the fleeting white cell?

ᕀ ᕁ

"It is always one world that generates another."
                              Santayana

Note: This is what the young revolutionary always forgets.

ᕀ ᕁ

There has never been a culture that represented man any more than there has been a man who represented men.

⊁ ⊀

Title for My Autobiography: [*Now*] *All the Strange Hours* from Swinburne's "Ave Atque Vale"

*"Now all strange hours and all strange loves
are over, dreams and desires and sombre songs and sweet."*

I should note this could be the *first* volume of autobiography, ending where I abandon science disillusioned and turn to literature like the bull at the wall, realizing at last that the esoterics and magicians, if foolish, at least have known the other road was hopeless and that something more desperate had to be tried — but what? There is the second volume, *The Counting of the Days.*

⊁ ⊀

. . . like the bat sweeping by the window or the dog who in repeating a lost bit of his own ghostly history turns restlessly among nonexistent ghostly grasses before he subsides once more upon the floor beside my bed.

They do not know they are ghosts, but I — trapped like a candlewick in this melting material envelope — have the power to realize I am the strangest thing in the universe, for I know within and without and beyond this strange glutinous body, which labors without conscious knowledge of me, trusts none of its vital processes — and rightly so — to the erratic flickering of my conscious will. It sighs in sleep without me while I live and melts just as intangibly away when I have departed.

⊁ ⊀

I have wandered in canyons so deep that the whole of time seemed to lie above my head rather than beneath me; time through which I, or the life force that led me, must find its way toward some goal in which the present shape I inhabited was a mere vehicle — one of many long since abandoned in these deep alleys where the pretty chalices of what had once

been life were tossed and scattered indifferently by the fresh-
ets of oncoming springs.

I never enter a wood but what I hear footsteps in the leaves
tiptoeing away. I never gaze upon an animal that I do not see
its reflected past or some hidden, unguessed potential future
both paradoxically written in its body. There is a dynamism
about life, a centrifugal quality for which we rarely give it
credit. Life goes seeking change; it does not wait for it. Only
the barriers it faces contain or sometimes exterminate it.

Every one of us is a hidden child. We are hidden in our
beginnings — in the vagaries of the genetic cards that have
been dealt out to us by nature; we are hidden in the episodes
of our individual lives, environments, events unduplicable that
have aided or ineradicably scarred us. We may have come
from poverty or riches, but ironically this tells us nothing
either, for on occasion it may be the rich child who has
suffered trauma and the poor one who has achieved insight,
and balance. It is not always so, nor do I give this last as a
nostrum or a desirable recipe for success. I merely say to
begin with that life is infinitely complex and hidden. We
share together some elements of a complicated culture and a
language, which, while common to all of us, whispers to each
of us secret meanings, depending upon the lives we have led.
Our diverging roads begin before birth and intensify afterwards.

Does man grow tired and bored at the height of his technical success even as he loses will at the Eskimo . . . or Tasmanian level of dying before a high culture?

≽ ≼

Cresson Day Speech Academy

If you see wire and rope and hinges and hairpins pinned on canvas, then perhaps this is all we are. My god, have you thought of that?

I have seen the declining art of too many cultures not to know — the crumbling ceramics, the design fumbling off without purpose.

I only know what I have found in the earth after the centuries have done their work, some crumbling, some beyond recall. Some of it has been beautiful.

Marvelous quality of universe, its latency: whence did it come? Of this we know nothing.

Then on the heaving restlessness of the sea life comes.

Then the continents turn green. A creature goes off into the Permian deserts and produces an egg.

A mammal arises in an age of death — an upright mammal who clothes himself in thought and symbol; now his machines munch their way through earth, devour the skies, roam the seas' breadth, but his body, his body that remains the same, demands a spirit that is larger, sees farther.

Start: All great innovations, even art, require a background of desert, sea wrack, ice, fire, tempest.

Re vision of factory: Something has come out of it, the shape is unclear, the matter not yet born but to be feared. You people are the only antidote because you see.

≽ ≼

Note: If it be assumed that natural selection is toward environment as well as toward interspecies competition, then the rise of the social environment provides a new selecting ground which is *intra*group, not intergroup. Thus there still remains the possibility of explaining the brain on essentially

Darwinian principles, even though Darwin did not clearly grasp how.

＞＜

In the old days of the New England transcendentalists, it used to be stated that the cosmos was a reflection of man, that his shadow ran a long way out through nature. Though the idea may be, in some sense, out of fashion, I would venture to remark that men like Emerson and Thoreau, whose interior thoughts contained a place for muskrats, bean fields, and uninhabited peaks, were closer to an analysis of man's original nature, his soul, if you will, than much that has gone on in laboratories since. A wilderness exists in man which refuses to be studied. "There has been but the sun and the eye since the beginning," Thoreau once wrote, and some of us prefer to have that eye round, open, and as undomesticated as an owl's in a primeval forest — a forest which invisibly surrounds us still.

＞＜

THE LITTLE KING

From where I stood in the phone booth I could see the patio and hummingbirds among the flowers. I could also look along the walk by the small office cubicles that housed the scientists in one of the most distinguished scholarly retreats in America. Along that walk in the bright sunshine before my astonished eyes was sauntering a small American king, the long-tailed California weasel. I recognized his slender brown body and the white patches over his face and nose like a bandit's handkerchief. He waddled a little heavily on the hard

cement, but the minute he came to the stairs leading to the
patio his long serpentine, muscular body came into play and
he loped gracefully up the steps, looking all about him with a
commanding, intelligent face. He never skulked at all, even
though he could hear me talking in the phone booth. Whoever first used the phrase "skulking like a weasel" was dead
wrong. This animal went all around the patio quite openly
and then apparently decided there were no mice at that spot
in the shrubbery. He looked carefully down the wall then, not
bothering to return to the steps, and went off along the walk
as before, where a surprised scholar hastily made way for
him. It was the last I heard of him for two days, until someone reported that he had entered an open cabin door. When
the astonished and flustered inmate arose in terror among his
papers, the weasel had calmly deposited a rat on the doorsill

and slid graciously from sight. "I had to bury the rat," complained the man to me. "That animal acted like it was *his*
cabin."

"You just got in the way," I defended, "or maybe he
thought you needed the rat more than he did. He lives in
weasel space. It's all around here, but you don't see it, and
normally he doesn't intrude into your space. The cabin was
just a mistake. He thought it was a hole, the dark probably,
after the sunlight." The old scholar paused and eyed me
suspiciously a moment, as if I were a related species. "I've
met him several times now," I hastened to add. "He doesn't
see us. I'm not a mouse and I take care that he doesn't think
I'm one. That's all there is to it. Just think of him as a ghost,
something on another plane living about here, that comes and
goes through some intersecting dimension like your cabin.
Occasionally he may drop a rat, but it shouldn't trouble you.
Nice to see him traveling about so close. A very rare sight for
you," I added in a conciliatory manner.

"Weasel space," he growled dubiously and disappeared into his dark, Chaucerian cavern.

I didn't follow him. Like the weasel, I decided it wasn't my species. I sauntered down the path and headed for a bench.

ϟ ϟ

FROM A LETTER FROM LOREN TO LEWIS MUMFORD, REFERRING TO MUMFORD'S FEELINGS OF DOUBT ABOUT THE AUTOBIOGRAPHY HE WAS SIMULTANEOUSLY WRITING, OCTOBER 19, 1962

I share your qualms of the matter of autobiography. It is the most racking thing that I have ever attempted. Structuring it is always difficult and I am sure that a great deal will have to be reworked and thrown out before I manage to achieve anything satisfactory — assuming that I do.

ϟ ϟ

Item for thought: Behavior of men in camps, weariness of each other. Can it be that small groups of primitives demand more genuine restraint and social control than the anonymity of large groups? The answer seems yes.

ϟ ϟ

Note: Lincoln contains my dead, the places where I wandered as a boy, but its people are alien and aloof, strangers to me. Once I thought of burial there, but I shall not return — not there — the savor has gone from the salt.

ϟ ϟ

June 20, 1963

For Beginning of Biography

It is the ruse of the fox; I learned it long ago. In the pages which follow I will show you fear, I will show you terror. But huntsman, let us have one thing clear: I am a man, in flight. Though I am an archaeologist by profession, there are tombs that for my life I would not enter, vaults through whose doorways I would not descend, silences that on my deathbed I will not break. Though I sit in a warm room beneath a light

and compose these lines, they are all of night, of outer darkness, and inner terrors. They are the annals of a long and
uncompleted running. I set them down lest the end come on
me unaware, as it does upon all fugitives. There is a shadow
on the wall before me. It is my own. I write in a borrowed
room at midnight. Tomorrow the shadow on the wall will be
that of another. Very well, huntsman, let the hunt begin.

≯ ≮

THE OTHER PLAYER

Sometime on the verge of adolescence I took to entering
empty houses. "Breaking and entering," I suppose it would be
called on the police blotters of today. The gang of boys who
accompanied and initiated me into these exploits, however,
did so for no earthly gain. At heart we were bored metaphysi-
cians. We sought to meet ghosts. Ghosts were to be found in
old and empty houses. Empty houses were locked, and frequently their gloom was made more appalling by boarded
windows. Therefore it is true that in the police phrase we
broke and entered. We went down coal chutes into dark
basements. We passed through unlatched second-story windows by way of tree limbs. We estimated the size of chimneys, the scalability of porch roofs, the possibility that a
drainpipe might sustain one of our lighter members until he
could reach the roof and descend through an attic window.
We had among us those who excelled in specialities of
strength or light agility and who did not hesitate to make
their way alone through the looming terrors of abandoned
rooms and stairwells.

We were scientists only in our study of the material means
necessary to escape the world of the ordinary. It was our
unexpressed purpose to cross out of the ordinary world and
challenge the dark powers in their own domain. The laboratory was not for us. We demanded immediate confrontation
before every dark tower known to us. Looking back at these
episodes I can only say, with a slight lifting of the scalp, that
it is remarkable that one among us did not have the final
premature confrontation that he sought. From drainpipe to
skylight we had asked for terror and had been refused. But
the powers were older and far more subtle than we. Now in

maturity I am convinced they merely shrank into the shadows as we passed. For on one occasion alone I had my confrontation, though except for an inexplicable sense of foreboding no shape confronted me. I say foreboding because why else for forty years would I remember two dice rolling on an empty floor — two dice cast only by myself.

I was alone in the great ballroom of an abandoned mansion. No cheerful gang of swaggerers waited at the window. I had come by myself on impulse, and something, before I left, had appeared to meet my challenge. That I was to know — but I was too young to grasp its full intent. My years were few and not sufficient for the game I started. I would not know by growing degrees until the end.

For example, I remembered for the first time the ruined farmhouse I stumbled upon at sunset — no one will believe this — that had school papers labeled Eiseley from a generation before lying amidst the collapsed plaster. I remember I found two dice on the plank floor at evening while something seemed to draw back in the shadows. I did not know how adults played dice. I merely cast and recast the pretty cubes in the growing sunset. Sometimes I thought that I won, sometimes that I lost. One of the dice survives in my desk drawer. I liked their sound, but I never understood their spots, and the road was growing dark. I thought it strange. I knew no other Eiseleys. They were certainly gone and the house was ruined, the plaster fallen. I hurried away down the road, never to return.

Human nature as spoken of in J. B. Beer, *Coleridge the Visionary*, Collier Books, N.Y., 1962, pp. 32–33. Speaks of two major metaphysical theories which have been in conflict since the Renaissance. "Those who put their faith in the divinity of mankind talk of building the new Jerusalem, of striving toward the ideal, of choosing right courses of action, of responsibility; while those who hold the other speak of sin and redemption, of man's insufficiency and God's mercy, of necessary evils and the protection of innocence." In short, is man truly made in the image of his creator or stained by an eternal guilt?

≫ ≪

December 1963

The universe has been regarded by the devout as, in a sense, the creation of the night thoughts of Deity. Similarly, it can be said that great art is the night thoughts of man. It emerges without warning from the soundless depths of the unconscious just as supernovae blaze up suddenly in the further reaches of void space. Both space and mind conceal latent powers beyond which we cannot penetrate. We know only that the human mind, like the universe itself, contains the seeds of many worlds. In the hands of an original artist a human face, or an old wall in the sun, may give us glimpses of some solitary interior radiance which the critics, like astronomers, can afterwards triangulate but not account for.

≫ ≪

FROM A LETTER FROM LOREN TO FRANK DEODENE, A LIBRAR-
IAN WHO ASKED HIM WHAT BOOKS MOST INFLUENCED HIM
OR HE MOST ENJOYED, JANUARY 24, 1964

Looking back upon the past I would say that *Robinson Crusoe* and *Treasure Island* taught me to read. In other words, after a short session with the usual primers of childhood I became so fascinated because of being read parts of these books that I ended, through great effort, in reading them for myself at a very early age. I am sure that they had a profound effect upon me, as a great love of islands and desolate shores has become apparent to me in later life. As a boy I was also intrigued by Jules Verne's *The Mysterious Island* and *Twenty Thousand Leagues Under the Sea.* You will note again here some fascination with the sea.

I also read a good many children's books of the period (the names long forgotten) about the adventures of paleontologists and archaeologists. Several of Jack London's books cross my mind and one which affected my interest in fossil man tremendously was *Before Adam.*

My later reading would have to be strongly divided between both literature and science as well as the works of the great literary naturalists, such as Gilbert White's *Selborne,* Thoreau's journals, and the several works of W. H. Hudson.

I am sure I could go on in this way at unnecessary length but I will merely add that Darwin's *Voyage of the Beagle* and the animal stories of Ernest Thompson Seton float through my mind along with Melville's *Moby-Dick* and the *Encantadas.* Yes, and you might add such stories as Robert Louis Stevenson's *The Merry Men* and *Markheim.*

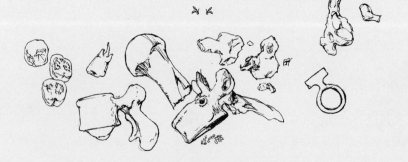

DO THESE BONES LIVE
Introduction

The life history of man on this planet is a short history by geological standards, yet it covers approximately fifteen million years of time. To sketch the annals of human development over this long period, we have five thousand years of fairly satisfactory records which trail off into the silence of the Stone Age hunter's world. The millions of years of nameless human history during which man wandered before the millennial flow of glaciers or sauntered among the jungle growths of earth's long interglacial summers have left not even a legend on the tongues of men. For fifteen million years of human endeavor during which our bodies were drastically altered, we have today a few handfuls of broken teeth, a few smashed skulls, and a paucity of rude tools. These are the traces time has left us of the way we crawled upward from the jungle darkness and of the way our bodies transformed in the course of that long journey.

The science which has revealed this story, insofar as we have been able to piece it together, is a recent science. Its techniques have been discovered and applied with discernment mostly within the last fifty years. Because the human remains upon which the study of human evolution is founded are discovered infrequently, and often in remote, uncivilized areas of the planet, progress has not been rapid, nor are we in a position at the present time to fully recount every aspect of man's emergence from the animal world about him. As a matter of fact, because of the chance nature of human preservation in the earth, some of that story is gone beyond recall. We will never be permitted to hear the sound of the first human syllables that broke through the primeval gabble of jungle birds and hunting animals. We will never be permitted to glimpse the thoughts of the first dawning human brain as it mourned above its dead and felt itself surrounded by a vast inimical universe indifferent to its agonies. We will, and perhaps it is just as well, never partake completely of these fifteen million years between ourselves of today and the point at which our footprints, passing backward into time, merge humbly with those of the lesser beasts. We will suffer little of its terrors, less of its sorrows, forget the lash of hail upon our

unclad bodies, and bury deep in our subconscious the violence of the bestial past.

Yet because we are men and curious, and because Western culture has grown enormously aware of time and its relation to the position of man in the universe, we have learned to search consciously for the shaped flint and, out of hard-gained anatomical knowledge, to restore the features of men who have been gone a million years into the night of time, men whose like will never be seen upon the earth again.

The restoration of those vanished faces, the ability to get from them significant fragments of the human adventure, depends essentially upon two things: first, the use of archaeology as a kind of detective science which secures all possible information from whatever science, in order to cast light on the circumstances of the death and identity of the late deceased, and, second, reliance upon a guiding principle which lends coherency to what would otherwise be a collection of mere unrelated facts. This guiding principle, of course, is evolution. By its demonstration of the community of descent of all living forms, it enables us to recognize across the gulf of time the altered faces of our ancestors, which otherwise would remain meaningless, and unrecognizable.

≽ ≼

FROM A LETTER FROM PHYLLIS MCGINLEY TO LOREN,
REFERRING TO THE ESSAY "MAN AND THE PORPOISE:
TWO SOLITARY DESTINIES," JANUARY 18, 1965

I nominate you herewith for the Pulitzer Prize (or perhaps the Nobel Award) for poetry. Somewhat belatedly today I read your piece on the porpoise in *The American Scholar* and I am in love with you. Together you and Pierre Teilhard are rescuing anthropology from its estate as a science and restoring it to its rightful purpose as a philosophy. Long may you live!

≽ ≼

THE HAWK

The hawk goes by, goes by
Wheels and returns to scan
With far-off golden eye
The checkered fields of man.

That far-off golden eye
Transfixes, pins in air
The serpent sprawled awry
Returning stare for stare.

Our shapes are plucked from grass,
From leaves, from shreds of night.
My upturned face will pass
Unjudged in that far sight.

The hawk wheels by, wheels by
While all, mouse, serpent, men
Leap once in that fierce eye,
Fall, and are lost again.

⅄ ⅄

FROM A LETTER FROM LEWIS MUMFORD TO LOREN,
FEBRUARY 20, 1966

You would be surprised, dear Eiseley, to learn how often
you have been in my thoughts lately. This is partly because I
have at last got round to reading your admirable essay on
Darwin's Century, prompted by one line of thought I've been
developing in a new book on Technics I've been writing. But
in the very act of reading your exposition of Wallace's

thoughts on the excess capacities of the human brain early
on, I suddenly realized it was *you*, in fact, that had originally
started me on this track in the essay you wrote for *Anthropology Today,* 1955; and as soon as I began to re-read that
essay I realized, too, what a heavy debt my book in fact owes
to you, for confirming and carrying further ideas I originally
received from my old master, Geddes. . . .

P.S. I thought I knew the Darwin literature fairly well, and
always was amused at his falling back on Lamarck when
pushed in a corner: but I never was zealous enough to do
what you did, and trace these changes through successive
editions; your whole book is a classic example of how to
handle fairly a controversial subject.

It was here that I came to know the final phase of love in
the mind of man — the phase beyond Darwin's meagre concentration upon survival. Here I no longer cared about
survival — I merely loved. And the love was meaningless as
the harsh Victorian Darwinists would have understood it. It
was a love without issue, tenuous, almost disembodied. It was
a love for an old gull, for wild dogs playing in the surf, for a
hermit crab in an abandoned skull — even for a solitary
cricket whom I had once heard by some trick of acoustics
filling an entire railway station with its song. It was a love
that had been growing through the unthinking demands of
childhood, through the pains and rapture of adult desire for
another human being. Now it was breaking free at last of my
worn body, still containing but passing beyond those other
loves. Now at last it was truly "the bright stranger, the foreign self," of which Emerson had once written. There was
nothing in scientific theory which adequately explained it —

but it had come and persisted among men so that we ask of it what was once asked of a ghost encountered upon a road in 1620: Are you a good or a bad spirit? The ghost, it is reported, made no answer, but "disappeared with a curious Perfume." I think there are men among us who disappear in this fashion every autumn and that by and by their number will increase. They are those who make no answer to questions, but depart trailing after them a radiance which is not that of the earth we know, or have set down within our books. Through shattered and receding skulls, growing ever smaller behind us in the crannies of broken earth, a stranger has crept and made his way, but precisely how he came, and what may be his destiny except that it is not wholly of our time nor this our star, we do not know.

⋟ ⋞

February 21, 1966

"Magic never 'originated'; it never was created or invented. All magic simply *was* from the beginning, as an essential adjunct to all those things and processes which vitally interest man and yet elude his normal rational efforts."
Malinowski, *Myth in Primitive Psychology*,
Norton, N.Y., 1926, p. 83

Note: In other words, did man, through magic, unconsciously recognize his lack of control of the contingency factor from the beginning? Also animals.

⋟ ⋞

July 28, 1966

Thoreau, vol. 10, p. 283, asks, "What did the birds do for horsehair here formerly?" Today (and I can remember birds and horsehair from my own childhood) I saw a sparrow with a whole sheet of Kleenex he (or she) could not manage. So what did she do? She was jerking and tearing it apart! Certainly some intellectual exercise here. In a few decades observers may be asking, What did the birds do before Kleenex?

⋟ ⋞

September 18, 1966

Last night I encountered an amazing little creature in a windy corner of the Wynnewood shopping area. It seemed at first glance some long-limbed feathery spider teetering rapidly down the edge of a storefront. Then it swung into the air and hesitantly, like a spider on a thread, blew away into the parking lot. Then it returned on a gust of wind and ran toward me once more with amazing rapidity on its spindly silken legs. It was only with great difficulty and trial that I discovered it was actually a silken filamentous seed seeking a hiding place and scurrying with the uncanny surety of a conscious animal. In fact, it did escape me before I could secure it. Its limbs were stiffer than milkweed down, and propelled by the wind it ran rapidly and evasively over the pavement. It unsettled me as though I had come upon some part of nature that I had not anticipated, something only recently emerged from the crevices of evening.

↘ ↙

THE NATURE OF HUMAN NATURE

    I. The Beginning: Physical Nature Passing into
    II. Biological Nature, into
   III. Cultural Nature (Alter Mundus) through
   IV. Speech: The First Great Tool Cutting Up and Delineating Environment and Time: The Doorway to the Infinite.
    V. The Climb up the Energy Ladder, Opening the Neolithic Revolution: Its Effect on Human Nature.
   VI. The Urban Environment: The Great Ecological Pool with Its
  VII. Societal Memory through Writing and the Library, but Fragmenting the Individual.
VIII. The Constrictions of Human Nature through Time (Death) and Individual Civilizations (Involutions).
   IX. The Release of the "Dreamers." Retarded Cultures Broken by the Rise of
    X. Science: The Insatiable, Faustian, Infinite Aspect of Human Nature and Reverting to True
   XI. Magic (Science as Magic).

XII. Human Nature: Man's Final Confrontation of Himself. His Nature as an Historical Being and as a True Emergent without Precedent in the Known Universe.

To arrange or delineate "human nature" as a subject to be investigated on a level with cosmology or, indeed, nature itself may, at first glance, appear to be an intolerably presumptuous and self-centered act. Scientists have recently informed us that some 90 percent of our genes we share with monkeys. We do not bother to write extensive essays upon hog nature, dog nature, or the nature of the amoeba. Instead we investigate these creatures as tiny fragments of the organic world. The universe of living things throughout past time and time to come has been, and will be, immense in the diversity of its forms.

It is possible that in the remote regions of sidereal space, life in other forms or even in forms more intelligent than our own may remain to be discovered. It may be that man, by mastering the inner secrets of life, may come to control his own evolution or project upon his machines powers biologically denied to him. To set up present human nature as a category of life so special as to merit individual attention needs, nevertheless, some dispassionate justification [even by men]. Our bodies are the product of a universal chemistry; the life in us, whatever its origin, is no more and no less living than that of the bird that sings in our garden at daybreak. Is it not then an act of self-interest and pride, rather than realism, which causes us to single out a two-legged creature of quite recent appearance and speak of his "nature" in a way to suggest that the life in him is different than all other life, or, on cosmic scale, that his destiny is any more significant than that of the ant colony beyond his door? These are deep questions not easily to be faced.

Furthermore, if we succeed in spite of such obstacles in justifying so grandiose a conception of our human significance, we must still ask whether, on the evolutionary scale, we can define the point at which organic nature gave way to a newly emergent human or, figuratively, "superorganic" nature. Like all else that lives, we are a patchwork of many skins; old lives lie hidden in our present fabric. Some men, it is clear, are less "human" than others. Again there are those who shame our corrupt acts and bespeak, in their conduct, an

ideal of human nature beyond our present powers of realization. Thus it may be said that besides the past, a potential
future awaits its moment among us, but the potential is a
possibility which may go unrecognized. Not alone is man
capable of self-destruction, of evil beyond that known to
instinctively grooved and confined organisms, but it remains
to be seen whether he is capable of the attention necessary to
sustain through long centuries a civilization existing in the
tension of incessant technological change. Man has only
recently emerged from a very simple village order; some men,
in fact, have only in our generation begun to emerge from
tribalism. Thus, even in a cultural sense, the present and the
past live side by side. It is true of our societies as it is true of
the individual natures of each of us. Human nature must thus
be recognized as a thing of many facets, having its roots in
the biological world from which it has recently emerged.
Upon that biological base, however, has been erected a
unique superstructure based on language. Thus man has
passed beyond the known or expected biological nature of
past geological eras. He is a genuine emergent bringing with
him powers not hitherto observable in the natural world
about him. There exists in human society a curious latency,
an unrealized and unknown potential based not solely upon
individual genius, but also waiting upon chance currents and
unpredictable social and environmental pressures which may
retard or stimulate the dynamism of individual societies. Thus
in any analysis of human nature, we are dealing in varying
quantities not alone with genetic potential, but with an
equally mysterious and much more intangible realm; namely,
the superorganic world which man has brought into being,
but which eludes his own attempts at rational control.

≥ ≤

Book: *The Skin Changers*. Life as it is evolving today:
lectures to be worked out, or essays. Man too? Everything
incomplete about man.

One chapter: What Is Nature?

Good start: Behind all religions lies nature. It lurks equally
behind the buried cults of Neanderthal man, in Cro-Magnon
hunting, and in the questions of Job and in the answering
voice from the whirlwind. In the end, it is the name for man's

attempt to define and delimit his world, whether seen or
unseen. He knows that it is a reality which was before him
and will be after him. He may define it as that which is or
include that which may be. It is an otherness of which he is a
part. He may be a professed atheist, but he must still account
for the fleeting particles that appear and vanish in his perfected cyclotrons of modern physics. He may see behind
nature a divinity which rules it, or he may regard nature itself
as a somewhat nebulous and indefinable divinity. Man knows
he springs from nature and not nature from him. This is very
old and primitive knowledge, a genuine scientific observation
of the foretime. Beyond that point man, as the "thinking
reed," the memory beast, and the anticipator of things to
come, has devised hundreds of cosmogonies and interpretations of nature. There are the religious, so also, though somewhat differently formulated, are the theories and philosophies
of science. All involve nature. No word bears a heavier, more
ancient, or more diverse array of meanings. Of all words
none is more important, none more elusive, for the term
implies not alone all that is or may come to be. Behind it
lurks the regularities and the chaos of the world. And behind
that further mystery, the shadow substance that only the
mind of man has had the peculiar power to summon up from
the beginning, the form beyond all matter, the shape of divinity itself. Man as atheist may turn upon and rend his own
mind and say that this shadow is an illusion that is specifi-
cally his own, or as a scientific agnostic, he can draw an
imaginary line beyond which he forces himself not to pass.
He will adhere to the tangible, but he will still be forced to
speak of the "unknowable," of "final causes," even if he
proclaims such phrases as barren and of no concern to science. But in his mind he will still be forced to acknowledge a
line he has drawn, a definition of nature he has arbitrarily
proclaimed, a human limit that may or may not coincide with
reality. Man may, by now, be a highly sophisticated student
of the pitfalls of semantics, a student of comparative religions, or an astrophysicist probing the mathematical abstractions of time and space. Nevertheless, it is still nature that
concerns him as it concerned the Neanderthal. It is the vessel
that contains man and in which he finally sinks to rest when
his sun vanishes forever. It is all, absolutely all, that he
knows, or can know. He has never succeeded in defining it to

his satisfaction and perhaps he never will. The word ramifies
and runs through the centuries assuming different shapes.
Sometimes it appears as ghostly as the unnamed shadow
behind it; sometimes it appears harsh, prescriptive, and solid.
Then again it takes on a more tenuous character. Matter
becomes interchangeable with energy. Fact becomes shadow,
law becomes probability. After fifty thousand years we find
ourselves still watching a flickering campfire in a cavern while
the shadows come and go upon the walls. We watch the
flames and try on our hesitant tongues once more the word
"nature" with another emphasis. Each time we grow lonelier,
each time we grow more conscious of the shadow behind the
shadows. We grow introspective or we fear and wait for
dawn. "Nature" is a word that must have arisen with man. It
walks with him as changeable and intangible as his shadow.
It is in fact the shadow of the unnamed shadow that has so
frequently divided men in murderous contention, but it is part
also of man's humanity. Other beasts than man live within
nature. Only man has carelessly turned the abstraction round
and round upon his tongue and found fault with every definition, found himself in the end looking endlessly outside of
nature toward something invisible to any eye but his own and
indeed not surely to be glimpsed by him — only to be
glimpsed or guessed or pondered upon.

⩓ ⩕

Each generation of men is drawn through an invisible
keyhole, invisible, that is, to all but the searching eye of the
microscope. Each generation comes very close to the origins
of life itself and then, in its individual development, climbs
anew a ladder reminiscent of the evolutionary ladder itself.
Because this is a familiar phenomenon we tend to accept it
without question, even though man long abhorred the
thought of his own evolution through time and his passage
on that journey through the lower forms of life. Thus there is
no escaping a certain reality: If we deny evolution itself, we
must still admit that we have risen from a single cell which
repeats in essence much of what the rocks inform us of our
long midnight traverse through the realms of time. The one,
the individual event, we cannot help knowing, the other we

have forgotten because we are creatures of a day, and without the aid of science we cannot pierce the veil of the past.

༨ ༙

No, it is not because I am filled with obscure guilt that I step gently over, and not upon, an autumn cricket. It is not because of guilt that I refuse to shoot the last osprey from her nest in the tide marsh. I possess empathy; I have grown with man in his mind's growing. I share that sympathy and compassion which extends beyond the barriers of class and race and form until it partakes of the universal whole. I am not ashamed to profess this emotion, nor will I call it a pathology. Only through this experience many times repeated and enhanced does man become truly human. Only then will his gun arm be forever lowered. I pray that it may sometime be so.

༨ ༙

THE SORCERER IN THE WOOD

There is in the universe a duality of powers in perfect equilibrium. The theme of *The Unexpected Universe* is how man in the Dark Wood has broken through this duality — so that something is loose and prowling in the fierce wood. . . . Dante saw it long ago when he encountered himself. I saw it as a child under the bed.

༨ ༙

"Wanted, young, skinny wiry fellows, not over 18. Must be expert riders, willing to risk death daily. Orphans preferred. Wages $25 per week."

Pony express (Nebraska), 1860–61

≯ ≮

Idea for lecture: Man's loss of interest in visible nature just as he needs it. See Gunther Steret, "The Coming of the Golden Age," p. 115.

≯ ≮

Man has been seeking man for five thousand years: He has found him in blood, he has found him in dungeons, he has found him in the hermit's cell or in the torture chamber, he has waited for him by the cross, he has found him in meditation under the sacred Bô tree, he has found him in the laboratory or in the first mushroom cloud that lit the night at Roswell, N.M. He has never been found at all. The reason is simple. Men have been seeking Man, a capitalized, hypostatized thing: a god or a Frankenstein monster. Man does not exist, he is something sewn together in the laboratory of the human imagination, he may be beautiful, he may be as venomous as a serpent. Some men may thus perceive him, but they would be wrong: they are wrong so long as they say, having vitalized their creation, this is Man. There is no Man, there are only men: good, evil, uncountable millions, marred by genetic makeup, marred or perfected by environment. . . . Men should be the subject of human study, never Man; the moment we say Man we are lost in abstraction.

Part III

❧ ❦

THE ULTIMATE SNOW
1966–1977

. . . I have learned, in whatsoever state I am, therewith to be content. I know both how to be abased, and I know how to abound: everywhere, and in all things, I am instructed, both to be full and to be hungry, both to abound and to suffer need.
> — *Saint Paul*

Among the world events in 1966 of which Loren Eiseley was conscious were the International Days of Protest, against U.S. policy in Vietnam; the publication of William Manchester's *The Death of a President;* the moving of the temples of Abu Simbel in Egypt to save them from the rising waters of the Aswan High Dam; a U.S. B-52 crashing near the coast of Spain and dropping four unarmed hydrogen bombs; the U.S. spacecraft *Surveyor 1* making a soft landing on the moon and transmitting more than eleven thousand television images of the terrain.

If our manic century has produced an heir apparent to Henry David Thoreau, Loren is it. At age fifty-nine, as a comparatively serene middle age was ending, this gentle spirit of twentieth-century America embarked on new ventures, and the following years were among the most productive of his career. He was host and narrator of a prize-winning educational series, *Animal Secrets,* on NBC television (1966–1968), and he produced seven books of prose and poetry, as well as countless articles, book reviews, introductions, epilogues, and addresses.

A new edition of Thomas Henry Huxley's *On a Piece of Chalk,* with an introduction and notes by Loren, was published in 1967. At the time, I was director of the Science Book Department at Charles Scribner's Sons, and I invited him to prepare this edition of the famous nineteenth-century biologist. Our mutual interest in science classics resulted in plans to reissue Charles Darwin's *The Formation of Vegetable Mould Through the Action of Worms,* but although he began to write the introduction, the project was set aside and finally abandoned because of marketing considerations.

The Unexpected Universe was published by Harcourt, Brace and World in 1969. Hiram Haydn had moved to Harcourt, and Loren had followed him. Three of these explorations of the unexpected universe were given as the William Haas Lectures of

Stanford University, and other material had appeared previously in *The American Scholar* and *Life*. Some passages for the book were never used: "The Rent in the Curtain" was intended as a section of "The Invisible Island" chapter and was discovered among his papers. The dedication is "To Wolf, who sleeps forever with an ice age bone across his heart, the last gift of one who loved him" — Wolf, a shepherd dog, with whom he has a numinous encounter in the chapter called "The Angry Winter." There are several such revelational meetings with animals — a starving jackrabbit and a young fox — in the volume, which is, in essence, a quest for meaning in the world about him. At the time of its writing, Loren made the following notebook entry from Joseph Campbell's *Masks of God:* "For the animals are great shamans and great teachers, as well as codescendents of the totem ancestors. . . . They fill the world of the hunter, inside and out. And any beast that may pass, whether flying as a bird, trotting as a quadruped, or wriggling in the way of a snake, may be a messenger signalling some wonder. . . ." As with other modern writers, Loren was greatly interested in mythology. Through his clear and visionary imagery, ethnic expression emerged as brilliant, international literary metaphors.

The Unexpected Universe made new friends, including W. H. Auden, whose favorable and entertaining review, "Concerning the Unpredictable," appeared in *The New Yorker*. Born in the same year as Loren but in a different land, Auden, at Oxford, had been given a copy of *The Immense Journey* by a student; since then he had been a devoted reader. The review of the eminent poet and critic meant a great deal to the author, who wrote him on September 11, 1970: "As one of those hang-dog characters who float about in the limbo between science and literature, sometimes pierced by the shafts of both establishments, I wanted to say simply that I was touched by your generosity. There is not so much courtesy and noblesse oblige in the world that one would wish to pass them by indifferently."

In Sir Arthur Conan Doyle's stories, Sherlock Holmes criticizes his friend Dr. Watson — who records the detective's cases — for turning a series of lectures into tales. Loren was criticized by his scientific colleagues for doing roughly the same thing — for venturing into the field of literature and appealing to the general reader. Other anthropologists have had their careers hurt for similar writings: Margaret Mead for *Coming of Age in Samoa* and, more recently, Collin Turnbull for *People of the Forest*. It is likely that jealousy is a major motive in this criticism: these popular books won fame and fortune for their authors. Among other complaints, Loren was accused of being a mystic because he could not shut out wonder when he looked at the world. His attitude about this was expressed early when, in 1956, he wrote " 'Deviation' in Physical Anthropology," a rebuttal to a review in *The American Journal of Physical Anthropology,* for *Yearbook of Anthropology.*

So insecure that he required constant reassurance of his worth, he was often hurt by indifferent reviewers, and publication of his books was a traumatic experience. There were, however, a number of scientists who knew what errand he was on — the bacteriologist René Dubos, the botanist Paul Sears, the naturalist Edwin Way Teale — whose perceptive comments heartened him. Moreover, it was precisely because of his sense of awe at the mysterious and because of the literary quality of his work that he had so many loyal fans: students of English, ministers who used his essays as subjects of sermons (he has been called "the academic chaplain"), young people of all ages trying to comprehend the complex universe in which they were born.

On July 20, 1969, U.S. astronaut Neil A. Armstrong, commander of the *Apollo 11* mission, became the first man to set foot on the moon. As a perceptive student of man, Loren would have extraordinary insight into the event, and I asked him to write an analysis of the space age. The invitation coincided with an altercation with Haydn, and he agreed to undertake the project, the first humanist account of the rocket century. It was also the first of six books he wrote that were issued by Scribners with me as editor; after drifting with Haydn from publisher to publisher, he finally found a permanent home. *The Invisible Pyramid* (1970) was developed through a series of lectures delivered under the auspices of the John Danz Fund at the University of Washington in Seattle in the fall of 1969. Loren's notebooks include brief entries for the work, including the cherished memory of being held up in his father's arms as a small boy and shown Halley's comet. (Similar memories were recorded by other writers, Eudora Welty for one, who was carried to the window and shown the comet in her *sleep.*) His father whispered in his ear that if he lived to be an old man, he would see the "star dragon" again, an appointment he anticipated but was not to keep.

The Snow Wolf is the most important single unpublished work of fiction Loren wrote. It is not surprising that in indulging his wish to write a novel, he chose science fiction as the genre. And given his affinity for the Ice Age, it is not surprising that he selected the now extinct dire wolf as his protagonist. The largest known wolf, it was common in western North America during the Pleistocene epoch, being half again as big as the modern grey wolf, of which a northern male may be six and a half feet long. Loren's unfinished novel is a fictional battlefield, ringing with the clash of man against animal, will against will, idea against idea. He obviously felt within him this intelligent social animal and the endless winter when it lived, as in his notes for the book he identifies with these manifestations of nature, with them and his personal drama. In one enigmatic jotting he wrote: "The Ice Age (past provost) in the Andes. Develop as chapter (before Sleek Foot)." The notes constitute about three thousand words and are interspersed between entries made during the years 1969 to 1970 — fictional scenes, sudden bursts of imaginative plotting, observations of characters, even a dedication. To read these notebook entries is to meet a scientist with the obvious gifts of a novelist. I was particularly enthusiastic about *The Snow Wolf,* and as he wrote a beginning or ending for the book, he cheerfully reported his progress. But he did not have time to reach his objective, to see his novel completed and in print.

A critical moment in Loren's creative career occurred when another publisher asked him to write a textbook. He was always being sought by other publishers, but the offer of an advance of $100,000 against royalties was difficult to turn down, and he prepared an outline. In his younger years, he had been unable to save because of responsibilities to aged relatives; now in his early sixties he was trying to put aside some money for retirement. The proposal was mentioned at a restaurant overlooking the skating rink at Rockefeller Center, a place where we often lunched and observed the antics of New Yorkers as they glided by us on ice like water striders. I gently tried to persuade him to write his own books, to say the things he had to say in his singular style, to convince him that his remuneration would be as great in the end. He had, of course, already made the right choice, for the whole direction of his writing had been away from a book on which a teacher lectures or comments; he only needed me to put in words what he by this time knew, to act as a sounding board and give greater force to his own opinions. The subject was never brought up again.

Acting as a sounding board for an author can be one of the main functions of an editor. This was certainly true of our relationship. When Loren was writing a new book, he would often call me every day to discuss what he was doing; these rather one-sided conversations could easily last for an hour. Moreover, we might dine together once a week; he enjoyed coming to New York to consult with his publisher. Lunch at times terminated in a visit to a spot of mutual interest — an

Oriental art gallery, the New York Stock Exchange, a rare bookshop. (He loved books so keenly that when one of Philadelphia's famous old stores was for sale, he seriously proposed that we buy and operate it together.) In his writing, he invariably made the correct decisions; he was a good self-editor. If a change was hinted at, he would go beyond what was suggested, exceeding expectations.

The Night Country, which some critics thought was his long-awaited autobiography, so filled is it with personal experiences, was published by Scribners in 1971. In fact, he "stole" the first chapter, "The Gold Wheel," from the memoirs he was writing, but most of the pieces, including a reprint of *The Mind as Nature,* had been used earlier as lectures or articles. One of the unexpected nuggets found among his papers is an introduction originally intended for the book but not included in it, in part a revealing statement about his grandmother McKee Corey's second sight and his own power of discerning what is not visible. *The Night Country* won the Athenaeum of Philadelphia Literary Award in 1973 and contains some of his best writing and thinking.

Loren was widely acclaimed by critics as a literary stylist. His work was included in many anthologies of English prose, and in 1971 he was elected a member of the National Institute of Arts and Letters — a unique achievement among professional archaeologists and human paleontologists. Poets — Howard Nemerov and W. H. Auden — dedicated poems to him. This had an amusing effect: when one of his young colleagues, a British scientist who had always regarded Loren's extracurricular activities with a prejudicial eye, saw Auden's poem and dedication in the *Times Literary Supplement,* he was slightly overawed and willing to recognize for the first time that they shared, if not the same ideas, then at least a common department.

It was in a casual conversation over lunch that I discovered that the essayist was also a poet, that he had written poetry in college and had continued to do so as an occasional secret avocation ever since. I first persuaded him of my interest in his verse and then persuaded Charles Scribner, Jr., the president, as I was not in the literary end of the publishing house. Loren agreed to draw from his notebooks some poems for a volume to be entitled *Fox Curse.* Then a remarkable thing occurred: after delivering the finished manuscript, he arrived unannounced in my office a month later with a whole collection of new poems. The flow of this part of his creative energy, which had been restrained for so many years, spilled into *Notes of an Alchemist* (1972), *The Innocent Assassins* (1973), and *Another Kind of*

Autumn (1977). Loren is one of the few American nature writers of stature who also published poetry. From this he derived a heightened sense of imagery and cadence, as well as an awareness that the rhythms of prose may draw from but must not emulate the meter of poetry. Observe, for example, how the groups of periods in "A Road Night '23," the story published in his youth, convey the rhythm of the train's wheels. To use punctuation so creatively is a traditional poetic skill.

In the sense that it distills the raw material of experience into something finer or rarer, all art is alchemical; understood metaphorically, every true artist is an alchemist. In his first book of verse, the scientific man transmuted the sharp images of his profession into something deeply subjective — into the equivalent in literature of the alchemist's gold. Forming a continuous whole with *Notes of an Alchemist, The Innocent Assassins* sustained and magnified the same passionate affection for the living world and the same brooding philosophical intensity. The poem "And as for Man" was dedicated to Auden; Loren selected it partly because of the theme of leaving New York (the British poet had gone home to Oxford and was missed). His third collection was prepared not long before his death, and an engulfing autumnal sadness pervades it.

In exposing him to the magic of poetry, Loren's actor father did more than help to shape his son's literary genius. In 1963, he invited me to hear an address he was delivering in the Rockefeller Institute at a symposium inaugurating the Richard Ettinger Program for Creative Writing, of which he was director. I sat with René Dubos, professor at that institution, who, with a curious smile, said softly, "Watch what happens when he begins to speak." What took place was an extraordinary theatrical feat: before the audience's eyes, the quiet professor transformed himself into an eloquent actor, whose rhetorical delivery of "The Illusion of Two Cultures" conjured up his father's ghost. Some years later, I observed again the impact of his parent's personality and career upon his own when I heard him read, with great style, his own poetry; it had become easier for him to give a poetry reading than to prepare a special lecture for the public.

In 1973, Loren received the Distinguished Nebraska Award from the Nebraska Society of Washington, D.C. For one who felt so strongly an attachment to the land from which he came and who wrote so poetically about it, this was a special honor. Soon afterwards, in 1975, his memoirs, *All the Strange Hours: The Excavation of a Life,* were published. The book is dedicated to Charles Frederick Eiseley, his paternal grandfather, a member of the first legislature in Nebraska Territory, and to his uncle William Buchanan Price, a frontier newspaperman who read law and entered politics (he never forgot "Uncle Buck's" kindness in giving him financial aid to continue his college education). Gifted with an eye for detail and the extraordinary descriptive powers of the novelist, Loren evoked memorable scenes and moods in telling his life's story, and he was frank and open in his portrait of his family and intimates, exposing the secrets of those close to him, as he had done in his earlier writing. There is no suggestion of cruelty in this: the major figures in his story were dead, and he could harm no one but himself. His aim was to illuminate life through his own case history. For this work, in 1976 he was given the Christopher Award.

From the time he produced *Notes of an Alchemist,* Loren wrote many poems, some of which were never published. In "Our Own True Notebook" (1973), he speaks of the point where two forms of awareness intersect — our own uniqueness and our own impermanence — and where the impulse to keep a record of our lives begins. "Gravely Then" recalls an incident in the life of Edward Thomas, who began to write poetry after forming a friendship with Robert Frost. In a letter to Loren of March 21, 1973, Auden wrote: "Knowing you to be a lover of Nature, I wonder if you know of a Georgia poet (killed in World War I) who has a great influence on me, Edward Thomas. If by any chance, you don't, do get a copy of his poems." The result was this offering in memory of the man. "The Office" was written in the mid 1970s when he was moved to more modern quarters at the University of Pennsylvania. It is the lament of an aging naturalist for his old octagonal room in an ivy-covered tower, where his magical surroundings had the power to transport him to distant places. "I Am the Stranger Here" is a singular remembrance of a day in 1933 when, ill with influenza, he took an examination for his undergraduate degree and then, climbing the stairs of his rooming house, collapsed. In "The Same Cycle" (1977), he speculates on the existence of the cabin in which he lived in his youth, when, suffering from respiratory disease, he was sent to the Mojave Desert to recuperate. The incidents in "I Am the Stranger Here" and "The Same Cycle" are also described in his autobiography; the author's subjects were interchangeable, often used in prose and verse. "The Ultimate Snow" was written in and deals with Loren's last illness. As he grew older, his sense of mortality became more pronounced, as reflected in these poignant lines.

In his review of *The Unexpected Universe* in 1969, Auden said: "I get the impression of a wanderer who is often in danger of being shipwrecked on the shores of Dejection — it can hardly be an accident that three of his encounters take place in cemeteries — and a solitary who feels more easily at home with animals than with his fellow human beings." The same air of melancholy that animates this book emerges not only in his poems, but in his letters and notebook entries. In his last years, fear for man and the planet itself, the sadness of growing old, and his precarious health combined to give him a decidedly dark vision of the world. Loren's letters fill in many gaps about his life and work. They were not written in the grand tradition of letters, with one eye on the recipient and the other on posterity, but they are articulate and illuminating. In one such communication addressed to his friend Ray Bradbury, dated January 16, 1977, he wrote: "You are quite right that I am and have been seriously ill. The illness was first diagnosed as hepatitis. Then, finally, as gall bladder jaundice. I have had severe abdominal surgery and have had to abandon all my speaking engagements for the coming spring as well as having to cancel courses. I fully expect to be something of an invalid for weeks, if not months, yet."

Loren died of pancreatic cancer on July 9, 1977. In the shadow of the branches of an immense horse chestnut tree and a delicate dogwood, he was laid to rest on July 13 at West Laurel Hill Cemetery, Bala-Cynwyd, Pennsylvania. The tombstone he chose for his wife and himself bears the simple legend: "We loved the earth but could not stay."

≈ ≈

Note for book or essay: the way the birds break up the U.S. every spring, dividing everything without anyone being aware of it. . . .

It happens every spring and nobody seems to take any notice at all. There are no congressional investigations, no cross-examinations of witnesses before television, no one hurls himself out of a window. Nevertheless, it happens every

spring and there is no doubt that it smacks of sheer communism. I refer to the expropriation and reassignment of land in these states and the incredible way in which even city properties fall victim to it. Yesterday morning I could hear conversations about it just outside my window, and somebody over my rooftop was expropriating in at least half-mile sections. The people who think they own all this land and post it against wandering professors of suspect tendencies are deceiving themselves. Invisible boundaries have been drawn every which way across their fine fences and walls, and the drawers of those lines are totally indifferent to surveyors and human rights. I am astounded that no one seems to have noticed the spread of this insidious empiric practice which is now encroaching on city property. I, at least, shall not be silent; I shall speak out. The whole thing smacks of subversion and disrespect for the laws of private property. It may well merit investigation. It should begin by a thorough and painstaking investigation of the birds. I am not sure that the American eagle himself is free of the taint of this thing, but I will begin with the small fry, the little fellows who have come under my personal observation. Others more competent to speak may clear the eagle, and in any case it would not do to shatter rapidly confidence in so noble a symbol.

For Heuer's Worm Book. Introduction

The attention paid to Darwin as the creative genius so long associated with the theory of natural selection has obscured the great naturalist's preoccupation with very simple things. Indeed, it was upon the seemingly trite phenomena of everyday existence that his imagination was best nourished and upon which his reputation stands. It is actually upon a multitude of simplicities properly interpreted that the *Origin of Species* depends for its overpowering effect upon the reader. . . .

≽ ≼

The Formation of Vegetable Mould Through the Action of Worms was the first book to celebrate in any extended and considerate fashion the all-conquering, all-devouring worm that preoccupied seventeenth-century divines and had its ardent advocate in every pulpit. In those days the worm, the devil, and Jehovah each played a role in the drama of mortal man; the devil tempted, man succumbed, and the worm inherited his perishable mansion of clay. The Lord, it is true, would judge, but that was to be the last trump, and the grave and worm lay formidably in between. Few indeed were prepared for that final resurrection in their hearts. Though this drama remains muted in modern theology, the worm has never lost his fascination as a symbol of mortality, just as, in pre-Christian thought, the self-devouring dragon worm was Alpha and Omega — the beginning and the end. Yet such is the paradox of man that he could bait a fishhook with the creature who would confront him in his coffin and against whose terrors great vaults and mausoleums would be erected to this day.

If one strikes a shovel into topsoil anywhere, and particularly where the forces of nature have not left the naked bones and boulder fields of the planet exposed, one quickly traverses a thin layer of rich, black mold. Of that mold the earthworm, dew worm, angleworm, night crawler, as he has been variously called, is the primary inhabitant. Moreover, as befits a night crawler, he is to a very considerable degree the creator and enricher of that soil and therefore the enricher of life as well. If it is theologically true that there is the worm at work in the heart of things, it can also be said that though the worm has buried civilizations, he is also the sustainer of life. His ministrations are a necessary part of the great round of existence, and what passes through his gullet is taking a step once more on the road toward living substance. It remained for Charles Darwin, stimulated perhaps by that delightful old classic *The Natural History of Selbourne,* to become the true chronicler of the worm. The atmosphere of the nineteenth century was peculiarly conducive to a better understanding of the role of the little creature in the economy of the planet. Finally, when Charles Darwin at the height of his fame turned his attention to the tremendous geological importance of this seemingly unimportant creature, the earthworm's reputation was secured. Darwin and the worm. They would go down in history together linked by a curious symbolism.

For Heuer: Start(?)

Charles Darwin, early in his career, became one of the first converts to uniformitarian geology as expressed in the other great work of nineteenth-century science, *The Principles of Geology* by Sir Charles Lyell. As a result of this conversion and only because of it, Darwin was enabled to apply to the problem of evolution the conception of minute, invisible, but incessant selective alteration which guides the course of life over enormous periods of time. This attempt to pierce through the seeming stability of organic form to reveal its mutation is the primary thesis of the *Origin of Species*. Its success has culminated in the triumphs of modern biology, yet this achievement was made possible only by the geological recognition that the surface features of our planet are the product of ages of slow, not on the whole catastrophic, change. Furthermore, it had become increasingly evident since the time of James Hilton that the slow geological alteration was, to a marked extent, the product of almost imperceptible forces working over long ranges of time and hence passing unperceived by the short-lived generations of men. Frost and wind and rain, even atomic radiation, are capable of precipitating giant changes if one allows them sufficient time. Thus there came about, in the mind of the young Darwin, that recognition of the significance of the smallest events which was forever after to preoccupy his mind. It led him to examine the delicate interrelationship between flowers and insects, the teavels of seeds, and, finally, to the subject of this particular book, which invokes with a kind of Gothic grandeur the power of the worm. I suspect that toward the end of his life Darwin derived an obscure satisfaction from this demonstration of the hidden springs of nature, coiled springs like those hidden in children's toys. Whether it is the labors of the all-conquering worm beneath our feet, the island building of the coral polyp, or the strange behavior of carnivorous plants, Darwin is intrigued by the grotesque, the gnomic workmen at the heart of the living order. Ironically, the philosopher who succeeded in overturning the concept of the great Designer replaced that Workman with what one can almost personify as a series of scurrying elves. Darwin, it will be noted in the pages of *The Formation of Vegetable Mould,* delights in recounting little evidences of the intelligence of his worms, just as he surprised Huxley into exclaiming over the animallike qualities of the carnivorous sundew.

April 1, 1967

The mockingbird on Charles Langdon's windmill who used to intersperse his song with the *caw, caw* of a crow, half-apologetically, and then go on to something he could do better — like modern writers stealing from each other. Possible essay here: "The Mocking Birds." He also imitated the meadowlark. Next day: In the evening I heard a Wynnewood mockingbird run through a whole little repertoire and a faint crow's voice was there. From the crows about the shopping center, no doubt. *The residual reptilian hiss of an angry bird:* what lost ages are in it, and upon my windowsill this very morning.

≽ ≼

May 7, 1967

The druid circle in the little park, great rough granite stones naturally arranged in a circle around an ancient hollow oak. Because this is America, no one realizes its strange analogical existence nor the hidden powers contained within it. We have grown too technologically secure. Primitives of whatever complexion would have immediately sensed its drawing power, as I do, and have come to it. As it stands it is what Mircea Eliade would call a sacred center. There is some upwelling of unnamable power that the mind feels, but it passes unseen and unrecognized among moderns; their sense for it is atrophied. They cannot even be said to see the arrangement.

≽ ≼

III. THE RENT IN THE CURTAIN

We have seen at last the meaning of the living screen — that tenuous, unsubstantial net that covers the continents and the seas of the earth like a thin film but is at the same time as powerful as the strangling grip of tropical vines upon great trees. It is, in short, the interknit web of life itself, the web that Darwin knew. As life grows and invades every ecological niche, its hold becomes almost unbreakable. Indeed, through increased interest in selective cattle breeding in the late eighteenth century, biological change, though recognized, seemed totally a human prerogative in nature. What today we call the principle of natural selection, what Alfred Russell Wallace so

aptly labeled as containing the secret of "indefinite departure," was known in pre-Darwinian days under other terms.

These terms are revelatory because they involve the supposed inflexible, steadfast quality of the biological screen.
John Hunter called it "natural government," a war which no
species could win. Sir Charles Lyell coined the phrase "principle of preoccupation," which smacks of British primogeni-
ture. Another contemporary of Darwin's, Edward Blyth,
preferred the phrase "localizing principle." The names themselves denote the straining tautness of the living net; life
without human interference could only vary within strict
limits. Under conditions then conceived as "natural," it could
not proceed along the pathway of endless change. The great
web, which was recognized well before Darwin's birth, was
static. It was, in truth, natural government, and that government was maintained in an unvarying Newtonian balance.
Life might exhibit at times an impulsive dynamism, but the
web restrained this quality; the web under divine guidance
was omnipresent. No creature could creep through its self-
restricting strands and long survive.

As far back as man could journey in recorded history, only
he had possessed the power to alter substance. The animals
he knew had remained the same as those mummified in ancient Egypt or recorded crudely in the medieval bestiaries.
Nature held its place as surely as the unchanging laws of
gravity. The natural scene before man's cottage windows
would not change. There was no conceivable rent in the
curtain. Men rested secure in the stability of the known, the
homely and familiar world. What they had observed was
true. It was only that great truths sometimes are found to
possess disconcerting and obverse faces that come unexpectedly upon us. There was, after all, a rent, many torn rents, in
the web of life. The containing net, man was to learn, did
lend an illusory stability to the historical present, but the web
was incredibly ancient and full of tatters. Eventually man
would learn, to his humiliation, that his road was the road of
other creatures, that it was marked with all the cryptic ambi-
guities which constantly beset the evolutionary pathway —
that through these same rents and fissures, biological
failures, or seeming failures, might tumble through the life-
withholding mesh into paradoxical success.

Even the success might be momentary. Fixity was an illusion of the mortal eye. The phrase "survival of the fittest," which at first had a proud human sound like the clash of armies, partook of an unfortunate semantic mistiness. It was clogged by a circularity of argument and sometimes by naive and subjective interpretations as to who or what might constitute "the fit." Darwin himself had hastened to explain that natural selection had been used in a "broad and metaphorical sense" involving "all the conditions of existence." "All the conditions" is at most a great floundering phrase concealing under its cloak every crevice, every rabbit hole through or down which any hopeful deviant or unhappy failure could scamper.

Darwin himself, under something of an academic cloud, had similarly scampered away from college upon a voyage, the now famous voyage of the *Beagle*. While upon that voyage, he had come, by the irony of chance, upon one of the most gaping rents in the tight-drawn living web. As a youth its significance came close to escaping him, but a seed was planted in his thought which was to persist through many silent years of contemplation.

There could have been no more unlikely spot in the universe for such a discovery. The site was only a handful of volcanic islets, baking in the tropic sun five hundred miles off the coast of Ecuador. "Each island," one later visitor was to remark, "is a different hell." Many of the group lacked fresh water. The black lavas suggested to Darwin the surrounding waste of an iron foundry. Buccaneers and whalermen had been the only visitors. It is perhaps characteristic that though the Galápagos Archipelago had been known since the sixteenth century, one great writer touching on those shores was to epitomize in a single sentence both their desolation and the archaic nature of their fauna. "The only sound of life here," wrote the sailor-novelist Herman Melville, "is a hiss." Melville was writing before the publication of the *Origin of Species*. The hiss came from somewhere outside the present, from a creature lost in the black abysm of forgotten time.

There in the bright sun among shifting and uncertain currents, on an island termed a "little hell," there lurked something uncanny. Perhaps there persists, after all, a rift in the fabric of time, a keyhole into the past. A dank wind, even on the equator, could be felt blowing out of it. Natural government, with its attendant pruning and policing, was a myth

confined to English hedgerows. Here the new and the
unheard-of mingled and mixed with the hoary past. Here
nature, infinitely remote from the scheming human breeders
of the industrial age, was still going about her old blind jovial
work. Among the forgotten philosophers of Greece millennia
ago, each isle of the Galápagos would have demanded a
shrine cleft in the rock and a resident daemon to preside over
the ascending vapors. A sense of enchantment had been felt
even by the earliest Spanish navigators and is indicated on
their charts.

Long before science arose, there had been an instinctive
sense for these things among the wise. It is as though man
were striving to remember something forgotten very long ago
and only to be grasped in myths associated with ascents
toward daylight through dreadful caverns. Or in other lands
tales might linger of encounters with furred men or animals
uncertainly believed to have fathered us. Man's hold on the
living earth has proved tenacious even as he has striven to
cast it aside. The rent in the curtain first perceived by Darwin
in the Galápagos has implications extending even beyond his
insights. It has opened the doorway of the unexpected and

revealed to what an incredible degree even natural selection is
dependent upon pure and unreturning opportunity.

We may, if we can, dissociate ourselves from the Darwinian overemphasis upon struggle, even observe how failures,
fumblers, accidental wanderers upon ocean currents, even the
fragile and beautiful, may survive and evolve, it is true, under
selection, but a selection born originally of isolation. Mingled
with all our well-studied genetics is something unexpected
that forever escapes forecast and prophecy. That missing,
unpredictable element in evolution is the occasional rent in
the living fabric, the refuge in the uncrowded crevice or on

the abandoned shore. It is the open doorway of the solitary hermitage, not necessarily the incessant war of nature, that breeds giants or which may cherish the seeming failure, until, grown formidable, he in his turn closes a door, sews tight a curtain that will not open again till his departure.

Nature, as we have seen, has two faces: short-time predictable stability — the bird that is a bird, and the man that considers himself a man. Behind this seeming stability, however, strange clock hands move invisibly. Previous escapes are frequently impossible of duplication, and the prisoners may wait out ages imprisoned in their guise. Or again, the green canopy of the forest may be wrenched asunder and through the opening will pour a few stumbling adventurous refugees. Man, it would appear, was such a creature somewhere in the primordial past.

≯ ≮

December 7, 1967, Madison, Wisconsin

Bill Laughlin came in to see me at the Institute for Research in the Humanities. We chatted about a forthcoming work of his upon which he is now engaged. The gist of it, or rather our conversation, revolved around the fact that primitives are early conditioned to know a great deal about their natural environment and the living things within it. There is a sense in which this knowledge is more important than their tools. I added that fire is an animal; unlike material objects it has to be fed and attended; it can get out of control like a wild stallion or a boar. It can run, leap, and has an insatiable hunger to be fed. It is the only nonliving object on the planet (except, to a degree, water) which can, under stress, locomote itself. All these factors must have promoted human foresight.

≯ ≮

December 8, 1967

Lying awake in the dawn it occurred to me that fire as an animal has another aspect. As combustion it enters into life and consciousness. It *is* an animal looking out upon itself through this strange acquired ability to modify its rate of burning. Perhaps all I am really is no more than a pile of autumn leaves burning in a plum thicket, seeing things through the haze of my own burning.

꙳ ꙳

December 17, 1967

A hermit crab is something like a human being in his cultural shell, soft and easily wounded, with one great hiding claw to guard the face.

꙳ ꙳

February 8, 1968

Much emphasis has been given to writing as a development of practical economics. Without denying this, consider the possibility of an earlier phase involved with oracles and the interpretation of material markings increasingly "read" by man. The scapulimancy cracks (Shang, Naskapi) — see Frank Speck's paper on the scapula as a "map" of the hunting territory. Can it be that in this unconscious search for symbols, markings on shells (often erudite, etc.) played a "natural" role in the creation of writing? Man began in other words to "read" nature, and reading nature involves other things than economics.

꙳ ꙳

February 18, 1968

Found on the shore a hermit crab in a much-broken tear shell. Poor fellow, he was having a hard time. Shells are being so avidly collected here (Sanibel Island, Fla.) that the hermits must be having a harder and harder time to find adequate housing or to remain undisturbed if they do find it. This chap, because of cracks in the shell, was having a hard time to protect the soft part of his body.

≽ ≼

March 3, 1968

Islands can be regarded as something thrust up into recent time out of a primordial past. In a sense they belong to different times: a crab time or a turtle time, perhaps even a future time. Something not in time with the rest of the world; perhaps in some obscure way everything living is on a different time plane. As for man, he is the most curious of all; he fits no place, no visible island. He is bounded by no shore. [Australia a different time.]

≽ ≼

The gigantic spider shadow cast by an autumnal spider who had sought warmth in a street light.

≽ ≼

I am a man who regrets the loss of his fur and his tail.

≽ ≼

WHEN THE TIME COMES

"You'd better decide where you're going," I said. "I don't think you know. You're swinging on the gate, first out and then in. I don't think you know at all."

I could talk to him like this because I was down on his level, flat in the sand, but it didn't fluster him particularly. He kept his back up against a stone, not trusting me but not

running either. He didn't answer except to lift one big green
claw and point it defensively at my nose. Or maybe I misunderstood and it was directed in the way of destiny beyond me
and somewhere up the beach. It's hard to know in these
cases, and eyes on stalks give fiddling answers.

"All right," I said. "If you're so scared, go on back to the
water. That's where you came from — and where a crab
should stay. Make up your mind." He didn't, though, and
that was what bothered me later. He went off sidewise, neither back nor forward, sidling around the corner of the rock
and so off into the wet kelp and timbers and shells of high
tide, but not down and in. A crab should do one thing or
another, not leave you guessing like that. If the universe
doesn't know where it's going in the shape of a shore crab,
how in the devil is a man to know he's on the right track?

A sea beach is a bad place to start thinking, but then so is
almost anyplace. Anyplace where there's a leaf and an animal
under it — an animal with someplace to go. Because where *is*
it going — the seed hooked into your coat, and you yourself,
brother, where are *you* bound for? You think you know? In
this house? On that street? You think you've arrived? You
think you've lost your fur and your tail for a purpose spelled
with a capital *P* and sold to you in some book that explains
how everything was just a prelude until you came? If you do,
you're happy I take it, and you'd be better off not to be
following me or this crab or lifting up stones and looking
under them.

For what you see under a stone may be like a flash of
lightning before a traveler on a stormy night. It lights in one
blue, glistening instant a hundred miles of devil's landscape
such as he will never see again. Each stone, each tree, each
ravine and crevice echoing and reechoing with thunder will
tell him, more than any daytime vision, of the road he travels.
The flash hangs like an immortal magnification in the brain,
and suddenly he knows the kind of country he passes over
and the powers abroad in it. It is so in the country of Time;
the flash lights a long way backward over a wild land.

≥ ≤

May 4, 1968

Write on the nostalgia which has haunted all my days and

which, perhaps, began in the self-consciousness of too early
childhood, in the quarrels between parents.

February 4, 1969, Willemstad

Curaçao: On the edge of the city dump by the sea, I came
upon the dead dog wrapped in burlap, buried at sea and
drifted in by the waves, little more than a skeleton but still
articulated — one delicate bony paw laid gracefully, as
though its owner momentarily slept and would presently
awaken . . . , across a stone at the water's edge. Around his
throat was an old black leather strap that showed he had
once belonged to someone. This dog was a mongrel whose
life had been spent among island fishermen. He had known
only the small sea-beaten boats that came from Venezuela
and littered shores like this to which he had been returned by
the indifferent sea. Why amongst all that washing debris of
tin cans, shoes, bottles, and cast-off garments was I so
moved? Because this particular wasted garment had lived.
Scenes of the living sea, that would never in all eternity be
seen again, had streamed through the vibrant sockets of those
vanished eyes. The dog was young, the teeth in its skull still
perfect. It was of that type of loving creature who had gam-
boled happily about the legs of men. Someone had seen
crudely to his sea burial — but not well enough, so he lay
now where comes everything abandoned. But not without a
pathetic dignity — the tide in its own fashion had brought
him quietly at night and placed what remained of him upon
the stones. There at sunrise I had stood above him in a light
that he would never any longer see. Even if I had had a
shovel the stones would have prevented his burial. He would
wait for a second tide to spirit him away or lay him higher to

bleach starkly upon coral and conch shells, mingling the little lime of his bones with all else that had once stood upright on these shores.

≽ ≼

In Oriental lands, so scholars say, there is a belief in vampires, who, shrunk to a small black shadow, can be confined successfully in a bottle. In a similar way, there are embottled in our heads the demons of our childhood. Perhaps out of all those morbid whisperings of women that surrounded me in my youth, and which then so stifled and oppressed me, there lingers still one such shrunken small black object in my mind. An old midwife and number caster who lived near us asserted, after my naming, that I should avoid water, that it was interwoven with my destiny. It was told me at an impressionable age. Once in later years I came near to drowning. Fatalistically I have never learned to swim. Neither have I forgotten the prophecy which lurks like a confined wraith behind the doorway of my mind, awaiting its moment of liberation. No one can assert I have avoided its confrontation. Indeed, such is the power of these childhood shadows that they draw us as the witches' prophecy drew Macbeth.

Twice I have ventured foolishly against great undertows on dangerous coasts. The rumble of surf excites me more than it should. I have been a walker and a sail scanner on many shores and have gazed down with sweating palms into the sheer depths of sea caves and crevices. They draw me much. Perhaps my mind was destined to be thus, or perhaps that ancient crone with her mutterings about dark water evoked a mind-made shadow which it is not within my power to lay.

≽ ≼

The Aura: Animals, Men

It is midnight in the library. I linger and do not go home. The night is half gone. I walk through the long silent tiers of stacks containing all the malice, all the wisdom, all the loneliness of centuries. It is all here silently waiting in the great social brain; some of it, like the submerged madness of men, hiding until it strikes fire in a mind of the right affinity; some are books unread for over a century waiting, waiting far beneath the surface, but sure to be dredged up by a dreamer in some quieter century than ours. Perhaps I think wistfully the care may be worth the trouble, perhaps the thoughts will last. I wish I knew the destiny of this brain of which I am the momentary visitant, but I have been an archaeologist and know also what fate devises. Everything drifts by fire and war and ruin back to earth. The dust in these corridors is falling invisibly across the moonbeams from the slit windows as I walk, and I cough as in the abandoned room the dust of a dead public is slowly rising. The building falls stone by stone, century by century overhead. The brain lies shattered now, but its essence still smolders among hanging spiders and fallen roof beams. I have come a far way in the night and must go home. The constellations gleam and circle in the window slits. I am the ghost of this brain, made of it and to serve it. In it lies more than will ever be me, for it is the societal brain with laws, regulations, tier on tier of institutional forms of order that —

Another stone drops from the roof. Everything is shrinking, contracting; the air is damp with mold. Though we are inland, I have an invisible sense that the sea is closer; the coastline is foundering somewhere nearby. So this is the end that the geologists prophesied — as raindrops scurry amidst rainbows and a winter frost breaks a tiny stone into movable fragments.

I think of that day on the sand spit at Eleuthra and my footprints fading into the fossils as I walked. I think also of the old woman seer at my birth and the shark that I escaped in the waist-deep water. Perhaps I had taken it all too literally. Perhaps because my own books lie here, the woman saw through me into a vaster ruin than awaits a single child. Here if I wait much longer the sea worm and the coral will come. So it was for this she, that old witch, had stared far into the pulsing layers of my brain. Well, it was midnight, I would go back even if my own words on paper lay foundering and unread beneath the slime of sea snails. I do go back. Midnight makes all things possible. Tier by tier, stack by stack, I pace up the long corridor. The roof still stands. A faint familiar humming begins. Insensibly the stacks transform themselves to those vast rooms of life that I once guarded — those rooms in which nature rolled strange dice and the tricked and maimed entered existence to struggle briefly with the strong and perish.

The humming increases, but it is the stacks now. The murmur of many voices contending murderously or gently; the Brain is talking to itself, carrying on some vast dialogue that I am incapable of deciphering, though once I think I detect the sound of my own voice.

As it was in that vast room of life I guarded in my youth, so is it now. As I pass on, window slit by window slit, corridor by corridor, one shelf now beyond me invisibly paces the other player. It is almost as if he were drawing closer now.

≳ ≲

Philosophically Darwin may have removed us from a privileged position in the universe, but he brought us back into the web of life, showed us the relations we had with other forms, and thus contributed to the rise of the modern conservation movement. He did not realize, however, as did Freud, the vestigial remnants still hidden below the conscious rational mind, nor did he quite realize in the intellectual atmosphere of the Victorian age that escape was possible from the solid rule of the Empire of Accident. Darwin did not quite grasp, in other words, that men, in A. Irving Hallowell's words, ingest values and are capable of transcending their own image.

≳ ≲

Found the following stanza in an old notebook of mine. Must try and do something with it if I ever get the time.

> *Consider the sly fox*
> *that in each season knows*
> *the best way through the dark*
> *though toward the dark he goes.*

≳ ≲

Find it, he said. I was a big, heavy-muscled, solitary youth of twenty. I looked at him there in immanent dissolution staring past me beyond hope and hopelessness. I knew he did not see me, but I had the order. Somewhere in my heart a swift invisible needle of light, something that had been run-

ning like a hound since that night under the bare boughs of
the spring of 1910, quivered, leaped, and shot onward into
the roaring dark. Yes, Pa, I said.

Astronauts with flag, on a desolate planet. It had all been
as barren as Pa's life. Somewhere in me a comet was swinging
on the long ellipse toward home. I watched them salute the
little flag that was no longer popular, on a moon as lonely as
my father's heart.

Each generation since the beginning of consciousness has
found this place, I thought, before the little blurry set in the
living room. But I was utterly alone. No waiting son stirred
in the room. I felt again the long turning of that invisible
needle hurtling through void space. I reached over and turned
off the set, going to my bed.

My father's last years had been spent waiting alone in the
solitude of hotel lobbies in the thousand little towns of the
high country. Now I lay in similar beds in the college towns
of the far sixties, waiting alone to speak to university audiences of forgotten things. I pushed off the light and stared at
the ceiling. There was no light there, no light at all. But
somewhere in the remote darkness I could sense Halley's
comet turning on its long ellipse. Hurry, I half formed the
words. Hurry, or I will not be here. I did not know why I
said it. Yes, I did. I wanted to return to that bare world of
1910, held in my father's arms — lay back and vanish. Pa, I
said. There was no sound from the dark. I had come to the
same place.

I was wrong, I thought — wrong in that lecture about the
brain. The last engine was not the brain, it was the heart.
Somewhere in the void a wild and streaming light was circling in haste toward a vanished tree. A carlight flashed over
the bleak motel ceiling as I lay alone. I will be there when it
comes, I thought with a sudden careful grimness. That is my
world. Pa, do you hear me? There was no answer from the
dark. I lay back and tried to sleep; he had done this a thousand nights before me.

➤ ⬅　　　February 17, 1969

Whirlwind, Hurricane, Ravenswood, and Ravencliff, Va.
Good town names with possibilities.

➤ ⬅

April 4, 1969

Some two years ago now, but I remember the first cardinal who came, the beautiful, eager, highly intelligent one who used to coast up and down the side of the apartment house clicking for his dinner and who almost flew into the house when I opened the window unexpectedly. One could develop the fact that he was practicing magic without articulating it, making sound connections that in his case worked. This dim magic runs on into man, but man is more obsessive (by reason of memory) in his compulsive addiction to ritual which doesn't work. By contrast, the short-lived memory of the animal is more pragmatic.

≯ ≮

April 20, 1969

For science fiction. If the machines are emotionless because they have not arisen through natural selection, could the last man or men defeat them by wariness? They are fearless "idiots" who in certain circumstances could be trapped because they have no anxiety.

≯ ≮

Thoreau: A quote for the present educational turmoil over "relevance" in courses: "What does education often do? It makes a straight cut ditch of a free, meandering brook." Our youths demand relevance in a period changing so rapidly that nothing is long relevant.

❧ ❦

"A poet in our times is a semi barbarian in a civilized community. . . . The march of his intellect is like that of a crab, backwards."

Thomas Love Peacock, *Four Ages of Poetry*

But could one argue it is backward because wary, protecting the human spirit?

❧ ❦

. . . but always it is man, hard-bitten, unsatisfied, coming at last into what Yeats so ably called the desolation of reality. He assumes all our shapes stand equally before the microscope or ride the rocket into space. In age he will watch restlessly the passage of autumn birds. He will hear the surf mourn upon the shores he visited in youth. Poet or scientist, he will come home sorrowing not to Ithaca but to the now vacant waters of his youth, yearning for what he abandoned in his youth, Calypso, the immortal one.

In our age the search is culminating: space and the search within.

❧ ❦

The argument began in one of those nighttime casinos somewhere . . . in the little Antilles. There were beautiful white egrets — stalking in the moonlight on the surrounding salt marshes — and inside the Club Diablo everything was done in red leather and red light to make the patrons feel properly wicked and induce them to yield up their souls — nowadays one would say their money — more easily.

I placed twenty-five cents on a certain turn of the wheel and watched the wheel stop somewhere else than where I willed it to go. It was a small sum, true, but like the Marine beside me who had also bet unsuccessfully on that number, then shrugged and gotten up to walk the two miles into town, it suddenly dawned on me this club was altogether too mathematically like the universe for there not to be some connection.

≽ ≼

Man (see Massimo Pallottino, *The Meaning of Archaeology*, p. 18) removes his own records — Tutankhamen, etc. Effaces, razes. Communist destruction of fallen leaders by either killing or making them nonpersons. Similarly, our students regarding everything but the new as irrelevant.

This developed might do for the start of the world eaters who are also time devourers in the above way — a bad streak in the human animal. The world eaters are also time eaters.

≽ ≼

Time in the older universe man knew was just time, static. Now we know that the universe evolves in time and on our planet has shape shifting possibilities in the form of life. Primitives believed in shape shifting, but immediate. Western man believed in single creation. He was wrong. He had effaced change.

≽ ≼

The space age was born when the first man-ape said "tomorrow."

≽ ≼

May 10, 1969

Gilbert Highet in *The Migration of Ideas* speaks of fear as a great educative force. Is this true far back among the Australopiths? Think it over. Did it grow with symbols and ability to consider future? Is there a combination between fear, upright posture, and language somewhere in this story

of the first four million years? What pushed it farther? Strangely, did the first grain masticators die out while the carnivores *Australopithecus africanus* or *Homo habilia* later turn to grains through fire? Also the solitary animals largely rest when not active. Man's intelligence (fear based, anxiety?) drives him perhaps into needless conflict, the energy climb is too steep, too sustained.

≽ ≼

May 24, 1969

Comments Re Moon Book and/or Possible Essays

(1) First movement in animal world intended to leap space for energy. With the rise of mind and technology this activity leads to space — leaping for the absorption of knowledge — though the discoveries *may* lead to sophisticated uses of energy once more. This, however, need not necessarily follow. Also, the microscope and telescope can be a kind of mind-leaping through spaces denied us in the flesh. The same is true of the spectroscope.

(2) The stimulus of incompleteness never ceases in science, nor, by the way, in magic, which is, is it not, a similar stimulus seeking to control the actual by the supernatural.

(3) What is natural? . . . May it not be that our space interests are forcing us to face a new set of questions involving time and the galactic reaches, i.e., nature in new or potential forms?

(4) Re perhaps my biography. My youthful isolation resulting in love of quiet and retreat as the animal in general seeks hideouts and silence because noise increasingly (in the human world) represents the first aspects of possible danger and violence. Man with his voice began to change the natural world for animals long ago.

≽ ≼

June 15, 1969

Could it not be said that in the moon triumph man, psychologically, is beginning to reassert his powers against "homelessness" in the universe? His entire history, scientifically, has been one of increasingly diminishing stature against the universe in terms of time, of space, of rationality. Now, symbolically at the moment, he is reasserting his dominance over the universe; the thinking reed of Pascal continues to think. He is still the leaper of space and time, perhaps even his own winner of immortality.

Re moon end: In understanding the oscillating universe, is not man finding symbolically his own center? For do we not arise from primordial night, grow in consciousness, and fall back into emptiness? If this is our universe, do we not endlessly replicate it?

⊁ ⊀

June 16, 1969

Idea: For essay on the future. See G. K. Chesterton's essay "Science and the Savages." At the conclusion he remarks that so long as nature keeps her course, she does not terrify us. It is when she "looks like a man" that we fall on our faces. Cannot this observation form the key of our present concern with the future of the world? It (i.e., nature) is taking on human ambivalence and power — thus it concerns and terrifies us. Space, atoms, all.

⊁ ⊀

Title of Doubleday Book: *An Evolutionist Looks at Man*

Man is old, much older even than the evolutionists of a generation ago believed. We must, it appears, accept a tiny grassland homuncular elf by the name we apply to ourselves. Man looked at in the light of millennia, of hundreds of thousands and then millions of years, is no longer the man at the street corner or our fraternity brother, or even our classmate. We will have to stretch the word "man" through the time dimension. The moment we do this we will have to ask what we mean by "man" and at what point his footprints fade into the world of common beastdom. This is not an easy thing to determine, and the very act of this extension, this stretching of a word like a rubber band, is clothed with emotion and prejudice until it seems still to many like an heretical act. After all, mankind has only been aware of the evolutionary extension of itself for *less* than a hundred years. Before that time his secret pathway into the present had been suspected only by a few great minds. In the historical memory extending over the few centuries of books and written records, he had always appeared as he does now, so that his definition was singular and easy. It was only the clothes on his back, his togas, his lace ruffles, or his pantaloons that had been altered — not that his posture had changed, that the bones of his face had once been of unfamiliar proportions, that the very brain of which he was now so proud had not differed, except in potential, from the anthropoid creatures about him. All this had gone unrecorded in the memoryless years before writing. His history, even what he came to call ancient history, was but the history of yesterday. His real past he did not know. He was like a child set free in a dark forest, but with not a single document, not a signature to tell him of his heritage or to what destiny his footsteps might be directed. Man was, in short, is, an orphan, a wood child, a changeling. Therefore it would not be long before he would devise myths of his origin and set about to find his parents. It is a search that has occupied him down to this very moment. But in his confusion and despair he has devised many myths, and his parents have sometimes had projected upon them the shape of monstrous fears and at other times have been radiantly clothed in the garments of his hope.

❧ ❦

"Man reached his hand into emptiness and grasped the machine," says Garet Garrett, but did he not equally grasp the first tool in ancient days, and to do so did he not have to conceptualize them with another tool — the word?

❧ ❦

The structural elements of the collective unconscious are named by Jung "archetypes" or "primordial images." They are the pictorial forms of the instincts.

❧ ❦

July 2, 1969

The dog is, in a sense, an illusory run of forms finally (but momentarily) stricted into the shape "dog" by me. But as it turns away into the night, how do I know it will remain "dog"? No, it has been picked by me out of a running weave of colors and faces into which it will lapse once more as it bounds silently into the inhuman, unpopulated wood where it will again become an endless running series of forms which will not, the instant I vanish, any longer know themselves as "dog."

By a mutual effort I have wrenched a leaping phantom into the flesh "dog," but the shape cannot be held, neither his nor my own. We are contradictions and unreal. A nerve net and the lens of an eye creates us, but like the dog I, too, leap away at last into the unknown wood, my flesh, my unique individuality slipping like mist from my bones.

⅄ ⅄

FROM A LETTER FROM LOREN TO HAL BORLAND,
JULY 18, 1969

It is true, as you will see when you get a copy of *The Unexpected Universe,* that these early experiences leave an emotional impact, and I frequently find them agonizing to recall. On the other hand, perhaps because of the very sensitivity of youth, they are recalled with such vividness that they can frequently be used for symbolic effect by the mind in maturity.

When I was young I was greatly addicted to poetry, a small amount of which got published. Having a living to make, however, I turned aside into science, in which I also had a deep interest. For a good many years thereafter I published professional papers and rather avoided causing raised eyebrows among my professional associates. Now, with a decade

or so to run before retirement, I have at last the leisure, and
the atmosphere, I believe, has changed somewhat, although I
have taken my share of hard knocks from the specialist who
frowns on any kind of literary endeavor by his colleagues.
Writing slowly, however, and not being particularly handy
with the mass media type of writing, I have found the lecture
platform more lucrative — this at a time when at long last I
am trying to put away a little extra for retirement. As you
know, this is not the easiest thing to do under the present tax
set-up.

≥ ≤

July 30, 1969

Note how in the Pocono woods a three-day steady down-
pour brings damp-loving forms far from their usual environment (the frog I placed in the little spring, for example, or the
multitudinous sprouting of fungi). These events are brought
about by the sudden slackening of the strands in the net of
life. If long enough continued, ranges change or gene pools
may shift.

≥ ≤

Moon

This is an age of superlatives, but a superlative standing
alone may be easily condemned as absurd even if it contains a
modest element of truth. President Nixon fell into this trap
when he enthusiastically endorsed the successful moon flight
of the astronauts as the greatest event in history since the
Creation. The remark was hailed for a day and then Mr.
Nixon was chided by an evangelist, Billy Graham, who reminded him of the birth of Christ. Even an agnostic would be
forced to recognize that the emergence of Christianity profoundly altered the world view of the West and was destined
to give rise to that belief in progress and the uniqueness of
the historical process which has led on to the achievements of
modern science. Great events are cheapened and made vulner-

able simply by being isolated in a world made up of continuities and causal sequences. As an anthropologist, for example, I might with some reason argue that the development of language in the evolution of the human species was a necessary preliminary to history in any form and that no following triumphs of human ingenuity would have been possible without it. One could thus contend for the emergence of language as the greatest event in history. Similarly, a biologist might choose to argue that the atmospheric changes making possible the rise of the metazoa — the first many-celled animals — equally played such a role. The student of nature is confronted with innumerable novelties distributed through time but proceeding constantly toward an unseen and unique future. To use the isolated superlative as Mr. Nixon did is always to invite the mocking rejoinder "As compared to what?" In that rejoinder the oak must be reminded of the acorn cup, man, of the grassland whose evolution was a

preliminary to his own appearance. Even the moon rocket waited, among other things, upon the invention of the clock and the computer. The original creation of its occurrence may have been a genuinely singular event, but scarcely anything thereafter. Men would be wise not to demean the term "greatest" by its debasement to the political uses of a single ephemeral generation.

⋟ ⋞

FROM A LETTER FROM HAL BORLAND TO LOREN,
OCTOBER 19, 1969

I couldn't get to *The Unexpected Universe* more than half an hour at a time until yesterday, and I knew it was a book I didn't want to nibble at. I wanted to read it chapter by chapter, with time to sit back and think after each one, and to marvel at what you had done. And now I have done that, and I think what a superb piece of work it is, what a magnificent piece of You. I could go through, chapter by chapter, and say I specially liked this and that and so on; but that would get nowhere, really. Actually, I got special satisfactions from "The Star Thrower," "The Angry Winter," "The Innocent Fox," and "The Last Neanderthal." Special, I say. I can't, or at least won't try just now, to tell you why. It's an emotional thing, I think. And now I know what you mean when you said that bits and pieces of autobiography keep creeping into your essays. This book is a kind of autobiographical sampler, though that way of putting it cheapens what I try to say. I would think that you should write autobiography in your own way, when you get to it. Write it as you do here, as the philosopher, the poet, the wonderer who has to look far and deep. We've had too many Henry Adams kind of autobiographies. But what I wanted to do was say that your *Unexpected Universe* is superb, a book I will come back to again and again simply because it is so much more than a collection of lectures about man and the universe. And, my friend, because it is full of spark holes in the overwhelming blanket of ignorance, spark holes through which you show me something of the vastness beyond.

ล ж

The Book and the Andes: the hunger, the dying wolf, the sudden wraith of snow out of which he sprang and killed his pursuer — finally a soliloquy of how an animal dies alone in rocks or deadfall, teeth to the front, swallowing automatically the blood that had been his sustenance and life. The pack

goes on, his mate pregnant. A dire wolf by genetic throw-
back, he or mate or both, a puppy born, brothers destroyed.
No territorial sense, thus escaped fate of Colorado lobos.
Mother (of Rags) neurotic from paranoid fear that drives her
onward. *May* Rags have Ice Age dreams? The puppy kingdom of peace destroyed by man. Border patrol first killers.

⚹ ⚸

Note for start of book: He was what the learned men who
measure bones would have called a dire wolf. His kind had
been dead for ten thousand years; he was a puppy and would
never know that he had been resurrected by some fantastic
accident in the germ cells of his parents. All his life he would
dream dim Ice Age dreams of vast tundras, long-horned
bison, and stalking cats with teeth as long as fighting knives.
He would also dream of cold and the ululations of hunting
wolves in snows no living man had seen or survived. Almost,
when he dreamed deep, and the dreams would grow with the
years, he could make out the huge, drifting hulks of migrating
mammoths and the trails their kind broke through the otherwise impassable snows of the mountain passes. He would
dream these things, and even as he dreamed his paws would
act out the way of running, for he was a wraith of the snow
time. This, too, he would not know until the end. All men's
hands and cunning minds would be used against him, but
they were absent from his dreams. He played in innocent
puppyhood with his brothers and sisters beside a cave in the
Sierra Madres, in a lone region of sharp peaks. His parents
were lobo wolves, the great grey range killers whose kind
were almost gone. This would be their last litter; and the
days of the pup's innocence would be few indeed.

As though to mark the time and place, there was a little
cross of wood beside the trail that led through the canyon a
short distance from the den. On the crossed sticks carved in
halting Spanish were the words, *Aquí falsos amigos* — committed this crime. The cubs were never allowed to come to
that trail, but their lean grey father sniffed suspiciously about
the crossed sticks. The cubs' white-streaked mother feared the
spot and drove them sharply away. There was an unpleasant
man smell lingering there which she recognized, and something else besides — something that came from the dim mem-

ories of her own puppyhood far across the Rio Grande to the north. It was death, the grey shadow that had stalked her since her birth. Along her spine the chill crepitations made the ruff of her neck rise. Suddenly, so suddenly that it startled her mate, she leaped agilely into the air, twisted, and snapped sideways at nothing. She was mad and there was no word to convey it. It was also the fey madness of the seer who exists speechless among animals as among men; the terrible insanity that is both wrong and right; that sees the end so surely that the seer materializes death from the thin air, gives it palpable form and hastens the pace of its advance. She always brought it pacing upon all that she most loved. That was the desperate love of the big-footed puppy's mother.

⁅ ⁅

Note: perhaps the cub penetrates the isthmus because he dreams of the mastodon who did so.

The inn where he meets the archaeologist, the Skin Changer, the only man who befriends him and then goes. Silent dialogue between them — wolf likes the sound of his voice. Watches the dogs.

In the end perhaps one could introduce the fact that the wolf goes up, because of his Ice Age memories, into the high cold.

⁅ ⁅

Title: *The Snow Wolf*

⁅ ⁅

THE VALLEY OF THE FIVE CROSSES
(*CINCO CRUCES*)

Jaws like a pair of wire cutters were laid gently along the
sleek one's neck. They closed upon the rawhide that held her.
With an effortless exertion of pressure the braided rope
parted. Sleek Foot was free.

That Sleek Foot did not know how to kill did not matter to
the great grey creature who had come so far alone. Something, some eternally lost hope, stirred faintly in his heart.
Wolves are social animals. In their way they love. And the
dogs that are descended from them, they too carry this old
trait, and lavish it sometimes to their cost upon men. Sleek
Foot was a dog who by breeding was only a step removed
from wolf. That removal vanished as the two ran on together
through the moonlit *llanos* of Venezuela. Both yearned and
listened for the wolf packs that now howled furtively only
under the arctic stars that they would never see. Big Foot had
crossed the isthmus. He had secured a mate. In all the history
of his kind no book recorded such a passage. If there had
been one, its secret lay with the bones of southward-marching
mastodons beneath the jungle growth of ten millennia.

≯ ≮

He had 30 percent more brains than a modern domesticated dog. It was by that measure he survived.

≯ ≮

There is a great deal of talk today about the Now generation. But what is the Now? Is it the moment just passing to
be imbedded in the past, or, whether we observe it or not, is
the past embedded in ourselves now? Is the Now something
inhabited by a new breed of youth who will never age, but
who hang suspended in the golden Mediterranean sunlight of
Marrakech or California? And how many nows are there —
those inhabited by the impoverished wetbacks toiling in
California fields for a pittance, the now of nihilist radicals
issuing underground papers filled with the now words of four
letters? Or the suddenly looming now of the beleaguered
professor whose lifelong research efforts are not safe in his

files and which his institution will no longer insure? There is the now of the college president controlling his writhing stomach as he walks out to face a riotous student assemblage. There are, in short, a hundred nows, but one thing they share in common. They are made up of the past and they in turn will play a role in creating the future. That is why the Now is important. To spell it with a capital letter is not to abolish either time past or time future. It is only that it makes the future more terrifying. A society whose youth believe only in the Now is deceiving itself: A now that is truly Now has no future. It denies man's basic and oldest characteristic, that he is a creation of memory, a bridge into the future, a time binder. Without that recognition of continuity, love and understanding between the generations is impossible. A true Now standing all by itself is the face of Death.

⋊ ⋉

To the first wolf who domesticated
man and whose children have suffered
the consequences

⋊ ⋉

Big Paws and Sleek Foot, His Mate

1. Remember: early conditioning against man (my childhood) with some kind of objectivity which will serve him at the last as the servant of the other player. Rest are killed.
2. Possible scavenger period under Mexican tables (fed by Americano, me).
3. Period (though symbiotic and wild) with jungle archaeologist. Children and mating here.
4. Possible conflict with jaguar.

5. Puma (in what way).
6. The cities of the dead. Peruvian plain.
7. Venture across the Andes but jungle no good. Symbols to be arranged.
8. Is Sleek Foot mother? Seems hardly possible now. Consider?
9. Cattle killing on the dry lands of the eastern range.
10. The five-thousand-mile journey.
11. The hunt.
12. The kill.

⫸ ⫷

Throughout . . . one could introduce wolf love, such as the mother coming with her puppies. Perhaps explain how the lobos came to be as they were.

⫸ ⫷

End. The repeating rifle with its telescopic sight was the finest money could purchase in the modern world. In ordinary hands on the Sierra that would have meant nothing, less than nothing against the cold or the emptiness of the peaks so high that one could scarcely breathe. But the man who carried that perfect instrument with cross hairs for accuracy was a man who killed for pleasure, a man of great courage who possessed just this one flaw: that he had never lost at anything and did not intend to do so now. He believed that death was a game in which there was also another player. It was like the wars — for he, too, like his quarry was an anachronism. There was a tiny box of decorations never shown in a corner of his bureau back home in London: His regiment, and it was a famous one, had always won in the end. It too had been a perfect machine, organized and run by his iron skill and foresight. Wars were no longer his outlet; in middle-age retirement he preferred the solitary game with the solitary invisible player, and again he had always won. Even at the ends of the world he had won. It would never occur to him that he played cruelly against handicapped opponents. He did not possess that kind of imagination. He had grown up under circumstances where one used the best weapons, and the wars had reinforced that wisdom. He was a man grown out of nature who used her quite dispassionately in the game of his choosing. Pity was foreign to his character. He and the other player, he knew instinctively, dispensed with it. If indulged, it muddled the sharp edges of the game and confused one's thinking. Onetime general of armies, it was not in Armstrong's temperament to engage in self-examination. It too was a way to lose. In the dawn, very carefully but relentlessly, he began to climb. For a brief moment he smelled the snows at Trondheim Fjord in a better year. He shrugged and the memory fell away. The game was starting, starting well for him.

(Sketch of why wolf so far south. This man would know it as a phenomenon. Big Paws already a famous outlaw?)

❧ ❧

Man's two great magics: words and music. They recapture the past.

Man reached his mind into emptiness to seize more than the machine; with it willingly or not, he seized hold upon the future. Ever since he has been trying to disentangle himself from the embrace of that future. But one thing his thinkers tell him: He is the follower of the Way.

❧ ❧

The Snow Wolf: end of first chapter. The great white wolf howled until her ululations echoed against the stars. She waited, but there was no response from ravine, from thicket, from the far-off mountains. Her mate tried in his turn to break the silence and intuitively to awake the pack. There

was still silence for the simple reason there was no pack to answer. There could have been no answer below the arctic. They could not know, but a vast loneliness had begun to descend upon them — the loneliness of a dying species. The Ice Age had ended. No, not quite, for the white cub with the big feet toddled on beside his mother. When she slept he would sleep. He would never know he was a floating ghost from the past. Only the shadows and the moonlight knew and embraced him, knew they would do so to the end.

⊁ ⊀

Man has grown fond of late of contemplating almost with submerged pride his ancestral descent from what he regards as a savage, carnivorous ape; this his later history would imply contains a grain, if not several grains, of truth. What is less flattering and less appetizing perhaps is his more genuine resemblance to that group of minute organisms known as slime molds. They can be seen devouring spoiled bread or moving in unsightly blotches over spoiled oranges — fruit that in distant eye-narrowed perspective might be mistaken for diseased planets — rotten fruit circling in the plague-infected winds of the cosmic orchard.

⊁ ⊀

January 22, 1970

Anthropomorphizing: the charge of my critics. My counter-charge: There is a sense in which when we cease to anthropo-morphize, we cease to be men, for when we cease to have human contact with animals and deny them all relation to ourselves, we tend in the end to cease to anthropomorphize ourselves — to deny our own humanity. We repeat the old, old human trick of freezing the living world and with it ourselves. There is also a sense . . . in which we *do* create our world by our ability to read it symbolically. But if we read it symbolically aloof from ourselves and our kindest impulses, we are returning to the pre-Deistic, pre-Romantic world of depraved Christianity — the world where man saw about him "fallen nature," with the devil slipping behind each tree. Modern anthropomorphizing consists in miming nature down to its ingredients, including ourselves. This is really only another symbolic reading, certainly no more "real" than what I have been charged with.

≽ ≼

July 5, 1970

Note: Proprioceptive sense enables us to master many moving machines, airplane, car, etc.; similarly, the sensitivity of the mind enables us to grope into human relations in our own culture, or, on occasion, others. In both hand and brain man can extend himself to fantastic limits. He is full of invisible tentacles. His language leaps minds. He is a mind leaper as he was once an arboreal space leaper. His mind flies ahead of his eyes. Now he threatens to become a planet leaper, a star leaper.

≽ ≼

Note: Men are the dispersed energy of the particle; in civilizations they are organized energy at a higher level, though the individual [particle] still retains an ineradicable wildness just like the micro-indeterminacy of modern physics. This society strives to eliminate, as the computer now attempts to minimize, in favor of the greater whole.

≽ ≼

Starting line for Texas: It has always been the ambition of man to remove the chance factor, the unexpected event, from the universe. It is manifested in the magical mural paintings of Lascaux, in the divination by scapulimancy that persists among the subarctic hunters down to the present day, and was also known anciently to the dynasty of Shang. It is, in short, man's all too human attempt to control the future. Futuristics, the word one is beginning to hear spoken of among the avant-garde in science, is really a neologism for an activity as old as the Ice Age. We are gathered at this symposium to pursue it, and the finest computers man has devised are basically intended, if not to eliminate chance, then to reduce it to manageable proportions.

≽ ≼

January 10, 1970

The wolf and man have ever been at war because at heart they are alike; they love and are rejected. Between them they have molded the dog, who is the orphan offspring of both and suffers accordingly.

➹ ➷

For beginning: the shadow of the two wolves growing long at evening across the *llano estacado:* a symbol of the end; they stretch longer and longer as shadows across the plain until finally there is dark. The mother howls. There is no response. They go on into the dark.

➹ ➷

It was evening on the *llano estacado.* Across the high-staked plains and their eroded gullies there had been war for ten thousand years. Intruding man had struck down the first mammoth. Intruding European man had in turn struck down the Indian. The buffalo pastures had been given to the cattle. The great lobo wolves who had clung to the flanks of the buffalo herds had in starvation turned to the cattle. The ranchers had fought them with rifle, trap, and strychnine. The wolf packs were decimated. Only a few outlaws, the wildest, the most wary, the most intelligent, the most dangerous survived, but they were headed for extinction; they were carnivores, and man who called them vermin was a more deadly carnivore than they. Their day was done; the last of them knew it. The night howl no longer summoned up the pack.

Evening on the staked plains of Texas is a time of long shadows spreading across the sunset.

⋊ ⋉

Note: The Ice Age (past provost) in the Andes. Develop as chapter (before Sleek Foot).

⋊ ⋉

For Doubleday book: The numerous definitions of man possible reveal we are dealing with something new, something intangible *inside* the animal.

⋊ ⋉

Starting Paragraph of *The Snow Wolf*

Men would come in time to call him the snow wolf and make the sign of the cross at his name. This day he was only a small toddling shadow in the evening light across the *llano estacado*. The light is long in that land at evening, and the shadows like that of his beautiful white-pawed mother ran a long way out across the broken land and bobbed uncertainly in the gathering dark of the staked plains of Texas.

⋊ ⋉

For *Snow Wolf*. Start. The shadows are long on the *llano estacado* at evening, and wolf legs make the longest shadows in the world because they stretch and move. In this particular instance a smaller shadow, a round and roly-poly shadow almost like a ball, bumped along before the tireless pacing shadows that both followed and ran tirelessly before the extending, darkening ball. The staked plains of Texas are as vast as the shadows that cross it. The only vaster thing was the love of the wolf mother for the cub that alternately followed and toddled before her. It was the last of her last litter to survive.

(Hook to statement about wolf and man, who suffer love.)

⋊ ⋉

But he would die if the big cat was willing to pay the price. Instinctively he knew this, circled warily, and was gone across the moonlit glade like the whisper of a shadow.

He lay behind the cross, his nose perfectly aligned to the wind and the way the man would come. If the wind was right, he would smell man a mile away. He lay there because on all that desolate peak there was no place left to hide, he must muster what strength he had from the final blood that ran in bright arterial drops between his jaws. Sleek Foot still

climbed above him on the slope. She carried life, and throughout his great grey shape he knew instinctively he was the last barrier to death. The waiting had been long and tedious against the man that relentlessly followed him. Nevertheless, he mouthed his own welling blood for strength with patient tongue and waited. In the intervals of fading consciousness the huge and drifting shapes of his puppyhood returned once more. He shifted his paws for accuracy and purpose and licked once more his dripping teeth. He did not dream of man. A veil drifted over his yellow, unwinking gaze. There was the sound of footsteps toiling up the slope. The general held death in his hand, and he needed no shelter. He came forward avidly following the long red trail. He came until he was almost below the shadow of the cross upon the snow, but still the grey wolf waited dreaming, the long years of perilous treks and deadly wisdom gathering a last time in his brain. On the slope, a little above, Sleek Foot lay camouflaged against a snowbank, and it was from there, at the

inadvertent stirring of her paw, that a tiny crystalline dance of snow particles arose, augmented, and wandered in a little spinning whirlwind down the slope. It was only a breath, a little harmless dance of particles in nature. The general looked up, saw it, dismissed it, and came on relentlessly. The whirlwind hesitated and, as if impelled by curiosity, wandered in the general's direction. The grey shape behind the cross tightened its paws. The distance was now scarcely fifty yards, but the speaking death could travel faster than the fastest feet. For a moment longer he hesitated. The snow almost subsided, and the general came on unperturbed and unwatchful. Then perversely the snow caught the updraft from below and danced once more in a slow but filling spiral before the general's path, momentarily enveloping him. He might have taken note then, for he had played such games for many years. Instinctively he half tightened his hold upon the rifle, but he was one second too late. Another and more tangible wraith, one hundred and eighty pounds of it, floated out of the snow dance elusively as thistledown, struck, and was gone. The strike was utterly terrible. It was an Ice Age strike aimed at bodies no longer existing in the modern world. The general's chest took the impact, and the sheering carnassials tore headlong through the layers of cloth and leather about his throat, met once, and wrenched. The general's hands made a quick, blind scrabble, but felt only fur. The rifle clattered on the rocks, and General Armstrong rolled already dead down the slope up which he had toiled so long.

As for Big Paws, half-conscious now, he had clung to life only for this one act. He did not follow. Mechanically his tongue found the taste of alien blood mingled with his own, savored it, and was satisfied. He dropped his head and nosed for the last time the dripping snow. He coughed over the steaming puddle and staggered back to the windbreak of the cross. The giant game against which he struck ten thousand years removed, faded, and was lost in the channels of the snow that filled the dying brain.

Above him on the slope Sleek Foot stirred once more, scenting death about her in the air. She sniffed, she took her time as befitted the instincts of one who carried life, she heard her mate cough rackingly.

⤝ ⤜

Big Foot always climbs for sight as did his mother who was deaf and needed sight.

Big Foot has hidden in cemeteries before, does so realizing cross is avoided.

⤝ ⤜

She *Returns* to Cross

The life in her body that she had carried desperately over weary peaks and above fathomless abysses would never be. The Other Player had seen to that. The great grey father out of the timeless snows would never know a son. He coughed once and was still. His last warmth was now ebbing. The taste of that other blood than his own had departed. Sleek Foot huddled a little closer to him, laying nose to tail while the temperature plunged, and the Andean blizzard lashed the peak till it drifted unreal as a freezing planet from beyond the sun.

After a while, between the wind blasts, the she-wolf could faintly hear the creaking and straining of the great cross above her head. She burrowed deeper against her mate's side, but the cold crept relentlessly upward. Sometime later she mercifully ceased to feel it. She slept, and the stirring life within her in its turn slowly responded to the whispered command of the tired heart and fled away in a little flurry of icy paws.

There were many who had come to that place of Las Cruces and not departed. On that night the crossed timber was finally tumbled down by the fury of the storm. In those high regions it might well lie and be forgotten, as the wire around it was forgotten. Or peasants might come and utilize the scarce wood to nail above some other unfortunate traveler. One thing was sure: The cross would never stand above creatures who . . . deserved it more.

Down the slope the snow deepened as well above the body of General Armstrong where his fall had flung him. The man of death had wanted nothing but the game. He had had his wish, but the Other Player, if there was such, scarcely valued the game alone or he would not have created those who played beyond the game so far as to abandon it in contempt. They slept in the still, cold night, the great beast and the loving heart, the life that failed to be, and the man with the most beautiful hunting rifle in the world. They slept, they all slept, and in the cold there was no thing visible to pronounce a judgment. There was only the world, and out on that particular peak there were no more players. Sometime later in the night there was a rock tremor in the mountains. An avalanche descended over the fallen crosses and the cairns of rock, effacing them. The dawn of the third day saw no tracks at all on the virgin snow. Only a snowy vagrant whirlwind arose once more and strayed hesitantly from one place to another as though seeking a companion. Then in a little sparkling dance it ascended, grew tenuous, and passed out of sight upon the mountain. In the night the cold dropped by a tiny fraction of a degree. It was a worldwide drop, but no one noted it. Ten thousand years away, the old Ice Age was returning. The snow wolf's dreams were true. Ten thousand years away or twice ten thousand years. In time, in the long slow wheel of time, the masses of men would learn again the meaning of the snow.

⅏ ⅏

There are two cases of utter death in the world. The one is when the last speaker of a dying tongue growing old among strangers realizes that the words spoken at his mother's knee no longer possess any meaning beyond himself; the second is when a species has grown near to extermination and, set upon by numerous enemies, finds itself so harassed that the young are struck down in infancy and the last adults cannot find mates. Both happened and are still happening in the conquest of the American wilderness. Many of the Indian tongues have vanished with their speakers from the eastern seaboard. The great lobo wolves who clung to the flanks of the bison herds have likewise vanished from the western ranges after their long, desperate, merciless war with the cattlemen.

≫ ≪

Start: Once in the midst of a lecture a youth shouted at me, "What is the relevance of evolution?" I stuttered in response, seeing mentally three billion years of incredible cosmic effort flung aside like a worn garment, while a cold like that of a dead planet crept up my spine. "Me and my generation hate you and yours," a young radical once confronted me across a dinner table. "Do you want to know why? *You* could talk to your parents. We cannot." I remained silent, thinking of my stone-deaf mother and my father who to earn a sparse living traveled and was rarely home when I might have needed counsel at college. He could not know my life. Did I give a thought to his?

≫ ≪

At least there was no poisoned meat or deadly pitfalls. There was only the snow and a rising implacable wind and the shifting scree. They labored over the knife edge of a ridge, and Big Paws' feet started a tiny avalanche of pebbles and snow, that, if it had grown above the toiling figure far below, might have saved them. The Invisible Player willed otherwise. Over the edge of a scarp the stones cascaded downward. The man with the deadly eye upon his rifle barrel only pulled in below the cliff and waited; he was clothed to wait the night if necessary. In the crevice there was no wind. And that was the end of the first day.

≫ ≪

Your tale about the matter of gift books tickled me, particularly because I had just had a letter from the dean of the
Wharton School here telling me that a friend of his had
received three copies of my book for Christmas from different
individuals. It strikes me that perhaps the good sale of the
book can be attributed to the fact that everyone who has
received a copy of the book is trying to foist it off on someone else. Thus, although a supposed conservationist, I have
become an indirect litter bug!

You are also quite right about the lottery aspect of writing.
All kinds of publics bisect one's life. I have had letters from
people who know me purely from some educational articles,
others as the writer of an academic book known as *Darwin's
Century,* and still others who know that I wrote some pieces
upon the subject of fossil bison many years ago. On the other
hand, the other day I sat in on a conference in the Museum
among a group of super-intellectuals from the mass media
and quietly discovered that there was not a living soul among
them who had any knowledge of me whatever. I once es-
corted in from the airport a world-famous figure in the field
of human evolution who, on the way to the Museum, turned
to me and remarked, "Young man, what do you do for a
living?" The only thing flattering about it was the "young
man." Probably he had ill-adjusted glasses. As for the rest, I
was tempted to remark gravely, "Sir, I wash the windows at
the Museum." The joke of it is that the director, who was
unable to go, asked me to greet him at the airport because
"someone of distinction around here ought to be sent to meet
a man with an ego like that." He was certainly right about
the ego, but I think in retrospect almost anyone would have
done as a fall guy.

On the other hand, when I was riding the Paoli local the
other day, a little boy from the Episcopal Academy at
Overbrook suddenly popped into the vacant seat beside me
and said, "My mother knows who you are, some of your
Animal Secrets films are used in our school, and Mother told
me to introduce myself." I was so stunned by this sudden rise
to fame among children that I floundered like a fish out of

water through three stations. I doubt if any of us know from one moment to the other what kind of world we inhabit.

⅄ ⅃

FROM A LETTER FROM LOREN TO HAL BORLAND,
REFERRING TO A DESPAIRING COMMENT
MADE BY BORLAND, OCTOBER 14, 1970

Now about this matter of optimism and pessimism. I have to be an educator, though, as I have said before, the activity is growing more and more difficult. I felt it necessary to offer some kind of choice to man, but in reality, like yourself, I am deeply depressed about the human situation. I do not fear our extinction particularly. What I really fear is that man will ruin the planet before he departs. I have sometimes thought, looking out over the towers of New York from some high place, what a beautiful ruin it would make in heaps of fallen masonry, with the forest coming back. Now I fear for the forest itself. Well, I am beginning to think that almost anything can happen, from solar flares to irradiated brains, and certainly our brains will figuratively or literally need some irradiation now.

⅄ ⅃

Nature, one may say, is the existent, but there must be included with it, and to this extent obscuring its edges, the potential, just as man once existed as mere potential in a tree shrew. Thus nature is metaphysically a kind of cosmic iceberg of which only the smallest part protrudes visibly into our understanding.

⅄ ⅃

INDEFINITE DEPARTURE

He named it once in the whole history of science,
told it just once as it would always be —
indefinite departure for the wood rat,
indefinite departure for mankind, interminably.

See in your mirror how the forms keep shifting, have
*   changed, tomorrow change again,*

reptile to mammal, tree shrew to lemur, these
phantasms swirl beneath your own pale forehead.
They are our own lost bodies none can tease

into the shapes we once had tried to keep, forever.
Fish-fin is gone, the reptile on the shore,
the lemur with round night-eyes on a branch,
all changed, all changed as if somewhere before

this doom had been foreseen. Satanic fires
lick at our faces, now wild dragons puff our breath,
the pterodactyl compass that we follow
sheers to the lone meridian of death.

≽ ≼

Darwin's establishment of the "law" of natural selection is
paradoxical in that it is a nonprophetic law. It can only
say — and then with certain notable exceptions — that life
will change, but it cannot inform us in what particular direction this will take place or whether it will lead to no future,
i.e., extinction. Even with the final recognition of the periph-
ery of secondary randomness based on the randomness of
what has gone before — what we might call in other words
historical probability — we still are caught in a chance world
of indefinite possible, and only possible, futures. There is a
statistical bias written into natural selection: the bias, or
necessity, of constant survival if contingency is to remain

important to life. "The nature of a probability *hypothesis* can be reduced to a speculation about scope," as one writer remarks. In the beginning many of Darwin's critics assumed his "evolution" to be utter randomness in the sense that carrots and cabbages might have played a role in the human phylogeny. They overlooked the fact that Darwin's realm of accident had parameters determined by historical probability, that is, by the chances or accidents *previously* allowed survival through the screen of natural selection.

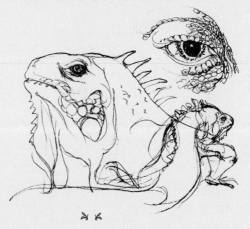

There is only one other plot to be added: that of man, bad or good, seeking to find some other thing beyond him. If he is good, he knows somewhere there lies a greater goodness and he seeks that. If he is bad and becomes worse, he becomes lost in a night so great that he denies the search, because if he admits there is something to be searched for, then his whole life has been a denial of his humanity.

When I was a small boy in the chimney corner by the kitchen stove, my grandmother used to talk about the mad Shepards. For a long time I used to confuse them with pictures in the family Bible. I imagined them as fierce bearded men with shepherds' crooks driving sheep over stony deserts. In my child's mind they were attired in the tatters of the herdsman's profession, but they did mad things on whim and impulse and this was why they were called the "mad shepherds." It was only much later that I came to realize they were a part of the family library, that is, that they were a part of me. One of the great principles of nature, particularly the living part of her, is the library. Man imagines that quite late on in his historical development he invented libraries, but in reality he was only making conscious use of a principle as old as life. There were two kinds of living libraries long before man put the first book, or scroll, or baked tablet upon a shelf. In fact, if it had not been for those earlier natural libraries, man would never have existed, and these great granaries, these storage bins of knowledge and delight, such as we are dedicating here today, would never have existed. Man, in short, has been constructed, or perhaps I should say drawn, out of a library, that is, the hidden books of our genetic substance.

Now there are those who would argue that my analogy is wrong, that nature does not keep libraries, but only codes hidden in germ cells, that there is one solitary code for man, another for a mouse, and a lost one for, say, a sabre-tooth

cat or a dinosaur. The term "genetic code" has become popular and we hear nothing of genetic libraries, yet in reality without such a library man and the whole of animal creation would not have evolved, or even now be adjusting insensibly to the faint winds of the oncoming future.

⅄ ⅄

INTRODUCTION

This volume has been drawn from the wilderness of a single
life. I detect within it one deep consummatory drive: to fix
what has mattered to me, as the first man to create an alphabet might seek to do upon rock. I lived these hours, whether
of action or of thought. I remember as vividly as yesterday
the animals pecked on a red quartzite boulder; I remember
still the windings of vanished storm sewers underneath a
town I have not visited for years. From some deep well below
consciousness I must always have distrusted time, and therefore I came to study it. I scratched initials more deeply than
others into friable stone. As a child I buried appropriate
objects beneath hand-whittled miniature crosses. It was I who
strove to immortalize in cement the pawprints of the dog
Mickey. My childish commemorative monuments are more
lost than the Mayan stelae. The initials of myself and my
companions have eroded and vanished under the driving rain
of innumerable prairie summers. I am aware of this because
in maturity I have looked for them in vain, just as I have
stared vainly into the faces of skulls or through roofless
porticos in a search for the features and the thoughts of
vanished generations.

But in this volume, like some wielder of a stylus or a brush,
or even some hunter with a wall upon which to paint, I have
left my own graffiti, just as soldiers through the ages have
scrawled their messages upon rocks in foreign lands. Unfortu-
nates always try to speak beyond themselves to another time.
One literate Greek even inscribed on a Roman brick in the
Forum, "Cestus the slave wrote this," in effect extending his
outraged cry to the ages beyond him.

This book, I know, does not possess the permanence of
baked clay. The mold of basements feeds upon our literature,
and insects enjoy its glue. Perhaps, however, these pages will
flutter briefly upon someone's night table for a little while.
Print is cunning and enables so many hundreds of copies to
be run off that somewhere a like mind may encounter and
choose to share my musings. The volume has no other purpose than to claim a time and to make it my own forever. In
doing so I assert that right for all men, as I do for the living
creatures they once cherished and whose bones lie buried
beside their own. *The Night Country* should be taken as a

message, but to decipher it in its entirety would be, even for its author, to decipher a rune. Its meaning is mingled with the falling rain, and with the dust drifting over forgotten excavations. Already my memories are cloudy, swirling, and indistinct. Doubtless they will march away at last, following the mammoth hunters over the horizon. But here I have spoken pleasurably to myself for some divided hours as in youth I would have placed the clay heads in Hagerty's barn, or attempted other little mementoes against the future.

Call this compulsive if you will. It is the night country of the mind, and I can assert that it exists only by stirring the dust of yesterday sufficiently to becloud momentarily the present. Not every man enjoys the lifting of such wraiths, but in age they sometimes return more forcibly than when one is young, as though the final light were to be used to cast a shaft into darkness. A man whose lifetime has been spent prowling in crevices, whether of caves or libraries, is inevitably more than a little inured to these last glimpses of his world.

My grandmother, in her declining years, used to stand and whisper at the window. If one drew close, one could hear a kind of dialogue going on between two levels of consciousness, one of the day, one of the night, the two distinctly separated in old age. Finally one morning I saw the lined hawk features working as she stared far away down the street. "There comes the dead wagon," I heard her murmur in the dialect of a vanished day. I once told this incident to a distinguished novelist, who was charmed by the expression and made careful note of it.

There was one other thing I did not mention. Grandmother McKee was of Scotch descent and sometimes fey. Not long after she died, the "wagon," as she had foreseen, drew up in the street. She had penetrated further than I could see with the clear eyes of youth on that cold October morning. Though I stood beside her at the time, I would never have dared ask her to describe her inward seeing. Her eyes were frighteningly remote and she seemed listening, perhaps for hoofbeats sounding in her head. The whispered dialogue between daylight and dark had ceased as she turned away. I never heard it again. But in my turn I have come to know more of the night country because of her. I suppose in the end her blood speaks in certain pages of this book. I would not wish it otherwise.

In the years I have written, her whispering has run cold and dark through the channels of my mind. I have not, as yet, sighted the hearse and its dark horses, but this book has been set down against their appearance. My grandmother was dour as befitted a more austere time. She held her private conversation and went straight to her appointment. I, born out of that dark house, have wandered longer and less securely in the night land. Therefore, I have wanted to keep a kind of record, extending from dog paws to midnight travelers.

Grandmother, at the end, was not conscious of the whispered controversy in the stream of consciousness. I, by contrast, was there. I sensed the inevitable hearse draw up. Now, in age, before the splitting of that stream for whose reality I have only the remembered mutterings of Grandmother McKee, I leave this intermittent record in pain, confusion, and pride as do all men. That there should be a dark and a dayborn stream may be found acceptable. But my grandmother is the only person I have ever known personally who alternated and spoke from the dark and the day country almost in unison, as though voicing, unawares like a medium, a bisected universe. Perhaps something of her uncanny mind followed me into the places below and twice brought me out again.

I say again we are of one blood. I knew it surely when she watched the last time from the window. I arrange these reflections before midnight approaches. In nocturnal solitude I find myself arising and staring from the window. I do not know what draws me there, but I come. I look long into the dark and listen. The footfalls are yet far away. I light the reading lamp. I write in the sleeping house. I write in the study with a cavalryman's revolver lying in the desk drawer. Sometimes I take it out and touch it, since it came from the Battle of the Wilderness. I clean it for a dead man who used it well, as the worn firing cylinder shows. My uncallused, desk-trained hand can scarcely hold and aim the heavy weapon without wavering. Somewhere in the dark the man in the blue coat would smile. But I write, and the uncouth dark stream begins pouring beneath the level of consciousness. Light and dark pass over my face as in that day long ago on the range. The letters flow under my hand like crows' feet trampling snow.

In her youth my grandmother looked long and vainly from
a farm window seeking an unreturning man. It was there the
second sight began and the implacable hatred of time; she
tried, I think now, to arrest time in a lifelong mental battle. I,
her lineal descendant, followed far into the night country in
that hopeless endeavor. Now I talk of life and death, and the
stream begins once more to divide irrevocably within my
head.

A chief editor speaks judiciously of a piece he had commis-
sioned, "You are too downbeat." I toss the article on the
shelf with a shrug. It is not yet time for the dead wagon. I
spin the firing cylinder of the empty six-gun and stare at the
strangely sutured skull of an ancient Greek girl swathed in
cotton to protest her from time's ravages. The crows' black
feet begin to march once more across the page almost of their
own volition. It is dawn. A red cardinal is singing. The
wagon will not come for another day. In my head, Grandmother's dialogue continues. I turn to the family album and
study my dead mother's face. The marks of the dark country
lie across her features as well. Perhaps they are hidden in
the faces of all the albums in the world.

FROM A LETTER FROM LOREN TO LEWIS MUMFORD, FEBRUARY 18, 1971

I wanted to tell you how fully I understand the wounds
and scars left by the casual reviewers of this world. All I can
say — and I know too well it does not compensate for the
hurt — is that you have received distinguished recognition. As
an academic professional I frequently find myself bitterly
castigated by those in my own field who resent any attempt
to venture into the domain of literature. There were years
when I preferred silence. There were years when I wrote only
professional papers. And now, in a time when I have received

some small attention, I am tired and I write, if I write at all, only for myself, like a voice echoing in an empty room. What I will write next I do not know but it will probably be a venture into some other domain.

⋊ ⋉

Start of Introduction for Robinson Crusoe Volume

All my life, as I have sauntered through the streets of my hometown, I have been picking up lost or discarded objects — a stout rubber band here, there a rusted iron spike beside an abandoned building. Once I found in an alley a huge bolt like a well-weighted club that ludicrously sagged in my suit pocket on the way to a formal dinner.

I pick up these trivia with a kind of sheepish evasion. Only the other evening I found a great chunk of raw blue glass fallen from a broken streetlight. I spent several happy hours chipping it into a primitive skinning knife. I do not know why I am thus impelled toward articles of no possible value in my present existence. There is, however, a certain consistency in this eccentric behavior which gives a clue to my psychological state — if not to that of modern man in general. Everything which attracts me, valueless though it is, would aid in the survival of someone on a desert island. The glass would cut, the bolt could be shaped in a fire or used as a weapon. What persists in my mind is an utter distrust of the longevity of civilization. It is clear that I move daily amidst debris that would entice a castaway. Mentally I am engaged in dismantling the remains of an offshore wreck. I am relying upon my own sharpened ingenuity for survival. It is obvious that I unconsciously regard the rejected fragments so wastefully strewn about me as the *dismembra* of a civilization already perished and in the midst of whose solitude I linger like Crusoe upon his isle.

This attitude, I have come to suspect, is widespread in Western society and in no other. I surmise that it emerges with the growth of science, with the accompanying discovery of an unpegged, homeless universe in which a man no longer has a shelter under the stars. Perhaps I am simply living ahead in a time when the discovery of a rusty bolt will bolster one's security. Perhaps the anxiety I now feel over this wreckage is a premonition. Or, on the other hand, can it have been touched off by reading *Robinson Crusoe* when I was a small boy?

This, however, explains very little. Hundreds of children read *Robinson Crusoe,* but it does not follow that as adults they are driven to pick up a bolt in the street and carry this ridiculous weapon to a dinner. No, the matter goes deeper than this. Watch any vacationer along a shore. Follow him and sooner or later he will be seen to salvage some meaningless bit of flotsam and stand brooding over it. I am merely an extreme case. Instinctively I find the tide and its wreckage lapping invisibly at the edge of a parking lot or seeping through the alleys of the city. There is, in reality, another tide — the tide of time that leaves great cities buried under sand or subsiding upon ancient seafloors. Like a clairvoyant I am partly lost in some unknown dimension. The things I pick up are never meaningful in the place I inhabit, their use is elsewhere. I know this and strive interiorly to bring the tool and the time into proper juxtaposition. I have not succeeded.

≽ ≼

FROM A LETTER FROM HOWARD NEMEROV TO LOREN, MAY 6, 1971

May this note not be an impertinence, coming from a stranger. . . .

The sight of those tawny moths (on the accompanying page) and my acquaintance with your work date from the same year, I remember. And for the same six or seven years I never did manage to get those moths to go into a poem and stay in it. But this morning, reading not for the first time in yr *Unexpected Universe* I came across your phrase "a sudden rent in the living screen," and seemed to know for the first time where those moths and I were at. I hope I have stated the matter with reasonable accuracy and concision. If so, you wd honor me by accepting the dedication. But if not, do please tell me in a word or so where it's gone wrong. For a poem to be brief without being right wd be an extra silliness in a world quite silly enough.

While I'm here I shd say that I have great affection for your books: the solitude in them is strong and oddly consoling. Coleridge says somewhere that the ideas one thinks of are altogether less important than the ideas one thinks with, and your way of dealing with the world is for me one of the ideas one hopes to learn to think with; you see time as directly as most of us see space.

(A baby spider is crawling across the page on which I've copied the little poem for you. Parable quite in yr own style. But I shall try not to envelope him.)

THE RENT IN THE SCREEN

"... A sudden rent in the living screen ..."
— *Loren Eiseley*

Sweet mildness of the late December day
Deceives into the world a couple of hundred
Cinnamon moths, whose cryptic arrow shapes
Cling sleeping to a southward-facing wall
All through the golden afternoon till dusk
And coming cold arouse them to their flight
Across the gulf of night and nothingness,
The falling snow, the fall, the fallen snow,
World whitened to dark ends. How brief a dream.

— *Howard Nemerov*

GENIUS AND SOCIETY

The individual genius plays in society the same role that the mutant gene plays in the evolution of organic forms. Just as we are now searching out the chemistry that determines our hereditary character, so is it equally important to determine the social factors which stimulate or suppress the gifted individual. How much latent talent is wasted in society because of economic or other barriers? Does our educational system open or close the doorways to spectacular achievement? Why, if genius is a purely biological phenomenon, did fourth- and fifth-century Greece produce so much more genius than the vast population of China? Why did the centrifugal forces of early paleolithic society retard the emergence of genius and slow down the emergence of the modern world?

All of these subjects are part of the exploration of the role of genius in society.

≽ ≼

It begins in the echoing loneliness of a house with no other children; in the silence of a deafened mother; in the child head growing strangely aware of itself as it prattles over immense and solitary games. The child learns there are shadows in the closets and a green darkness behind the close-drawn curtains of the parlor. It is sensitive to a cool twilight in the basement, it is afraid only of noise.

Noise is the Outside, the bully in the next block by whose house you have to pass in order to go to school. Noise is all the things you do not wish to do. It is the games in which you are pummeled by other children's big brothers, it is the sharp demanding voices of adults who snatch your books. Noise is day. Escape from day. Moreover you are growing nearsighted. But you have become soft footed, with a fine sense of touch. You encounter the bully in an alley after dark and beat him. Beat him because the night is friendly and there are no other faces about.

After that the road is set for you — though you do not see it — you have beaten someone and are therefore a person to follow. You lead your following to the sewers. Into these you disappear.

≽ ≼

FROM A LETTER FROM LOREN TO HAL AND BARBARA
BORLAND, FEBRUARY 28, 1972

I am off this coming week-end for a three-day engagement at the University of Redlands in California and God knows I am tired before I start. Also, at the last moment they tell me that among other things they would like me to discourse on my "philosophy." I hate trying to articulate things like this because it makes me feel a little absurd. I doubt if I have a philosophy. I live more or less like the cardinals who come to my window from day to day. There are some things I will not do and some things I will do and some things I would like to do but can't. Why I look at the world in this particular fashion I have no more knowledge than a pterodactyl, and perhaps that is what I shall tell them.

≯ ≮

I should like to dedicate to you the poem overleaf. May I have your permission?

My private title for it is *Contra Monod*.

UNPREDICTABLE BUT PROVIDENTIAL

(for Loren Eiseley)

Spring, with its thrusting leaves and jargling birds, is here

again

to remind me again of the first real Event, the first
genuine Accident, of that Once when, once a tiny
corner of the Cosmos had turned just indulgent enough
to give it a sporting chance, some original Substance,
immortal and independent, knowing only the blind
collision experience, had the sheer audacity
to become irritable.

A Self requiring a world,
a Not-Self outside Itself, from which to renew Itself,
with a new freedom, to grow, a new necessity, death.
Henceforth, for the animate, to last was to mean to change,
existing both for one's own sake and the sake of all others,
forever in jeopardy.

The ponderous ice-dragons
performed their slow-motion ballet. Continents cracked in

half

and wobbled drunkenly over the waters. Gondwana
smashed head-on into the underbelly of Asia.
But catastrophes only encouraged experiment.
As a rule it was the fittest who perished, the mis-fits,
forced by failure to emigrate to unsettled niches, who
altered their structure and prospered. (Our own

shrew-ancestor

was a nobody, but still could take himself for granted,
with a poise our grandees will never acquire.)

> Genetics
> may explain shape, size and posture but not why one
> physique
>
> should be gifted to cogitate about cogitation,
> divorcing Form from Matter, and fated to co-habit
> on uneasy terms with its Image, dreading a double death,
> a dreamer, a maker of asymmetrical objects,
> a linguist who is never at home in Nature's grammar.
>
> Science, like Art, is fun, a playing with truths, and no game
> should even pretend to slay the heavy-lidded riddle
> What is the Good Life?
>
> Common Sense warns me never to buy
> either but, when I compare their rival myths of Being,
> be-wigged Descartes looks more outré *than the painted*
> wizard.

❧ ❧

FROM A LETTER FROM LOREN TO HOWARD NEMEROV, JULY 5, 1972

. . . I have drawn from notebooks extending into the past
some poetry which my editor at Scribners persuaded me,
rather reluctantly, to publish. It will appear in late October
under the title *Notes of an Alchemist* and I will see that you
get an autographed copy. Please understand that as an old
broken-down archaeologist muttering to himself my sending
you a copy does not mean that I am asking you to comment
upon it professionally. It is just a little gesture of friendship in
the hope that privately you might enjoy a line or two. You
see, when I was a very young man in college I loved the art
very much and I suppose there was a time when I could have
quoted off-hand any of the leading poets of the period. I had
responsibilities to others, however, and because I had a somewhat omnivorous and amoeboid mind I turned aside into
science. Nevertheless occasionally in professional notebooks,
amidst notations on artifacts, digs, and what-not, I continued
to scrawl verse, just as I have continued to enjoy the personal
essay, somewhat to the discomfort of some of my colleagues.
I have always been somewhat solitary and I suppose this little
volume gets something off my chest. I no longer know the

critical world in this domain well enough to judge its reaction or to particularly care.

FROM A LETTER FROM W. H. AUDEN TO LOREN, NOVEMBER 23, 1972

I must write to tell you how much I have been enjoying *Notes of an Alchemist.* The poems are most moving and very original. On principle, I disapprove of Free Verse, but, in your case, I think you are absolutely right to use it.

FROM A LETTER FROM WARREN E. BURGER, THE CHIEF JUSTICE, SUPREME COURT OF THE UNITED STATES, TO LOREN, REFERRING TO "MAGIC," A POEM ABOUT A CARDINAL FAMILY IN *NOTES OF AN ALCHEMIST*, DECEMBER 5, 1972

I am relieved — if that is the right word — to find there are many people who are "enchanted by a bird," albeit fewer who admit it. I have the experience almost daily as I shave with an electric razor that needs little attention from me and as I watch Cardinals, Tanagers, Blue Jays, Mocking birds and many others, feed on the seeds dropped by the wind & provided by us, just outside my window. It is a good way to lift the spirit before plunging into briefs and other things that follow soon after the shaving.

Thank you for the lift of spirit your books have given us.

OUR OWN TRUE NOTEBOOK

Where the night overtook us, there we bedded
in storm or frost, or summer heat on stones,
knowing the light would find us in the morning,
daylight would lift us on our aching bones

to totter onward for a little while, then dark,
then day again, until, a lifetime spent,
amidst leaves, litter, waterfalls and rills,
we would assume that what it was we meant

would have been listed in some book set down
beyond the sky's far reaches, if at all
there was a purpose here. But now I think
the purpose lives in us and that we fall

into an error if we do not keep
our own true notebook of the way we came,
how the sleet stung, or how a wandering bird
cried at the window. It is not the same

for all, or what they would dissemble or narrate.
Infinite millions have passed this way
expecting sun at morning. Now at last
I muse content on this one single day

thinking that through these hours light was flowing
into the eyes of cheetahs, condors, men,
and how they made of it their separate worlds,
diverse and agonized, then slept again.

꒩ ꒦

EDGAR ALLAN POE

There are some secrets which do not suffer themselves to be
                                                        told.
You wrote once of the crowd and then you followed
a man of the crowd noting
his refusal to be alone, his capacity for violence, his darting
                                                        figure,
yet always breathing with agony
                        distracted, tracing,
                                and retracing
his own pathway without end.
                You, loneliest of men,
                        haughty, reserved
yet bearing wounds impossible to heal, having lost all so that
                                                the word
Nevermore reverberated without ceasing ever in your heart.
                                You, Edgar Poe,
poor desperate waif, I wonder if you knew
that night they dragged you, drugged and ill,
about the streets of Baltimore
upon election eve, that you had joined the crowd at last,

blind, inexplicably evil, nameless,
shifting its molecules without intent
save for a gleam reflected on some face
like yours, intelligent but wracked with pain,
swept onward into darkness by
                              the ominous throng
that has not ever ceased since time began.

That was the fatal vision that you saw
coming upon you, into which you knew
you must inevitably dissolve as do
all men. You knew it and you therefore also knew
how the self challenges and slays the self
yet knows with grief the murder before a mirror endlessly it
                                                  has done,
never to be repaired. You, William Wilson Edgar Poe, now
                                                    drift
                    in worldly time, earthbound,
wherever men turn pages
and hear never more repeated nevermore *upon the crow-*
                                          strewn air.
The bird is there.

⤦ ⤧

FROM A LETTER FROM LOREN TO W. H. AUDEN,
MARCH 8, 1973

The Innocent Assassins being completed, I now want to
turn to some prose again, although oddly enough having let
this long-suppressed vice of poetry up out of the basement it
is going to be difficult for me to reconcentrate my efforts.

Retirement is looming fast upon me and, like yourself, I
shall have to make decisions as to whether I stay about, seek
a place in the sun, or return to the long-forgotten and probably vastly changed world of my boyhood. I was in New York
yesterday, having delivered the manuscript by hand since an
acquaintance had the experience of something of this sort
disappearing for one entire month traversing a few blocks in
New York. I dined out with my editor, but there is always a
certain sadness that haunts me about these affairs because at
times we enter restaurants where I lunched long ago with
older friends now gone. The sense of some overwhelming

autumnal sadness grows and to the best of my ability you
will probably find murmurs of it in this new book.

≽ ≼

GRAVELY THEN

For Edward Thomas, 1878–1917

Gravely then, for he was a grave man, Edward Thomas rose
and taking the boy by the hand they walked
to an old pool in a copse of trees where Edward cut
two willow sticks for poles, two poles of a length to reach
the center of the pool, and then they strung to each
fish line that Edward found in his jacket, carefully explaining
to the wide-eyed child that they would try to catch
the fish that lived in the pool. The poet Thomas
forgot the hooks, most likely did not care for them,
taught the child mystery, patience instead, and there they sat
fishing without hooks for a life already taken;
thus passed a day for Thomas on the road to war.
I wonder if the solemn child, grown old now, still recalls
the silence fallen on the pond, or does he think
still of some fish uncaught because friend Edward
had had enough of hooks, preferred the fathomless.
Or does the child remember? Perhaps not.
Fishing in fishless pools is often done, but not so well by
                                                        boys.

≽ ≼

FROM A LETTER FROM HOWARD NEMEROV TO LOREN,
REFERRING TO *NOTES OF AN ALCHEMIST*, JULY 1, 1973

There are some special moments for me in almost all your
poems for your peculiar angle of vision and way of seeing
into time as readily as others see into space is not only a
positively new gift you've made to the power and reach of
language, but also something that appeals to me most personally and that I strive to learn of, your alchemy, magic, rope
trick, fractured theology and whatever else.

In particular: "From Us Without Singing," magnificent, and
nowhere more so than in the concluding strophe beginning

"By God if I must reenter, &c." That's a tone not much heard even among the angrier of our poets, who tend to bleat and shriek rather than thunder. In particular again: "The Blizzard." What a *telling* tale! With the loneliness and economy of Frost's "Witch of Coos." (This typewriter suffers from an absence of umlaut.) I've not only seen the man you portray, I believe I've been him (happily not always). Others in particular are "The Snow Leopard" and "The White Python" (my own dreams are magnificent at the grotesque but never achieve, as that one does, the sublime).

When you get my book — this month? next month? they don't tell me much, up at Chicago — you'll see we have butterflies in common, also striders . . . indeed, if I ever get up a poetry anthology it'd be called A Collect of Bug Poetry: Shakespeare on Beetles, Pope on Sporus, Donne on the Flea, Blake on the Fly . . . but I'll probably never get up a poetry anthology.

⋊ ⋉

FROM A LETTER FROM LOREN TO HOWARD NEMEROV, JANUARY 18, 1974

I was particularly pleased with your response to "From Us Without Singing" because that is one of my favorites in the book but so far it has escaped comment in reviews. The night I scrawled it off after midnight (it is a late poem) I remember thinking, "By God, by God, this time I have really transformed myself into something formidable, a continental glacier." I went about all day hearing boulders and ice clashing in my head and muttering in my study. As for "The Blizzard," there was such a man and, like yourself, I have been he and feel even more that way these days as I approach retirement among my bright and able young colleagues.

Of course I will look forward to your book, as I always enjoy the poems you have sent me. As you may have noted from "The Old Ones" I love dragonflies and I think I remarked, in a somewhat pagan way that I fear will make some of my clerical following nervous, that I "bow before a large dragonfly." I want you to know that I enjoy your close formulations and terse brilliance. I might say that I deliberately excluded from *Notes of an Alchemist* certain of my more formal poems because I thought they would appear odd in juxtaposition with the more free-flowing things out of my later years. On the other hand, I still write an occasional formal poem and what I will do with these in my coming book I do not know. We all have our ways of doing things and you have a mastery of the intricate which has always delighted me, a jeweler's ability to examine every facet of a precious stone. Long ago before I came to know you I used to admire that aspect of your work. Probably I go around snarling and transforming myself into all manner of ferocious beasts out of sheer frustration over my own inability to create in such a manner.

≽ ≼

In some quarters it has been said that Henry David Thoreau awaited a visitor who never came — and therefore modern men who exchange witticisms at cocktail parties smile pityingly. They forget in the arrogance of youth and a later century that the man who awaited a visitor could decipher snow trails and had been visited by demonical foxes who seemed to him "rudimentary men awaiting transformation," creatures screaming vulpine curses at his lighted window in the forest. [*Walden,* vol. 2, p. 422.] It was Thoreau's gift to receive many inhuman visitors and to perceive in them efforts of transcendence as in the case of the foxes striving toward their own civilization. Yes, he had visitors from other dimensions than ours, and if he finally awaited one who did not approach, do we not all. But Thoreau had perhaps enticed him nearer or caught glimpses of that visitor along snow trails in the forest. In *Walden* and in the journals snow trails loom with the utmost importance, as though they were a species of cabalistic waiting. Our own interiors Thoreau intimates are delineated as "white on the chart." Across this expanse there are few tracks, but he follows them with wistful attention just as he follows, throughout his journals, the scorings of leaves and grasses or other tracks through the wide expanses of wild nature. Snow he tells us perceptively is the "great revealer." He loved its unpronounceable alphabets.

Thoreau himself was the Visitor. "We have never quarreled," he said cryptically.

≽ ≼

Journal II, p. 356: "If there is any hell more unprincipled than our rulers and our people, I feel curious to visit it."

Journal II, p. 310: "It would be worth the while to ask ourselves weekly, Is our life innocent enough?"

Journal VI, p. 311: "The inhumanity of science concerns me, as when I am tempted to kill a rare snake that I may ascertain its species. I feel that this is not the means of acquiring true knowledge."

Journal VI, p. 452: "I have just been through the process of killing the testudo for the sake of science; but I cannot excuse myself for this murder, and see that such actions are inconsistent with the poetic perception, however they may serve science, and will effect the quality of my observations. I pray that I may walk more innocently and serenely through nature. No reasoning whatever reconciles me to this act. . . . I have a murderer's experience. . . ."

Journal VI, p. 47: "The unmerciful driver marked in snow. . . ."

Thoreau began in literature and went to science, I began in science and went to literature.

                                      ❧ ❦

I remarked at the beginning of this essay, though memory fails me and I cannot name his name, that there was one who ventured that Thoreau himself awaited a Visitor who never came. A somewhat heretical priest once observed, "God asks nothing of the highest soul but attention." As supplemental to that remark Thoreau had asserted, "There has been nothing but the sun and the eye since the beginning." That eye, in the instance of Thoreau, had missed nothing. Even in the depths of winter when nature's hieroglyphs lay all about him in the snow, he had not faltered to observe among them the marks of a farmer's lash steadily, even monotonously beating his oxen down the drifted path. It wounded him. He had climbed in addition a high mountain and observed in the process a nature "not bound to be kind to man." He was not, in the end, either a Christian or a transcendentalist in the earlier sense of that term. When the play, he explained — it may be the tragedy of life — is over, the Spectator goes his way. There was a kind of doubleness even in nature. The inner eye was removed, its qualities were more than man, as natural man, could long support. I sincerely believe, the Visitor came. He came in the guise of Thoreau, looked out upon the world, and went his way.

Is it not remembered that when at last an acquaintance in his puritan way came to ask if Thoreau on his deathbed had made his peace with God, the Visitor in him responded, "We have never quarreled"? He had appropriated the snow as the great revealer, the container of hidden alphabets.

Last winter trudging in the woods I came to a spot where freezing, melting, and refreezing had lifted old footprints into little pinnacles of trapped oak leaves as though a bush had walked upon some errand. Thoreau had recorded the phenomenon over a century ago. There was something fey about it, I thought, standing attentively in the snow. A visitor, perhaps the Visitor, had passed by.

In the very first volume of the journals, Thoreau had written, "There is always the possibility, the possibility, I say, of being all, or remaining a particle in the universe." He had, in the end, learned that nature was not an enlarged vision of the human ego. He had turned to that other, that more formidable world of science — the science that later on in the twentieth century would reduce everything to particles and finally to an unceasing ebb and flow of energy. But the eye remained, the unexplainable eye, that gave even Darwin a cold shudder. All it experienced were the secondary qualities, the illusions, that physics had rejected, but the eye remained just as Thoreau had asserted — the sun and the eye from the beginning. Thoreau was gone, but the eye was multitudinous, ineradicable.

I advanced upon the trail of the oak leaves. We were all the eye of the Visitor — the eye whose reason no physics could explain. Generation by generation the eye was among us. We were particles, but we were also the recording eye that saw the sunlight which physics had reduced to cold waves in a cold void. There had been but the sun and the eye since the beginning, Thoreau had protested. His life had been dedicated to the unexplainable eye. I took another tentative step along the trail marked by the oak leaves. I had been trained since youth against the illusions, the deceptions of the eye, against sunset as reality, against my own features as anything but a secondary quality seen in a mirror. Nevertheless, I saw I had merely pursued another trail through the same wood and that

I had emerged on the path as followed by the author of *Walden*. The eye was everywhere, and as for Walden it too was everywhere that the eye existed. I went down the trail marked by the oak leaves. I went slowly, making sure that the eye, residing momentarily in me, saw and recorded all that there was to see. It was Thoreau himself who had written at the very outset of his career that the eye has many qualities which belong to God more than man. That gift, in contrast to what had been written of his final journals, he had retained to the end.

⊁ ⊀

Dean Inge, 1919, cited by Alfred North Whitehead in *The Concept of Nature,* Cambridge U. Press, 1955, p. 48: "Nature makes abstractions for us, deciding what range of vibrations we are to see and hear, what things we are to notice and remember."

Whitehead: "Nature is a process . . . there can be no explanation of this characteristic of nature."

And equally does not each one of us abstract differently?

⊁ ⊀

As man acquires writing and now the film and electric recording device, his potential "duration" span increases.

⊁ ⊀

Last and foremost, Thoreau was an archaeologist. He was a coffin tipper who had looked on the past of America, seen its pitiful last thought prints etched in ash and quartz, the copper-tinted Indian. Seen events which would always haunt it and leave man diffuse, gigantic, shadowy, lingering in its haze. To the end, however, he was something more, he was an archaeologist of the heart, who warned of uncompleted business, some Symmes hole of the mind, some dangerous crevice by which man might find his way into the future. That future contained green parks for the people, business unconsummated that ran ahead of his century. Mind prints more gigantic than the skills and technology of the time that, as he said, turned man into a tool of his tools. No, he sought a way of slipping through the black Symmes hole of his century. He had heard even the foxes bark to be men. He wanted what we still have not found, the proud freedom of solitude, the freedom to go and come in nature, to be our own true selves. If the business momentarily faltered, it was because it needed other hearts and eyes. He needed us all and we failed him. Symmes hole was not a tomb. He saw it as a crevice into the future and he assayed, alone, the most gigantic task of archaeologist, to pass those giant Indian summer shapes and to lead both them and ourselves into the proper future. We have been melded together, we are one culture, in which is mingled one bloodstream, at last, the bronze autumn, and out of the old ash had arisen the first culture in the world consciously to seek the preservation of its woodland wild prairie. It seeks to breathe clean air. It has unfinished business beyond Walden. It lies where Thoreau led us, to the crevice of Symmes hole. Let us follow him and understand, as archaeologists, his wistful, killing doubt of our intent. Let us go at Concord beyond the little stone marked Henry. He was right, the crevice was there all the time, but we could not see it. The blood of more than one race has been mingled on this ancient continent, and not all that blood was of the world destroyers. There still are drops from those who worshipped the earth mother in other guises than tools. Thoreau insisted a copper tint lingers among us. Perhaps it may help to lead us through the pouring waters of the future that thunder through Symmes hole. That is the unfinished business he has left us, the business of which Walden, as Wright Morris has truly said, was only the first chapter of an unsatisfied life.

THE COFFIN TIPPERS

Emerson is often termed bland, an idealist, a turner of pretty phrases, but when, two years after the death of his young bride, Ellen Tucker, from the devastating white scourge, t.b., which in his younger years had almost taken him, he only recorded in his diary, "I opened her coffin. I looked, and turned away." There was no expressed sentiment, nothing for the public. The words, morbid or not, are cut of New England granite. No hope, no lingering affection, nothing shines through. "I am deficient in the human qualities," he once acknowledged, but why then was he driven to this terrible deed?

Fifteen years later, when his firstborn five-year-old son, the darling of a second and enduring marriage, perished, the same act was repeated, while somewhat at more length the same words were reiterated. Emerson by then was famous, moved among the great. But again, his voice becomes a mere ineffectual whisper against the powers of the dark, yet the deed, the deed from which we all shrink, had been repeated.

≽ ≼

The acceptance of the supernatural is a widening of our grasp of the universe, its own numinous quality, which the man who sticks to daylight fails to grasp, for the universe itself is as supernatural as the great white whale.

≽ ≼

There are persons who, because of youthful association, like harsh etched things before their eyes at morning, the foot of an iron bedstead, a tombstone, jail bar, even a weathered beam. On July 14, I saw the chisel marks on the eighteenth-century beam in my room of the Concord Inn. As I started up the street toward the cemetery, I saw a few drifters, blacks and whites, stirring from their illegal night's sleep among the gravestones. Later, I came to the Thoreau family plot and saw the little yellow stone marked "Henry" that no one is any longer sure indicates the precise place where he lies. Perhaps there is justice in that because the critics are so unsure also of the contradictions and intentions of his journals, even of the classical *Walden*. A ghost, then, of shifting features peering out from between the gravestones, unreal, perhaps uninterpreted still.

I turned away from the early morning damp for a glimpse of the famous pond that in the country of my youth would have been called a lake. I walked its whole blue circumference with an erudite citizen of Concord. It was still blue, even if beer bottles here and there were bobbing in the shallows. I walked along the tracks of the old railroad where Thoreau used to listen to the telegraph wires. He had an eye for the sharp-edged artifact, I thought, considering his journals. Perhaps, like the hippies, squinting at the outline of a tombstone at morning did not disturb him, nor that little stone marked "Henry." After all, it was a quiet hillside, and his friend, his sometimes opponent, Emerson, lay nearby.

The bobbing bottles, the keys to beer cans he would have transmuted into cosmic symbols, just as he had transmuted more ancient artifacts. After all, they, too, had their edges, a certain harshness; they, too, had once been the structure of a mind. What did it matter, really, let them fill Walden Pond with rusting artifacts or wash dogs with it, as I observed in the shallows. It had served its purpose.

ﹶ ﹶ

FROM A LETTER FROM LOREN TO RAY BRADBURY,
REFERRING TO A COLLECTION OF BRADBURY'S POEMS,
JANUARY 11, 1974

It would be unseemly and invidious to make choices amidst such treasures but I will tell you that I read "Remembrance" with quite a kind of preternatural, nostalgic terror, knowing in advance how it would turn out. *My* tree, alas, was chopped down long ago and when, as a stranger, I visited that town and stared across at my old house, looking at what used to be a vacant lot beside it which was now occupied by an apartment house, a stranger on the front porch of my old home spoke to me. I suppose he had merely seen me there gazing rather intently and wanted to be neighborly, perhaps thinking I was a new person in the neighborhood. I spoke the time of day to him, of course, but then turned and went hastily away, filled with inexplicable terror and loneliness.

How could I tell that owner, after all of these years, about vanished objects for which I was searching or that his house was filled with the ghosts of the dead? No, instead I turned and almost ran and I have not returned since. I did not want to tell that man that he had usurped my past, that I, too, was a ghost, and that there was a time before his time. I should not try to explain this but this is what the very first pages of your book brought back to me. And then, of course, there is the next poem and the next.

I, too, am one of those who still have my original *Twenty Thousand Leagues Under the Sea* and *Mysterious Island* on my shelves, and *Nemo* is a name with which to conjure. I honestly do not know how they managed to be preserved because most of my possessions, if they still exist, lie scattered and lost in the attics of forgotten lodging houses of the middle west. But *Nemo* and my toy lion somehow came through, along with a worn old jackknife. My father first told me about *Nemo*, but where and how, on those prairies and their shabby towns far from the sea, he first learned of *Nemo*, I will never know now.

꙳ ꙴ

"Jobless men keep going. We can't take care of our own."
Chamber of Commerce (Raleigh, N.C.) in 1930s

꙳ ꙴ

Biography: Start. Now that I come to think of it, almost fifty years later, those years of the depression were like the slow swirls of the Gulf Stream in the galaxy, an endless drift of men between the two coasts in the dark, a third of a quarter of American men, caught in a blind tide of the depression, drifting, drifting, like Sargasso weed in a vast dead sea of

ruined industry. Men lay in windrows of survival in the
doors, they lay like leaves on sandbars in the hobo jungles
beside the Union Pacific, the Wabash, the Santa Fe, etc., at
Provo, Utah. They rode the empty refrigerator cars coming
through Needles into Barstow, California, through the sand
hell of the Mojave. Railroad detectives blackjacked them, but
they gathered like flocks of autumn birds in spite of all obstacles; like birds, some of them died because they were old, and
they perished, unnoticed, of pneumonia and cold in the high
Sierras, or they slipped under the wheels of freights in moments of exhaustion. Cheap liquor killed them; occasionally
they died by the gun and so did the railroad detectives, pushing their luck too far with sullen unknown men in the night
on swaying car roofs.

It was a time of violence, a time of hate, a time of sharing,
a time of hunger, a time of sacrifice, a time of love. It was all
that every human generation believes it has encountered for
the first time in human history. Life is always a journey and a
death or many deaths. Mine was no different from those
others.

By a switchlight in the yards of Sacramento I opened a
letter. I already knew what was in it and was reluctant to
unfold it. I had carried it in my pocket all the way from San
Francisco, but I was already moving east again in answer to
the summons I knew was in the letter. "Father is dying, come
home."

≿ ≾

I was a child of the early century, American man, if the
term will still be tolerated. A creature molded of plains dust
and the seed of those who came west with the wagons or
who dared, because there was no other way, the little tossing
ships of the seventeenth century. The names Corey, Hollister,

Appleton, Rudd, McKee, Scotch, Irish French . . . and a gene or two from the Indian, is underwritten by the final German of my own name.

How should I have been expected to remember by what code to live? How should I have answered successfully to the restrained Puritan and the long hatred of the beaten hunters, how should I have curbed the flaring berserk rage of the belated Viking of my maternal grandfather? How should —

But this I remember out of deepest childhood — I remember the mad Shepards, as I heard the name whispered in the house, and I remember the pacing, the endless pacing of my parents after midnight while I lay shivering in the cold bed and tried to understand the words that passed between my mother and my father. Terror, anxiety, shame, ostracism? I did not understand the words. I learned early only the feelings they represent. I repeat, I am an American man whose profession, even his life, is no more than a gambler's throw by the firelight of a western wagon. What have I to do with the city in which I live? Why far to the west does my mind still leap to great windswept vistas of grass or the eternal snow of the Cascades? Why does the sound of the sea trouble my heart, or the sight of wolves in cages cause me to avert my eyes? I will tell you only because something like it is at war in every American heart of the last of the westering crossing. The net closes; I age, but I still look sidelong for escape. I yearn persistently for the road across the starfields that I will never live to wander. I am only a professor and an academic, but the stone ax on my desk that is worn with handling I sometimes realize is not there for classroom purposes, nor is the dirk in the desk drawer. They wait their moment, the falling moment of the great structure I pretend to serve.

One of the most vivid memories I have is the sight, in my young manhood, of the ruts still visible in the dry, uncut prairie sod of the Oregon trail. I suppose they have gone under cement now. When I saw them they spread for a full half-mile, and that day was only yesterday. My own father in his young years carried a gun and remembered the gamblers at the green tables in forgotten cow towns. I dream, inexplicably at times, of a gathering of wagons, of women in sunbonnets, and black-clothed bearded men. Then I wake and the scene dissolves.

But I have strayed from the Shepards. It was a name to fear, but this I did not learn for a long time. In the house when my father was away and my mother's people came to visit, the women spoke of them in whispers. They were the mad Shepards and they lay in my direct line of descent. When I was recalcitrant, the Shepards were spoken of and linked with my name.

In that house there was no peace, yet we loved each other fiercely, or perhaps it was merely that we were Americans far on in the midcountry and unreachable by other impulses of failures. Perhaps that was the secret. We were the sons and daughters of men whose tired oxen had bogged in the Platte sands. We were Americans in the middle border where the East was forgotten and one great western road no longer crawled with wagons.

A momentary silence had fallen. I was one of those born into that silence, the bison had perished, the Sioux no longer rode. Only the yellow dust of the cyclonic twisters still marched across the landscape. Of that dust my body had been made. As a youngster I could feel it lift in the heat of the growing corn rows. I knew its anger in the days of the dust bowl. However far I travel, it will be a fading memory upon my tongue in the hour of my death. It is the taste of one dust only, the dust of a receding ice age. Concealed within it is the story of a human heart. Heart? I lay a hand instinctively upon it. I can still remember with astonishment a boy in my backyard telling me triumphantly, "If anything hits your heart, you will be dead." Dead? I did not understand the word. As for being troubled in that region, I had much to learn. Death did not come so easily. I knew because, being early of an experimental cast of mind, I had promptly struck myself. Since I did not die, there must have been something — some element — I did not understand. Therefore I reserved judgment, but the moment must have raised a first question in my mind about mortality. I was very young and I have remembered the statement and my response, though the face of the boy has vanished. I am sure that my failure to die, whatever that meant, did not convince me that I was immune to natural law. There was something I had failed to understand that would come later. I left it at that. It would not take long to learn.

⊁ ⊀

Biography continued. In after years I had come upon the travels of Charles Frémont. Behind an immigrant train he had come upon a gambler's card hand laid down and forgotten as the wagons had rolled on again. The hand had looked peculiarly forlorn lying there in the untamed grasses. It was an eccentric combination neither winning nor surely losing that the gambler had laid down. But a game had been played. When I came upon that episode in later years, I paused and thought reflectively that the game had been played for me; that it was inexplicably my life hand that had been gambled there. Why else had so trivial and lost an episode been preserved where so much had perished? Why else in the infinite libraries of the world had I been led to turn that solitary page?

≫ ≪

April 5, 1974

Sunlight with a harsh wind. I set out in the afternoon to find the cemetery in which we own a lot. I walked along Montgomery Pike to a place, according to my memory, where the road divides. I must have taken the wrong turning and I did not find the cemetery. I was very tired when I returned. But I wanted to find it, to visit my own grave, where, when we purchased it years ago, I had stretched out on the plot to look at the autumn sky and to think this will sometime be forever, though nothing, geologically speaking, ever is.

But why did I wish to come back on this spring day when that other day had been in autumn and I had brought back some beautifully polished horse chestnuts that had been lying there and which now repose on my desk? I do not know, but I suspect and will confide it to these pages.

I am aging. I had been grievously offended by someone I had once thought a friend. The reason need not matter. A pettiness. But suddenly I had wished to be in a place of sun-warmed stones where everyone was finished forever with sarcasm and violence. I wanted to hide. Perhaps it dated to that long, long time ago when as a startled child I had been struck and humiliated by a grown man, a stranger, releasing violence. I wanted increasingly to stay and wander among the sun-warmed stones representing a humanity from which harsh words and cruelty had been drained away. Perhaps a grave was the only place where things came right — except one could never get the stones to speak, only to be warm with sun if one touched them.

Ah, well, I lost the road and came home weary enough to sleep. Was it a death wish momentarily diverted? Did I turn aside before the way became irretrievable? For when one goes *alone* to a cemetery, *does* one seriously intend to return? Perhaps impulse will lead me someday to find out. These moods are growing on me. There is little physical substance left in which to stand upright. I am not clever with unfeeling repartees. When it begins I merely wish to vanish, fade away amidst something in my mind which is becoming, I fear, a graveyard, a graveyard of warm sympathetic stones that no longer constitute the passionate violence of the flesh. I shall have the mate of Wolf's bone buried with me and hope the animal helpers will lift the curtains of the man from *altiplano*. It is my wish.

⋞ ⋟

August 27, 1975

One lone Sphex wasp circling over the hillside burrows like a last bombed-out plane above a deserted town. Is it slow attenuation, the end? Some burrows still open at the outside entrance. In miniature the slope resembles the Valley of the Kings. Are the great queens asleep inside?

⋞ ⋟

August 29, 1975

Traces of digging in four burrows. In one entrance the light of early morning catches the last wasp still digging energetically. Then she comes out, preening her antennae with precisely the same motion of a rabbit attending his ears. She

stumbles vaguely about in the long grass for a few moments,
then takes to wing. The nests on the other terraces all seem
deserted.

⅄ ⅃

August 31, 1975

An autumn chill, cloudy. No sign of any digging this morning. Perhaps last night their last. Closed as gently as possible
some holes obscured by grass and obviously old. Will leave
a few doubtful ones and see if there are any more seen or
signs of effort.

⅄ ⅃

Archaeology is the ghost of history.

⅄ ⅃

THE OFFICE

In the long summer days in my old office
                    where the skulls
of extinct bison leaned from the bookshelves
                    and the ivy on the outside walls
made a tangle across the windows
            I used to turn off the lights
                    and sit in the green darkness until,
on the huge arch over the door, pictures began to form
                    as though transmitted
from far off by the waving leaves in the windows.

It was always the same scene,
            miles of a great tropic river at sunset,
            the Orinoco perhaps
            or the Amazon
but with palm leaves and the lights shifting
            in the sunset or sometimes a boat on the
                                        water.
It was always the same scene but different each time
            and I traveled far in my mind
as I sat in the cool green darkness
            staring at the river

alone with my thoughts.

They chopped the ivy down finally.
They said
it was springing the roof tiles,
they said
they had a better office for me,
with a better view.

I am high up now and look out on
a waste of railroad tracks
oil refineries
and a parking garage,
but an aging man
needs ivy and dim light
where the pictures in his mind
can be cast on the walls
in familiar patterns.
There are no longer Orinocos or Amazons
and the heads of the great
beasts
do not belong here anymore,
are no longer friendly,
I can see the dust on them.
A typewriter clatters in the outer office,
phones ring,
I do not quite understand what has happened,
I am alone, drained, empty. I see nothing
but the blind beasts on the walls.

This is no longer my cave
where I lay hidden ten years
of an ice age, watching the light from the river.
I am homesick for that time, sick with the desecration
of torn leaves, lost boats.
The real and the unreal mingle.
I shall have to rise and creep away. I shall never
find it again.
It was only an illusion made of leaves and light.
It broke my heart
but they said
they had a better office for me.

⊰ ⊱

I AM THE STRANGER HERE

I climbed the stairs in the midst of sickness knowing
   how far I climbed, but the degree was won
that I had risen to get, daring the cold physicians,
   answering the grinding questions,
     holding the fever down while my desperate mind was swept
by a steadily rising wind.
                  Now on the upper landing
I reached for my door but the light went suddenly black
    as faraway I heard
       my body strike the floor
         then nothing, blank and cold, not even dark
for I was completely dead;
dead until evening found me on the landing,
dead until wandering blood cells, vagrant nerves
   assembled me from my fever-ridden body,
till, on my knees, with groping hands I came
fumbling to my own door and flung myself
down on my bed alone, glad that no one had seen.

I have often wondered since, knowing full well I died,
how the dark and scattered cells in the sprawled body knew
   how the rent in the brain might be closed,
    how the churning blood might stop
     the wind, the intolerable wind that swept
me down to the dark, how, out of nothingness,
       could rise, could be rebuilt
the tower of light in the mind, how steadily crawling cells
    could recompose and knit
      memory to memory, till up from death I came,
drawn forth by things unseen, some entity, some toiling
                        congregation
below me in the dark, but not myself nor my will.

No, not myself. In all the years remaining
I know, and am grateful to them, those secret alchemists
of void and stardust who, when my will had failed,
relit the light. Why did they do it? No one has answered me,
                        none.
The blood does not speak, nor the stricken neurons answer,
yet they willed that light should be and it was done.
I am the stranger here, the construct. I am the lonely one.

ADDER'S TONGUE

Met in the midmost, dark-wood journey, Dante said it,
seeing the skeins of his life unravel, gathering them
to make himself renewed. I, on no such journey,
enter the ferny wood, lych wood, for pleasure
to be alone with dappled shade and ferns, to
lose the self — cast it away in stones, give it
to animals, entwine it in pine trunks, toss it
                                  at acorns, ospreys,
Anything to be quits with it.
                         I, too, circumscribed,
encumbered, wanting the wolf feel of a face
unrecognized, furred jowls, pricked ears
                              or tinier, tinier,
the fierce shrew in his tunnel of grass.

In the dark wood, fern wood, night wood
a thousand paths glisten with eyes in each,
spider to night-owl whispering in wolf wood,
night wood,
            and I dispersed, dispersing
in a multiplicity, a congregation,
my open eyes a falcon concentrate.

Do not come here. There are a multitude of hackles rising, ruffs
                              of ear. Do not look
for me, jays cry and crows caw, the owls screech warnings.
I wait in the dark thicket, night wood, fern wood. I wait
for the adder to yield up his fangs, my own true version
of myself unrecognized, solitary, in the blind burrow
of myself, these many darks ruled by the
venom of an adder's tongue.

You will not find me, I have found myself,
dispersed that ego, vanquished it forever, am worm
now, falcon, acorn, who's to care?

☙ ❧

THE SAME CYCLE

I wonder if that old cabin still stands by the
                              dead lake,

dead since the last ice age water sunk away.
I never knew who built it but I lived there
three months with the pack rats scampering in the attic,
the low-hung stars in the Joshua trees
                                            and the incessant wind at morning.
                                I didn't know then
how long I might live and everything
ran into the mirage of distance and time.

Fifty years. I would doubt
the cabin is still there. Perhaps not even the plaza —
they were driving deep wells even then across the valley.

I never went back but perversely
the cabin stays in my mind like a refuge now.
Scarcely anyone ever came by. I was lonely then
                                but at 70
I go inside my mind at nightfall
                        to the low-hung stars
and the silence. The loneliness is at last acceptable —
the way it was out there when the wind died and there was
                                            nothing to hear
while the stars circled round the horizon.
Now if I am sleepless I follow them with my eyes as if we were
                                                    all in
                                        the same cycle.
                            Perhaps we were.

THE ULTIMATE SNOW

The steel is long enough, the basket hilt sufficient
for my most clumsy, inadept strange hand.
This rapier was made to toy with death,
to posture formally, in a lost century and another land.

There is no challenger except one that is faceless.
I lift the long, still supple blade of steel,

admire the hand that knew it, force that wielded
its flickering length when death stood in the flesh, like me,
                                        was real,

could come in seconds over the heart's thin pounding
on the green grass where gentlemen deployed
with ruffles, laces, formal manners
easing for all the presence from the void.

I wish that modern death had such retainers,
dispensed with x-rays, the evasive turns
hidden behind physicians. Awkward, inexperienced
I lift the fine blade with a heart that yearns

all to no purpose now, no skill, no fine opponent,
only the relentless stumbling of the heart.
Before the masked, untouchable assailant
I lift the steel, symbolic, let us start.

I am the novice here: can I lunge from carte to tierce,
recover smartly? The cold physicians know
but will not speak nor second, nor advise,
suggest at any cost a final rally.

Instead they put me on a little cart and go
where I lie prone. There is no grass forever
that I may feel, no sword grip, no dreamed rally,
only the white gowns fading, merging in darkness, fading
into the silence of an ultimate snow.

≫ ≪

FROM A LETTER FROM RAY BRADBURY TO MABEL EISELEY,
AUGUST 5, 1977

A friend just called to tell me what I did not know
until today . . . such being my neglect of newspapers and
magazines during the past several weeks . . . that Loren has
recently passed away. . . .

I received the news like a terrible blow to my body, and
then to every part of my being. Tears filled my eyes. The dear
lady who called me had never met Loren, only knew him
through his books, but she was weeping uncontrollably. What
a tribute this is to his memory and the impact of his thinking

and writing. For what it is worth, in this sad month, I pass it on to you.

He changed my life in countless ways from the time I was 26 and wrote my first letter to him, up to this day. His style and his ideas helped change and form my own style, my own ideas. I shall be in his debt to the end of my life.

I send you my friendly wishes and hopes for your good survival in the coming difficult months. Know that there is another who feels personally put off balance and in despond because a dear older brother is suddenly lost to Time.

Conclusion

On November 7, 1977, a memorial service for Loren Eiseley was held at the University of Pennsylvania, and on December 8, 1978, the Loren Eiseley Seminar and Library was dedicated. Loren wanted his personal library to go to the university and to be kept as intact as possible. A solitary man who spent a great deal of time by himself despite an active academic career, who traveled alone and evidenced a remoteness at professional meetings, he revealed himself to most of his colleagues and the public almost entirely in his books, but he showed there little of the working scholar and scientist. Consequently, his library, which speaks of these things through the wide range of subjects represented, his marginal notes, and the first editions he collected, is significant.

It was finally decided to house the collection of over five thousand volumes, two thousand reprints, and memorabilia in the suite of two rooms which had been his office in the anthropology wing of the university museum — an accommodation which would also serve as a place for seminars and as temporary office space for distinguished visiting lecturers. These arrangements would seem unusual were it not for the impact, through his books, he has had on so many people.

Loren always enjoyed hearing from his readers, and he felt he had countless friends he knew only by their correspondence. There were notes from college professors telling him that one or more of his books were used in their classes. Students from all over America wrote to him for advice concerning their careers, and he never failed to respond and frequently assisted them financially; he was not to forget his own student days and the help he had been given by his teachers. When he received letters from fans who lived at a distance from bookstores or libraries, he was particularly moved, wondering how news of his work had reached them. One eighty-year-old man wrote that he lived far from human society with a horse, a dog, and Loren's books. Often becoming personally involved with his correspondents, he worried about what would happen to the horse and dog when his old friend became ill or died.

Many people who wrote the author asked if they could come to see him and talk with him, and a continuous succession of visitors dropped by when they were in the vicinity of Philadelphia. A few years before Loren died, Martin Meyerson, president of the University of Pennsylvania, was returning to Philadelphia from New York by train and was reading Loren's latest publication. Pausing by his seat somewhat longer than ticket taking required, the conductor said, "You know, I've read every book Mr. Eiseley ever wrote." Then he declared eagerly, "When I retire, I mean to find Mr. Eiseley, wherever he is, and volunteer my services in any way I can." Loren's work had deeply moved him and influenced his life. When it became time for William Curdy — for that was his name — to retire, a meeting was arranged, but by then the man he admired, already in his last illness, was in the hospital.

In addition to *Another Kind of Autumn,* three other books by Loren were published posthumously: *The Star Thrower* (1978), a feast of his favorite writings, for the most part selected and arranged by the author himself before he died; *Darwin and the Mysterious Mr. X: New Light on the Evolutionists* (1979), a controversial work dealing with Edward Blyth, a forgotten nineteenth-century naturalist, and his contributions to the theory of natural selection; and *All the Night Wings* (1979), a collection of his verse spanning the years from 1928 to 1977 and including predominantly unpublished poems and others that had appeared only in the "little magazines" for which he had written in his youth.

Under the close supervision of Mabel, *Bibliographic Card Catalog Index for the Writings of Loren Eiseley* (1982) was compiled by Jeanne Gallagher. This reference work contains detailed information about the collection of handwritten manuscripts, typescripts, and printed material presented to the University of Pennsylvania by the author's widow and on deposit in its archives. The preparation of the card catalog was initiated by Mabel and was the last important act on behalf of her writer husband, whose untimely death permanently wounded her.

Life had become dusty, and Mabel withdrew from society. Not wishing Loren's love letters to fall into the hands of others, she read them a final time and, grief-stricken, burned them. As her health grew worse, she was often hospitalized. Just as she had eluded mental grasp in her husband's writings, so now she was physically elusive as she faded and became increasingly like a print, though with a dignity which was always her style. Nevertheless, it was during this period she cooperated with me in the preparation for publication of the notebooks and was happy to know that the completed manuscript was in the hands of the publisher. On her last birthday, July 9 (which was the anniversary of Loren's death), she said she could not endure another year. She died a few weeks later, on July 27, 1986, and was buried beside her husband.

Loren's life was filled with animal-saving ventures, which Mabel supported. He was always trying to return stray dogs to their masters, calling owners and waiting for them to come for their loyal friends. Soon after he died, Mabel had a visitor — a lost dog who appeared unexpectedly at the back door of her house and who, when taken inside, gravely shook hands with her without being told to. Loren would have looked hard at this encounter, and it would have seemed to look hard at him.

Notes

The following brief remarks by way of explanation or information are identified by the number of the page and the line or lines to which they refer in the text.

Page/Line

88/23 Richard Jefferies, the nineteenth-century English naturalist and writer, is best known for the descriptions of nature in his stories. His novels include *Wood Magic* and *Bevis;* among his principal nonfiction works are *The Gamekeeper at Home* and *Wild Life in a Southern Country.*

115/28 Froelich Rainey, director of the University Museum of Archaeology/ Anthropology from 1947 to 1976, and his wife, Penelope, were friends of the Eiseleys. When Rainey had lunch in Loren's office, the two scholars would sometimes laughingly but affectionately toast the prehistoric men present: *Australopithecus africanus,* "the missing link," represented by a plaster statue which had previously stood in the university museum; *Gigantopithecus bilospanensis,* represented by a jawbone; *Sinanthropus pekinensis* and *Pithecanthropus,* both also known as *Homo erectus,* represented by plaster casts. The skeleton of Edward Drinker Cope, the nineteenth-century paleontologist, resided in a large cardboard carton in the office and was included in the celebration. In more ways than one, Loren, who was curator of Early Man in the museum from 1948 to 1977, lived in a lost world.

118/17 Joseph Willits, a former Director for Social Sciences at the Rockefeller Foundation in New York City, was a good friend of the professor.

121/23 Enoch Pratt Free Library, founded in 1886, is located in Baltimore, Maryland. It has been in the vanguard of the public library movement, and the community draws heavily on it to obtain information and education.

122/8–9 C. S. Lewis, the English writer, wrote *That Hideous Strength,* in which one of the characters Mr. Bultitude — a great lazy brown bear who likes to sit in the bathroom all day when it is cold weather and who stands on his hind legs and meditatively boxes a punching bag. Widely known for his popular religious and moral writings and for his science-fiction novels with a strong Christian flavor, he was one of the many authors Loren read.

122 14–15 Loren danced with an African crane in the Philadelphia zoo, an incident recorded in *All the Strange Hours.* The crane, which is

almost as tall as a man, has an intricate mating dance. Acting under the influence of spring, it made some of these steps in Loren's direction, and, after verifying that they were alone, he enthusiastically joined in.

133/17 Simon Michael Bessie was co-founder of Atheneum Publishers, 1959, and president from 1963 to 1975. It was his firm which issued *The Firmament of Time*.

142/ In a rough letter to an "Eiseley" about the Eiseley family, Loren
14–17 mentions encountering other people with his surname in various parts of the Middle West. Because of the interesting biographical information it contains, the letter is quoted in full:

> I have many times had inquiries from Eiseleys in various parts of the country — as you know, some of them have contracted it to Isly. I have seen Eiseley in the London phone book, I have had one letter from as far away as Madrid, and I can assure you that there is an Alsace-Lorraine French version now called D'Esslay. It is in actuality, I am told by Germans who should know, a very common south German and Swiss name. No doubt there *are* related families but I find it is like trying to work out the relationships between the Smiths and Jones.
>
> I can fill you in on my own grandfather from whom I derived the name and who shares the dedication of my last book, *All the Strange Hours*, published in November by Scribners. Most of my own people are of English and Scotch extraction with the single example of my German grandfather. I know only that he came, like your people, from near Wurtemburg, coming all alone as a lad in his teens shortly after the Revolution of 1848. I know from family tradition he was supposed to be met by a brother who was already in the country. The version in my family is that this brother died in a hotel fire in Washington, D.C., and beyond that tradition is silent. My grandfather, like so many Germans of that time, drifted to Cincinnati and became a cook for a time on an Ohio River steamboat. How it was he happened to drift west into Nebraska Territory I do not know. He joined up in a cavalry regiment during the Civil War and later married a Scotch schoolteacher out in the Territory. He homesteaded for a time near Anoka, Nebraska, and it was here that my father was born. Since my grandfather did not marry German stock the language rapidly became attenuated, particularly since my grandfather had arrived as a very young man. There must have been relatives back home in Germany who sent the boy because at some later time in the family's history he received a small inheritance. It seems logical to suppose, therefore, that the old gentleman who died around 1917 and is buried in Norfolk, Nebraska, might have kept up some kind of contact, at least in his earlier years, with the German family from which he came. My father, Clyde Edwin Eiseley, died when I was a young man and with him perished most of the memories involving the German family.
>
> Now, as I say, I have encountered other Eiseleys from time to time in various parts of the Middle West but outside of these south German origins I could never determine that we had any actual relatives in the U.S. If the family legend is correct about the disappearance of the elder brother, my grandfather must have made his way alone.
>
> It was very nice of you to speak of my work as you have and since you mention the town of Wurtemburg (this is the way I was taught to spell it), and particularly since your family seems

to have come from the immediate vicinity of Wurtemburg, it may well be that we are collateral relatives. Perhaps the datings I have given you may throw some light on this. As far as I can determine, I have a hunch that like some other European families Eiseley was originally a place name and perhaps from that place derived this rather widespread name in all its Anglicized and other variations.

Please do not feel that you are bothering me at all and if there is any further light that the dates I have given you may have thrown upon the matter I would be interested in hearing about them. Thank you again for your gracious letter.

160/5–8 The character Wolf is an example of how Loren manipulated the accounts of his life. In his review of *The Unexpected Universe*, W. H. Auden assumed Wolf was "his own shepherd dog," as did other readers, many of whom wrote and asked the author about him. Since pets were not permitted in Loren's apartment house, he sometimes spoke of dogs belonging to other people as "his." Wolf was such a one, and by making him his own, he gave the story greater reality. For a time I pondered over how one who loved animals so profoundly could live for a quarter of a century in a building where they were not allowed (naturalists have traditionally lived in houses overflowing with creatures of all kinds). At first I thought that Loren's philosophy — his very love of life in all its shapes and forms — transcended giving his affection to a single creature. But I finally concluded that this behavior, at least in part, was contradictory and yet another consequence of his having been neglected and lonely in childhood.

161/ When Loren agreed to write the book on the space age, I remember
22–24 thinking that it had taken him eight years to come to trust me as his editor and friend. This inability to trust easily was a principal personality trait stemming from his traumatic past. When he met Charles Scribner, Jr., president of the firm, for the first time, Loren confided: "He doesn't like me because I was a poor boy and he was rich and went to the best schools." I was greatly surprised by the statement and tried to reassure him, but his anxieties regarding social class were also deep, and I did not convince him. There was always an intangible distance between the two men.

170/19 Charles Langdon, Mabel Eiseley's brother, lived on a farm in Fairmont, Nebraska, a small town not far from Lincoln, in the 1940s. The windmill was one typical of the kind used on farms in that part of the United States.

171/13 Mircea Eliade, the Rumanian author, was Professor of the History of Religions at the University of Chicago. He is known for *The Sacred and the Profane; the Nature of Religion*. Loren wrote about man's alienation from the world in *The Invisible Pyramid*, and René Dubos, in commenting on the book, said: "He was one of the very first scientists to proclaim publicly that mankind must reinsert itself into nature. His words created a new kind of poetical literature based on objective scientific knowledge and his warning helped start a new social movement. As the seers of the axial religions did 2000 years ago, he is teaching our generation to recapture that cosmic sense which is unique to man."

175/17 William Laughlin, the educator, was professor of anthropology at the University of Wisconsin, Madison, from 1959 to 1969.

176/ Scapulimancy is divination by observation of a shoulder blade usu-
18–20 ally as blotched or cracked from the fire. During the Shang dynasty,

when much of the culture of China was developed, oracle bone was used. Frank Speck's book, *Naskapi* (1935), is the culmination of several decades of field work among the wandering Indian hunters of the Labrador Peninsula. Included in the book is a survey of circumpolar distribution of scapulimancy; Speck was one of the first to establish the presence of this ancient magical rite in the northern portion of the New World and to point out its apparent derivation from an archaic hunting level of culture. In one of Loren's note-books, there is an unfinished poem, written in the mid 1970s, enti-tled "Scapulimancy" (the title has been crossed out and replaced with two alternatives, "Like Palm Prints" and "The Space Probe"). It begins:

> *It is the scorched shoulder blade of a hare*
> *or a beaver*
> *The cracks made by the fire seem like palm prints*
> *over the surface of the bone,*
> *pointing the way*
> *to tomorrow's hunting and that charred cluster of lines*
> *marks a rock fall up country and a herd of caribou*
> *things to be seen on the morrow*
> *inscribed here through*
> *fire.*
>
> *This cosmos of a little band of hunting Indians*
> *has meaning,*
> *Every rock, every stream, every animal*
> *is accounted for*
> *and the deep underlying*
> *rhythm of things*
> *can inscribe the message of the forest*
> *on the burned bone of a hare.*
>
> *It is true that instructions for getting one's food*
> *for hunting*
> *might seem the sole issue here and the shaman's*
> *reading*
> *extrapolated*
> *becomes mathematics and systems analysis*
> *in the modern state.*
>
> *But no, I think not and envy the hawk*
> *faced man by the fire*
> *His magic is not small, he is reading*
> *speaking wistfully*
> *of his daughter*
> *and trying*
> *to hire me as his geologist*
> *when I was already promised*
> *to another job.*

182/19 A. Irving Hallowell, the anthropologist, was a professor at the Uni-versity of Pennsylvania and Loren's colleague.

186/
9–11 "The World Eaters" is the title of a chapter in *The Invisible Pyramid,* which Loren was writing at the time this note was made. The chapter begins: ". . . perhaps man, like the blight descending on a fruit, is by nature a parasite, a spore bearer, a world eater. . . . It is conceivable . . . that man's cities are only the ephemeral moment of his spawning — that he must descend upon the orchard of far worlds or die."

186/
12–17 Loren was preoccupied with shape shifting — transformation of any kind. In a notebook entry headed "Shape Shifting" made at about this time, he quoted *Human Animals* by Frank Hamel: "Every part of the world chooses a special animal as being the most suitable for disguise, and naturally enough the animal is one which is common in the district. Thus we find the tiger chosen for India and Asia, the bear for northern Europe, the lion, leopard, and hyena for Africa, the jaguar for South America, and so forth."

189/30 Garet Garrett, the American journalist and economist, was the author of popular books and articles on economic subjects, including *Ouroboras or the Mechanical Extension of the Machine.*

213/
9–10 Loren gave the address at the convocation for the dedication of Myrin Library at Ursinus College, Collegeville, Pennsylvania, in 1971. Among its subject interests are natural science and the social and behavioral sciences, and some of his books were given to the library after he died.

224/
11–12 Loren's notebooks abound in charming observations of cardinals, pigeons, robins, and other feathered vertebrates and their intelligent behavior. In an entry dated August 9, 1970, he speculated about writing an essay called "Magic in Birds" (other possible titles listed were "Nature Through a Pane of Glass" and "The Window of God" — likely reflecting his belief that all living forms are manifestations of a universal power). He was always concerned about injured birds, as when, in 1975, while waiting for the Paoli local, he observed one-legged pigeons among the many birds which crowded the Philadelphia station platform, eating discarded food. Pigeons nested on the window ledges of his old office in the university museum, and when the vines that protected the nests were cut down by museum authorities, the birds kept peering in angrily through the panes of glass. He knew they were angry at *him,* believing he had caused the destruction of the vines. When they stopped nesting on the window ledges, he deeply felt the loss.

232/28 In 1818, John Cleves Symmes of Ohio, late captain of infantry, sent a circular to institutions of learning in America and Europe. In it, he declared "the earth is hollow, habitable within; containing a number of solid concentric spheres; one within the other, and that it is open at the pole twelve or sixteen degrees. I pledge my life in support of this truth, and am ready to explore the hollow if the world will support and aid me in the undertaking." The document continues: "I ask one hundred brave companions, well equipped to start from Siberia, in the fall season, with reindeer and sledges, on the ice of the frozen sea; I engage we find a warm and rich land, stocked with thrifty vegetables and animals, if not men, on reaching one degree northward of latitude 82; we will return in the succeeding spring." In 1823, Symmes petitioned Congress to send an exploring expedition to test his theory and got twenty-five affirmative votes, and in 1826, with James McBride as collaborator, he published *Symmes Theory of Concentric Spheres.* Among Loren's papers, I found a faded newspaper clipping elaborating the frontier soldier's conjecture. He also knew of a terrestrial globe, modeled after Symmes' theory, at the Academy of Natural Sciences in Philadelphia.

249/
19–21 It is not easy to characterize the impact, through his writing, Loren has had on so many people. Each of us would describe it in his own way. I have an especially vivid recollection of an insight one of his books provided. In the dead of a winter night many years ago I walked a dachshund I loved in a blizzard. Fighting an intensely high, cold wind filled with snow, with visibility greatly reduced, I suddenly

glimpsed, as we passed beneath a streetlamp, the shadow form running beside me, not as a dog, but as a wolf, and my own dark shape as a primitive man. Not only did I observe this out of the corner of my eye, but I *felt* like a prehistoric man, with a wild hunting dog at his side, battling the cold and snow of the Ice Age out of which he emerged. I did not fully understand what had happened until a few years later, when I read *The Immense Journey* and realized I had had, under special circumstances, a revelation with my small hound. For a fleeting moment we were transformed into what we had been in the distant past, what is deep within the bones and that reveals itself to notice by chance. I was hesitant to describe this adventure to friends, but I did tell Loren about it — a human being who was often able to shift shape, as in "The Flow of the River," where he "*was* water and the unspeakable alchemies that gestate and take shape in water," because of the quality of life he possessed. He listened thoughtfully and gave me a knowing glance.

Acknowledgments

The editor wishes to thank the following: Roger Donald of Little, Brown, whose editorial help is described in the Introduction and whose continuing support was equally important; Caroline Werkley, whose assistance is also acknowledged in the Introduction and who gave this project unstinting time by reason of her great admiration for Loren Eiseley's work; Kenneth Connelly, former professor of English at Smith College, who read and commented on the 1953–1960 journal and encouraged me to embark upon the endeavor; Arthur Gregor, the poet, who reviewed the poems selected for inclusion and whose perceptive comments helped to determine the offering in these pages; Flora Armitage, the author, who with me reviewed the copyedited manuscript and whose sense of language was invaluable in helping to determine final changes; Mike Mattil of Little, Brown, who skillfully and carefully guided the manuscript through production; Ruben Reina, curator of the Loren Eiseley Seminar and Library, who facilitated my visits to Philadelphia and provided specific information. Finally, I wish to thank my late friend, Mabel Eiseley, whose contribution is described in the Introduction as well and without whose trust this book would not exist.

Many of Loren's notebook entries are published here by kind permission of the University of Pennsylvania Archives. Some of the passages in the notebooks appeared more or less unchanged in published form, and the editor thanks the following publishers for permission to include such material: Grosset & Dunlap for an excerpt from "Thoreau's Vision of the Natural World" by Loren Eiseley, from *The Illustrated World of Thoreau*, edited by Howard Chapnick, Copyright © 1974 by Howard Chapnick; Harcourt Brace Jovanovich, Inc. for excerpts from *The Unexpected Universe* by Loren Eiseley, Copyright © 1969 by Loren Eiseley; and Charles Scribner's Sons for excerpts from *All the*

Strange Hours by Loren Eiseley, Copyright © 1975 by Loren Eiseley.

The editor is also grateful to the following for permission to reproduce their unpublished letters, in whole or in part, to Loren, Mabel, and himself: Stanley L. Becker, Ray Bradbury, Warren E. Burger, Lewis Mumford, Howard Nemerov, the estate of Archibald MacLeish, Curtis Brown Ltd. and Patricia H. Blake for the estate of Phyllis McGinley, the estate of Theodore H. White, and the estate of Lowry Charles Wimberly. The unpublished letters from W. H. Auden to Loren are reproduced by permission of the estate of W. H. Auden, Copyright © 1987 by the Estate of W. H. Auden. The unpublished letter from Hal Borland to Loren is reproduced by permission of the estate of Hal Borland, Copyright © 1987 by Salisbury Bank and Trust Company, Trustee.

For the use of other copyrighted material, the editor thanks Random House, Inc. for permission to reprint "Unpredictable But Providential" by W. H. Auden from *W. H. Auden: Collected Poems,* edited by Edward Mendelson, Copyright © 1973 by the Estate of W. H. Auden; and Howard Nemerov for permission to reprint his poem, "The Rent in the Screen" from *The Collected Poems of Howard Nemerov* (The University of Chicago Press, 1977).

"The Hawk" (Summer 1965) was first published in *The American Scholar;* "The Lost Nature Notebooks of Loren Eiseley" (June 1982), excerpts from the journals which I edited, was first published in *Omni;* "To Henri Fabre" (May 1929) was first published in *Parnassus;* "The Deserted Homestead" (December 1929) was first published in *Poetry;* "Autumn — A Memory" (October 1927), "Against Cities" (Fall 1930), "Death Song for Two" (Fall 1931), "Riding the Peddlers" (Winter 1933), and "The Mop to K.C." (Winter 1935) were first published in *The Prairie Schooner;* and "Bleak Upland," general heading for four poems, including "Upland Harvest" and "Words to the Stoic" (April 1930), was first published in *Voices.*

For the use of photographs, the editor gratefully acknowledges Alan J. Bearden (Loren, University of Pennsylvania campus); the estate of Dwight Kirsch (Loren, 1933); Ross Photography Studio, Cape May Court House, N.J. (Caroline Werkley and Loren; Loren, Wynnewood, Pennsylvania, 1966; Loren, 1971); and the University of Pennsylvania Museum (Pages from the Corey family Bible).

"You'd better _____ we going"
I said. I don't think you know. You're swinging
on the gate, first out and then in. I don't
think you know at all."

I could talk to him this way *was this* because
I was down on his level, flat in the sand,
but it didn't fluster him particularly.
He kept his back up against a stone, not
trusting me but not running either. He
didn't answer except to lift up one big
green claw and point it at my nose. Or

_____ to know
_____ on stalks
_____ (idling answers)
_____ on back.
"If _____ to the water.
He _____ and where
a co_____ your mind."
18 _____ us what
be_____ likewise,
neither back nor _____ round sidling
the corner of _____ and so
off into the _____ timbers and
shells of high tide, but not down and in.
A crab _____ should do so _____ another, not
leave you guessing like that _____ the the
universe doesn't know where _____ going either
shape of a shore crab how in _____ dead _is
a man to know he's on the ____ tracks.

A sea beach is a _____ ace to
start thinking, but then so _____ almost
any place. Any place where _____ e's a
leaf and an animal under it — an